Emma ADAPTED

PETER LANG
New York • Washington, D.C./Baltimore • Bern
Frankfurt am Main • Berlin • Brussels • Vienna • Oxford

Marc DiPaolo

Emma ADAPTED

Jane Austen's Heroine
from Book *to* Film

PETER LANG
New York • Washington, D.C./Baltimore • Bern
Frankfurt am Main • Berlin • Brussels • Vienna • Oxford

Library of Congress Cataloging-in-Publication Data

Di Paolo, Marc.
Emma adapted: Jane Austen's heroine from book to film / Marc DiPaolo.
p. cm.
Includes bibliographical references.
1. Austen, Jane, 1775–1817. Emma. 2. Austen, Jane, 1775–1817—
Film and video adaptations. 3. English fiction—Film and video adaptations.
4. Film adaptations—History and criticism. 5. Television serials—Great Britain.
6. Television serials—United States. 7. Women in motion pictures.
8. England—In motion pictures. I. Title.
PR4034.E53D5   791.43'6—dc22   2007006820
ISBN 978-1-4331-0000-0

Bibliographic information published by **Die Deutsche Bibliothek**.
Die Deutsche Bibliothek lists this publication in the "Deutsche
Nationalbibliografie"; detailed bibliographic data is available
on the Internet at http://dnb.ddb.de/.

Cover illustration by Donald Hendricks (used by permission of artist)
Cover design by Sophie Boorsch Appel

The paper in this book meets the guidelines for permanence and durability
of the Committee on Production Guidelines for Book Longevity
of the Council of Library Resources.

© 2007 Peter Lang Publishing, Inc., New York
29 Broadway, 18th floor, New York, NY 10006
www.peterlang.com

Printed in Germany

For Stacey

Contents

Acknowledgments ix
Introduction. 1

Chapter One. Austen and Adaptation 5
  A Question of Worthiness 5
  The Problem of Adaptation 9

Chapter Two. *Emma* and Literary Scholarship 21

Chapter Three. The Early Television Versions (1948–1972) 39
  Analyzing the Transposition Adaptations 39
  The Judy Campbell Screenplay (1948) 44
  The NBC Kraft Television Theatre *Emma* (1954) 54
  Vincent Tilsley's Screenplay & the "Lost" Adaptation (1960) 62
  The Glenister-Constanduros Version (1972) 73

Chapter Four. *EMMA* A.D. 1996 85
  The Two Recent "Period Piece Adaptations" 85
  Douglas McGrath's *Emma*, starring Gwyneth Paltrow 87
  The Lawrence-Davies *Emma*, starring Kate Beckinsale 105

Chapter Five. *Clueless*: Emma Woodhouse
Becomes Cher Horowitz 125

Chapter Six. Overview 141
  Emma on Film: Male and Female Perspectives 141
  Adaptations in the Classroom: Final Thoughts 149

Notes 153
Appendix: Adaptation Reference Guide 177
Bibliography 183

Acknowledgments

My mother chose to name me after the Cathedral of San Marco in Venice because she had been moved by its beauty. Consequently, I had always assumed that I was named after Saint Mark himself, the "Patron Saint of Writers." Expecting to take full advantage of my connection to such a holy personage, I would sometimes, over the years, pray to San Marco to help me out whenever I had a serious case of writer's block. As far as I can tell, he never did. And I just found out why this evening. As it turns out, he's actually the patron saint of notaries.

Notaries.

It figures.

Since Saint Mark wasn't of much help to me in writing this book, I was indebted to a great many earthly helpers, who urged me to press on during my darker moments of agony and indecision and sloth, and who helped make this book what it is today....

First of all, I would like to thank Donald Hendricks, of *Legacy Designs* and www.paperdolls.com, for lending his talents to this project and gracing the cover with his superb illustration. He is both a wonderful artist and a joy to work with

I also owe a large debt of gratitude to Nadine Ollman and James Hala of the English Department, and Marie-Christine Masse of the Foreign Language Department of Drew University, for their encouragement and support, as well as for their valuable suggestions for revisions. Without them, this book would not exist.

Special thanks to Sue Parrill, author of *Jane Austen on Film and Television* (2002), who graciously sent me the screenplays for the 1948 and 1960 *Emma* adaptations during the early days of my research, granted me permission to quote extensively from her scholarship, and agreed to review the manuscript upon its completion. Also helpful in tracking down elusive sources were Rosemary Hanes, Zachary Joseph

Balian, and David Reese of the Motion Picture and Television Reading Room of the Library of Congress, Madison Building, who arranged a special viewing of the rare, 1954 *Emma* for me. Joanna Di Pasquale, former Web Administrator of *The Elmer Holmes Bobst Library* at New York University, was invaluable in helping me navigate NYU's rich collection of material on Jane Austen. And thanks to John Nelka, a knowledgeable and gregarious librarian at Alvernia College who overcame his own personal dislike of Austen to help me find several key sources. To Gerald Vigna, Dean of Arts and Sciences at Alvernia, I owe many thanks for showing strong Italian-American solidarity by helping me get this book published.

Thank you Elizabeth Steele, Regional Coordinator of the Eastern Pennsylvania-Delaware Valley Region of the Jane Austen Society of North America, for agreeing to review my manuscript. Thanks also to Denise Kohn for granting permission to reprint passages from her excellent essay, "Reading *Emma* as a Lesson on 'Ladyhood': A Study in the Domestic Bildungsroman," originally presented in *Essays in Literature*; Macomb; Spring 1995. I would also like to thank those writers who have tackled the subject of adaptation theory and the *Emma* film adaptations before I did. Your work has been a joy for me to read, contemplate, and write in response to. I can only hope that my humble thoughts may be of interest to you, and that you feel that I have responded to your work in the spirit of collegiality and respect.

And to Jane Austen, my favorite author, who described Emma as "a heroine whom no one but myself will much like": *You are not alone. I like Emma Woodhouse, too. Thank you for writing such perfect novels.*

On a personal note, I would like to express my love and thanks to my wonderful wife Stacey, to my supportive parents, Cathy and Ted, and to my brother Brian, all of whom helped me, personally and professionally, in more ways than they know. I would also like to offer a heartfelt thanks to Michael Shugrue, Professor Emeritus of The College of Staten Island, for his support and input. Finally, I would like to thank Mitchell Sherry, who was the first of my friends to encourage me to embrace a life of creativity, love, and thoughtfulness. I love you all and I couldn't have done it without you.

Marc Edward DiPaolo
March 16, 2007

Introduction

In 1995 and 1996, three filmed versions of Jane Austen's Regency-period novel *Emma* reached movie and television screens: *Clueless* (1995), an American production written and directed by Amy Heckerling and starring Alicia Silverstone that modernizes the story by setting it in a present-day Los Angeles high school community; *Emma* (1996), an American film written and directed by Douglas McGrath and starring Gwyneth Paltrow; and *Jane Austen's "Emma"* (1996), a British television production written by Andrew Davies, directed by Diarmuid Lawrence, and starring Kate Beckinsale. Aside from a 1972 BBC production starring Doran Godwin, a live 1954 American television production, and three additional television adaptations from both sides of the Atlantic that no longer exist on film, these 1990s era films are the only cinematic retellings of the novel.[1] They emerged as a part of a 1990s popular revival of interest in Jane Austen that was spurred on by the blossoming of an independent film community interested in making more films for and by women.[2]

The effects of the creation of a cinematic Austen canon are still felt today in academia, since the films have garnered great critical attention from literary scholars and adaptation theorists. While recent adaptation theorists, who often write from a cultural studies or a cinema studies perspective, tend to be enthusiastic about the quality of the films, both as adaptations of revered "mother" texts and as autonomous works of art, literary scholars who write about the film adaptations tend to be more conflicted in their views. For example, many literary scholars have expressed concerns that the films ultimately rob Jane Austen's works of their integrity and independence by "cashing in" on the author's artistic currency. Also, such scholars often express fears that film studios market literary adaptations to the less-informed moviegoer as audio-visual retellings of the originals that act as narrative experiences equivalent to reading the source novel.

As a literary critic and film aficionado with an interest in adaptation theory, I hope to provide a more even-handed approach to examining the Austen adaptations than has generally been seen in the past. Aside from John Wiltshire, who assumes a very fair scholarly position on the issue of adaptation in *Recreating Jane Austen* (2001), one of the most impartial judges of Austen adaptations is Monica Lauritzen, who published a study of a 1972 BBC adaptation of *Emma* long before the 1990s popular revival of interest in the author. In her book, *Jane Austen's Emma on Television* (1980), Lauritzen offers a fair evaluation of the strengths and weaknesses of the *Emma* miniseries:

> As a work of art the *Emma* serial is different from the original. It is weaker in some respects but also stronger in others. Because of these differences, the watching of the serial cannot replace the experience of reading the original. But it may stimulate and enrich the reading, and also attract new readers, who might otherwise never have found their way to Jane Austen's masterpiece. (154)

I would submit that what Lauritzen found to be true about the 1972 adaptation of *Emma* can also be said of the three filmed versions that followed during the 1990s, as each of these films offers an intriguing interpretation of Austen's text that can inspire fruitful meditations on the themes of the original.

Admittedly, Jane Austen narratives have sometimes proven to be more difficult to transplant from print to film than a first impression might suggest. After all, Austen gave greater attention to developing her characters' inner lives—their thoughts, feelings, and voices—than she did to describing their physical appearances and their observable actions. She also spent little time detailing setting and scenery. Therefore, one might assume that her books would translate poorly into a medium that (at least in the case of mass-marketed Hollywood films) tends to emphasize image, movement, and a style of operatic melodrama that often grants primacy to plot over characterization. And yet, all of the films based on her novels thus far have garnered more than their share of serious praise from members of the film community, and the three different adaptations of *Emma* are particularly worthy of note, especially since they are so different from one another and in their relation to the book.[3] In effect, each individual film can be read as a critical assessment of the novel by the film's director, and can be used to bring to life in dramatic form the vastly divergent readings of the novel that have long been put forward and debated by more academic textual critics.

In addition to making interpretive and critical connections between the films and the novel, I will offer examples of how the films, usually in an attempt to commercialize the story or to make it more "filmic," deviate from the book, and will determine to what extent these deviations retain the spirit of the original novel. For example, while *Clueless* is the film that comes the closest to finding a cinematic equivalent of Austen's "free-indirect writing style," it is also the film that alters the book the most by changing the criteria by which Emma evaluates worthy mates for herself and her friends.[4] Instead of judging men's eligibility by uncovering their noble lineage, land holdings, and annual income, she is primarily concerned with men who possess the liberal values of the sexual revolution while being free from the behavioral excesses that lead to drug addictions and sexually transmitted diseases. The film *Jane Austen's "Emma"* featuring Beckinsale rewrites Knightley as a progressive socialist. This change necessarily creates a cinematic world far different from the one in the original novel, in which the prevailing Regency-period class structure demanded that Emma's relationship to her lower-class friend Harriet "must sink" by the closing pages. The McGrath film featuring Paltrow casts Emma as an even more liberated figure than she is in the book (for example, she would never steer her own carriage because her father would insist that James be her driver and protector), but the important consequence of that alteration is that it masks the real reason for her hostility towards Miss Bates, Miss Fairfax, and Mrs. Elton presented in the original story—her fears of social displacement. The kinds of textual divergences I have cited above, often seemingly small, have great thematic import to the films. Alterations to the original appear throughout each of the films, and it is in a close examination of these alterations that I will be able to determine where the films make interpretive assumptions about the original text.

In Chapter One, *Austen and Adaptation*, I will offer a discussion of the often skeptical outlook literary critics have presented on filmed adaptations of classics in general and Jane Austen adaptations in particular. This section will close by suggesting some preliminary ways of looking at the films, from a stylistic and cinematic perspective, as a first step in analyzing the adaptations. Chapter Two will include a general overview of recent criticism of the novel *Emma*, and a discussion of specific readings, contemporary and traditional, that are relevant to the issues that the films raise.

Chapter Three features a detailed examination of all five of the adaptations of *Emma* that were made for British and American television between the 1940s and the 1970s. These adaptations were reviewed in Sue Parrill's book *Jane Austen on Film and Television*, but have not been discussed in detail elsewhere. In examining these earlier adaptations, I will be able to place the discussion of the 1990s adaptations of *Emma* in a broader context, since I will be discussing them as parts of a complete body of work that includes all of the versions of the novel ever put to film.

Chapter Four will turn its attention to the two films made in 1996—*Emma*, and *Jane Austen's "Emma"*—offering interpretations of them as readings of the novel. Chapter Five will examine how *Clueless* simultaneously acts as a reading of the novel and as a satire of the social values of 1990s America. The overview found in Chapter Six will examine all of these readings together to ascertain how filmmakers have presented Jane Austen and her novel *Emma* to the lay public over a period of several decades, and will determine what trends can be found. This section will also offer suggestions as to how future adaptations of *Emma* might improve upon those already produced by positing what an ideal adaptation of the novel should hope to achieve.

Austen and Adaptation

A Question of Worthiness

The film world still awaits a cinematic recreation of Austen that translates her satiric perceptions of society into cinematic terms a modern audience can respond to, yet without losing the heart of what has made her works endure. No film has yet been made worthy of Austen.

—John Mosier, "Clues for the Clueless" (251).

W hat does it mean for a motion picture adaptation of a classic work of literature to be "worthy" of its source? Since Jane Austen has become my favorite author, I must confess to nurturing certain feelings of protectiveness towards her when viewing adaptations of her work, and I have wondered to what extent they have committed a form of literary "crime" by meddling with her original. For example, while I very much enjoy the film as a whole, I am practically offended by the fact that the *Pride and Prejudice* film with Greer Garson and Laurence Olivier alters the ending of the novel to rob Elizabeth Bennett of her victory over the villainous, upper-class Lady Catherine De Bourgh. In making Lady Catherine into a benign figure who approves of the union between her rich, landed nephew and the socially inferior Elizabeth, the film considerably undercuts Elizabeth's heroism.

To that extent, I view this movie, and many other adaptations, with a divided consciousness. There is the part of me that watches the film as one who will always be loyal, first and foremost, to the "mother" text, and there is the part of me that wishes to view the film in its own right, and see what it is trying to achieve, artistically and socially, by retelling an established narrative. Although few of the

Austen devotees who have written about the film adaptations have acknowledged a similar mental divide, Rebecca Dixon is the one who appears to be the most frank and unapologetic about it. The title of her 1998 essay, "Mis-Representing Jane Austen's Ladies," seems to speak for itself, since its primary concern is indicating all the ways in which the 1990s crop of Austen films incorrectly portray their female leads. And yet, Dixon begins with the following disclaimer:

> [I]n spite of the dismayed nature of this article, please understand just how much I enjoyed each of the recent Austen-based productions. *Persuasion, Pride and Prejudice, Sense and Sensibility,* and *Emma* are all delightful visual and audio experiences. Beautiful settings, witty and lively dialogue, lovely costumes, clever irony, and more—overall, they're all well done....If an Austen-based film appeared in theaters, I saw it at least once and later purchased it on video....I *like* these films. Allow me to articulate my fervent desire that movie makers will continue to make such fine films.... (44)

Of course, many literary critics are not as conflicted as Dixon concerning the artistic merit of Austen adaptations. Naturally, for those who see the Jane Austen films (or any other adapted films for that matter) as generally poor in quality, there is no conflict to resolve— the films are terrible, need to be renounced, and that is final. But a conflict is created when, on some level, the literary critic recognizes some artistic merit in the film. Then the question remains, what kind of relationship does the adaptation have to the source novel? Could that relationship be viewed as anything but parasitic if the eventual determination is that the original is "better" after all? Interestingly, despite his conclusion that the Austen film adaptations are failures from a purist perspective, Mosier offers some intriguing meditations on these very questions:

> Besides providing a certain level of intellectual entertainment, the primary objective of good adaptation, like that of any good interpretive reading of a text, is to make viewers return to the text and reconsider it anew. Probably the most successful adaptations of literature to film are those which cause the viewer to conclude, after having returned to the text and evaluated the reading that the film has delivered, that the filmmakers have a point, an interpretation which deserves a hearing. This interpretation need not be all-inclusive for the compressed length of a film does not permit comprehensive coverage, nor does the nature of the medium. However, it must carry insights that together provide a valid understanding of the original text. (228)

The working premise that Mosier outlines above is quite valuable as a starting point for this discussion of adaptations of *Emma*, although I would maintain that the individual *Emma* films meet Mosier's own criteria more successfully than he allows that they do. Nevertheless, Mosier makes several insightful criticisms of the 1990s films that are important to take into account. For example, he is particularly critical of the casting of the films, especially of Mr. Knightley, who is usually too young, and of Emma, who is often played by a slim, fair-haired actress when the book describes her as "handsome" —a word that signifies a voluptuous figure and suggests darker hair.[1] Mosier is also correct in observing that the films do not go far enough in recreating the specific 18th century context of the original story, in which the rising middle-class challenged the sovereignty of the landed establishment forces of the time. These legitimate complaints concerning the films are difficult to challenge, and similar objections to the fidelity of the movies may be found in the writings of other Austen devotees.

Although not a literary scholar, *New Yorker* film critic Anthony Lane based his poor review of Douglas McGrath's lush, fairy-tale-style adaptation of *Emma* on an intriguing scholarly premise—film versions of Jane Austen novels consistently fail to capture the right dramatic tone precisely because even the most learned readers of the original novel have difficulty identifying Austen's tone themselves:

> In a way, you feel sorry for McGrath and his designers; they have to decide on a tone and stick with it, whereas the atmosphere of the original resists any such definition. You can spend a lifetime reading Austen and still be unable to place her: Is she affectionate or flinty? Does her tolerance float free, or does it exist to peg back her anger? McGrath turns her into a proto-Dickensian—Emma's infuriating father, in particular, becomes a Mr. Bumble figure, all plaintiveness melted into joviality—but there is an equally strong case for revering her as the last of the Johnsonians. No burden weighs more heavily on a writer's shoulders than that of being much loved, but something unreachable in Austen shrugs off the weight. Only a fraction of this ambivalence is available to a film like "Emma"; McGrath has opted to make things nice and snug, but in so doing he dooms us to sit through the movie sighing for the lost astringency of the book. (76)

Here again, an insightful criticism leveled at an *Emma* adaptation seems truly damning. Similar objections were raised by other Austen scholars, both to the fidelity of the 1996 McGrath film as well as to textural and tonal liberties taken by other Jane Austen adaptations made around the same time. One of the foremost evaluators of the Hollywood dramatizations of the 1990s, Carol M. Dole, suggests that the films as a whole cater too much to the American myth of "class-lessness" to deal seriously with the class issues that concern Austen.

Whether the objection is to casting, to tone, or to dramatic representations of class issues, essentially, the critical consensus is that the films romanticize and misrepresent the original texts.[2] For example, they emphasize the marriage-plots at the script level, make the male love-objects more appealing than they are in the novel, eliminate the most liberal and feminist-oriented dialogue from the text, and they misrepresent the social context of the Regency period in which they were written by depicting the society as more democratic than it actually was.

A great many of the criticisms included in the writings mentioned above are valid from the perspective of an Austen scholar who is interested in making sure that the version of the text that the public is most familiar with through the film medium is an accurate reflection of the original. To the extent that I agree with these criticisms, and that I believe they are important to keep in mind, I will be preserving many of these arguments in my discussions of the various film adaptations of *Emma* by quoting extensively from critics who view the films as fundamentally unfaithful, commercial piratings of Austen. However, I will try to qualify these complaints as often as I can by judging the films on their own terms, as readings of the novel rather than as complete recreations of the novel. As Derek Paget writes in his essay comparing the Jane Austen film adaptations to the movie adaptation of the contemporary novel *Trainspotting*:

> Discussion of film/TV adaptation of novels is often troubled by the vexed question of fidelity to 'prior texts' deemed to have inherently greater cultural standing. Inevitably, the 'not a bit like the novel' argument is often heard (along with its extension—'not as good as the novel'). Such arguments are more stridently heard when the work of classic authors is at issue. It almost seems to constitute a kind of perverse pleasure for those jealous of canonical literature's supposed superiority to continue to argue for the primacy of print. (131)

Perhaps the best solution to the "vexed" questions of fidelity and artistic merit is provided by a decision, made at the outset, to avoid thinking of the films in such starkly evaluative terms. Austen scholar and adaptation theorist John Wiltshire has advanced one such alternative way of looking at film adaptations and their architects. In *Recreating Jane Austen* (2001), Wiltshire suggests that, in the case of each individual adaptation, the "scriptwriter and filmmakers be understood as readers, and that one advantage of all such revisions is that they make public and manifest what their reading of the precursor text is, that they bring out into the discussably open the choices, acceptances, assumptions and distortions that are commonly undisclosed within the private reader's own imaginative reading process" (5).

Wiltshire's philosophical approach will prove especially useful to this discussion as it will enable me to examine the films as readings of the source novel, and not as pale reflections of it. Although Wiltshire is not the only scholar who is attempting to change the parameters of the discussion of adaptation, there is a sense in which the debate concerning adaptation has yet to be resolved, and there are still a great many critics who find this widespread process a highly questionable popular phenomenon. Assuming, for the moment, that the prevailing view of adaptation is skeptical, I would like to begin my discussion of the Jane Austen adaptations in particular by offering an overview of the traditional objections to the feasibility of the adaptation process in general.

The Problem of Adaptation

Until relatively recently, the weight of scholarly opinion has been against the feasibility of film adaptation, and the objections to the enterprise have been particularly convincing because of the stature and eloquence of the skeptics. Virginia Woolf famously balked at a movie version of *Anna Karenina* because it merely showed Karenina as a plastic image on silent film and utterly failed to make manifest her thoughts and feelings. As Woolf observed, "the brain knows Anna almost entirely by the inside of the mind—her charm, her passion, her despair" (Geduld, 88–90). Therefore, the portrait of "Anna Karenina" being projected onto the screen before her evoked no recognition whatsoever from Woolf. Indeed, in so failing to capture the spirit of the novel, this film version of *Anna Karenina* seemed too far removed from the original to warrant calling itself by the same title. Many adaptations, before and since, have fallen just as disastrously short, calling into question the validity of the entire project of adaptation.

In *Aesthetics and Psychology of the Cinema* (1963) Jean Mitry convincingly framed the argument against Hollywood film adaptations of classics in this fashion:

> Adaptation to begin with (whether of plays or novels) was no more than a guarantee of quality which the reputation of the work adapted was supposed to lend the film. The cinema's claim to be art depended on the amount of art injected into it. Though distorted by translation, the original work retained its potential power even when it was being caricatured, impressing the stamp of its quality on the film it inspired, giving it the necessary aesthetic warranty but inevitably pointing up the congenital inferiority of an art totally dependent on it. (326)

Later on in the chapter, Mitry made a grudging concession that David Lean seemed to be one of the few filmmakers who could prove him wrong, since that particular auteur had demonstrated unique artistic skill in transforming some of the novels of Charles Dickens into legitimately great motion pictures. Therefore, while Mitry seemed, on balance, to be skeptical of the feasibility of a film being crafted that does justice to its literary predecessor, he posited that it was at least possible for a filmmaker to craft an adaptation that

> through an art of effacement, renunciation, scrupulous fidelity to the original work and, though incapable of translating the deeper meanings and providing aesthetic equivalences...[is] at least capable of producing a worthy reflection.

> The most notable successes in this genre have been David Lean's films adapted from *Great Expectations* and *Oliver Twist*. The images seem to jump right out of the pages of the novel and, here and there, it is possible to recognize little flashes of Dickens' style and manner. (329)

Mitry is not alone in identifying these films as worthy of Dickens' original novels, but they appeared to be (to him, at least,) the exceptions that prove the rule, since Mitry alluded to few, if any, other directors who were as successful as Lean at adapting films.[3] Writing more specifically and less generally, Mitry's primary objection to a film's ability to transpose a complex novel to the screen is his sense that films have a narrative structure to them (and a sense of narrative time) that bear a closer resemblance to a short story than to a novel.

Films seemed to demand, by their nature, that every single scene advance the plot, that every object on screen have a clear-cut function in the story, and that archetypal characters played by "stereotyped" actors would advance the simple narrative to a logical conclusion. Thought could not be effectively conveyed, nor could emotion, stream-of-consciousness, or abstract principles.

Although himself kinder to film adaptations than most, Seymour Chatman has correctly identified what is possibly the greatest obstacle to transplanting a classic story successfully to the screen. Texts enable readers to mentally visualize the physical details of the story in any manner that they wish. Readers are limited only by their imaginations when they conjure mental images of the setting and the physical appearances of the characters. However, in watching a film, audience members are limited to visualizing what the casting director, the set designer, the costume designer, the director, and the director of photography have chosen for them. Therefore, anyone who sees a film version of a book after reading it finds that their visualization of the story, and their power to make the story their own, has been challenged and limited by what plays out on screen.

> In verbal narrative, story-space is doubly removed from the reader, since there is not the icon or analogy provided by photographed images on a screen. Existents and their space, if 'seen' at all, are seen in the imagination, transformed from words into mental projections. There is no 'standard vision' of existents as there is in the movies. While reading the book, each person creates his own image of *Wuthering Heights*. But in William Wyler's screen adaptation, its appearance is determined for all of us. (101)

The irritation created by the cinematic visualizing of the world of the novel is even more greatly enhanced by the casting of specific actors to play beloved literary characters. In many cases, the fame and performance style of a given actor further interferes with a reader's personal vision of how a particular character should look or behave:

> Some characters in sophisticated narratives remain open constructs, just as some people in the real world stay mysteries no matter how well we know them. Therein perhaps lies the annoyance of enforced visualization of well-known characters in film. The all too visible player—Jennifer Jones as Emma Bovary, Greer Garson as Elizabeth Bennet, even a superb actor like Laurence Olivier as Heathcliffe—seems unduly to circumscribe the character despite the brilliance of the performance. Where the character is simpler, 'flatter,' the problem is less acute: Basil Rathbone is easier to accept as Sherlock

Holmes because Conan Doyle's character is more limited to begin with. The predictability of Holmes' behavior (his power to collect clues, his teasing of Watson) is agreeably matched by the predictable appearance of the actor. (Chatman 118–119)

Traditionally, scholars who have examined film adaptations have seen such problems as insurmountable and have sided with Mitry's assessment that filmmakers should make movies from whole cloth rather than adapt them from other sources. For example, George Bluestone, author of the landmark 1957 work *Novels into Film*, concluded that film adaptations are formalistically and fundamentally different from the novels they are adapting and are inferior art. Contending that novels are more about an exploration of the thoughts and emotions and films are more of an exploration of observed reality, Bluestone writes that:

[t]he film and the novel remain separate institutions, each achieving its best results by exploring unique and specific properties. At times, the differences tempt one to argue that filmmakers ought to abandon adaptations entirely in favor of writing directly for the screen. More often than not, the very prestige and literary charm of the classic has an inhibiting effect, shriveling up the plastic imagination. Like Lot's wife, the film-maker is frequently immobilized in the very act of looking over his shoulder. (218)

And yet, even Bluestone, whose tone was strongly skeptical, expressed hopes that someday the adaptation process might be better understood, and that some great motion pictures might one day be inspired from written material:

As long as the cinema remains as omnivorous as it is for story material, its dependence on literature will continue. The best one can hope for, then, is a minimal awareness of that metamorphic process which transforms pieces of fiction into new artistic entities. Once that process is understood, the alchemist's firing pit will surely yield less disappointing lead; it may even yield surprising deposits of gold (219).

Notably, Bluestone wrote this passage in 1957, and there was a sense at the time he was writing that motion pictures were still largely looked down upon by the academe. Despite the fact that marvelous and innovative films were produced each year by Kurosawa, Fellini, Hitchcock, Bergman, and numerous others, there was a popular assumption at the time that films could not be considered "art." Fortunately, that assumption is more and more being called into question, especially as independent and mainstream films continue to be released that redefine the boundaries of cinema and what audiences expect from it. Ever since its initial release, film critics have argued that *Citizen Kane* proves that movies have the potential to be as rich and as complex as novels. Therefore, I would argue that Bluestone failed to anticipate the potential of the filmic medium, and did not anticipate that a motion picture such as *Lost in Translation* (2003) would be capable of achieving the kind of psychological subtleties of characterization and non-traditional modes of storytelling that it does. And, once it is possible to assume that a film can have artistic merit, and that it can have a "novelistic structure" instead of a "short story structure," it becomes less absurd to assume that a film can—at least in some manner—be "worthy" of the culturally treasured source novel that it is based on.

In the years since the publication of Bluestone's book, an array of adaptations has been produced that strive to achieve greater fidelity to the source material through longer running time (the three-hundred-minute television miniseries *Pride and Prejudice*), more extensive use of voice-over (the Douglas McGrath *Emma*), race-appropriate casting (Laurence Fishburne played cinema's first black *Othello* in the 1995 film), and greater attention to historical accuracy in set-design and costuming (the Lawrence *Emma*). In the face of these excellent films, Mitry's objections on the basis of abstract principle and essentialism don't appear wholly credible. Indeed, as Morris Beja, author of *Film and Literature: An Introduction* (1979), indicates, "When we place less emphasis on some abstract sense of theoretical properties and consider the real world, we cannot avoid the recognition that important filmmakers have in fact adapted novels into films which are themselves valuable and distinguished, and occasionally masterpieces" (79).

And Beja is only one of many voices that runs counter to Bluestone's. In fact, in recent years a growing number of critics have appeared who have defended film adaptations. They have asserted that, despite the differences in storytelling modes between a film and its written source, one must not always conclude that the novel is superior because it came first and because film, by its very nature, is a lesser medium intended for the uneducated masses (Beja 34). In addition to Beja, some of the writers who have written in support of the

project of film adaptation, both recently and in the past, are V.F. Per-
kins, F.E. Sparshott, Joy Gould Boym, Andre Bazin, and James Griffith. Griffith, for example, explains in *Adaptations as Imitations: Films
from Novels* (1997):

> if we allow that viewing a film usually does not permit the full
> representation of a novel's events, we acknowledge a phenomenological
> difference as fact; such acknowledgement does not then force us to conclude
> that adaptations are also always simpler, for we cannot assume shorter is
> simpler. The actual difference in this instance leads to no deductive
> judgments for all adaptations. Individual adaptations may actually be
> simpler, but others may be as complex as the original novel or more
> complex (35).

In the introduction to his book *Film Adaptation* (2000), James
Naremore posited that most of the writing done on the subject of literary adaptation "tends to valorize the literary canon and essentialize
the nature of cinema" (8) while it should be more eager to "ask more
interesting questions" (9). For example, Naremore observes that:

> We now live in a media-saturated environment dense with cross-references
> and filled with borrowings from movies, books, and every other form of
> representation. Books can become movies, but movies themselves can also
> become novels, published screenplays, Broadway musicals, television
> shows, remakes, and so on…and, on a theoretical level, the problem of
> sequels and remakes, like the even broader problem of parody and pastiche,
> is quite similar to the problem of adaptation.…
>
> Notice, moreover, that all the "imitative" types of films are in danger of
> being assigned a low cultural status, or even of eliciting critical opprobrium,
> because they are copies of "culturally treasured" originals. (13)

Despite the dubious reception that these films still garner from
certain quarters, they remain a Hollywood constant, especially in the
past several years where all of the innovation in the industry appears
to come from the independent film community and the mainstream
pictures rely conservatively on proven markets—which means audiences have been inundated with sequels, remakes, movies based on
video games and old television shows, and adaptations of recent and
classic novels. Fortunately, although the reasons for the recent wave
of adaptations may have more to do with profit margins and bottom
lines than art, many of these films that are commissioned by the studios are helmed by artists with a genuine respect for the source mate-

rial and a desire to create the best possible film adaptations.⁴ As Mosier suggests, the most successful of these film adaptations not only stand on their own as great works of art, but inspire us to return to their source and read it again with a fresh insight into the story and its characters. I feel safe in singling out for praise the stunning 1997 A&E production of *Jane Eyre* featuring Samantha Morton and Ciaran Hinds, and—more importantly, since it is the central subject of this book—the excellent adaptations of *Persuasion* (1995), *Mansfield Park* (1999), and *Emma* (1996).

This line of argument may seem too evaluative in nature, but it is in the tradition of adaptation theory to select particularly successful film renderings of classics for distinction. The individual films that are chosen sometimes vary from critic to critic, but it seems reasonable to suggest that the general quality of film adaptations has improved in recent years, especially when one compares the films listed above to the kinds of loose adaptations which were filmed in the early days of cinema, which included a poorly conceived *and* unfaithful version of *Moby Dick* (1930, dir. Lloyd Bacon) in which Ahab, played by John Barrymore, slays the white whale at the end and goes home to his true love.

Generally speaking, the pioneers of serious adaptations of classic literature over the past few decades have been Masterpiece Theater, Merchant and Ivory, A&E, and Miramax. These films have received their share of criticism over the years, but Griffith offers a strong defense on their behalf in *Adaptations as Imitations* (1997). Griffith notes that some critics use the terms "Ivoryesque" and "Masterpiece-Theater treatment" to "demonstrate that films, which supposedly cannot be faithful to novels, fail when they nevertheless remain faithful to the novel" (229). He counters this attack on "'slavish' fidelity" by noting that, given the excellence of *Brideshead Revisited*, *Howard's End*, and other works produced by these companies, he "cannot see how these terms can stand as insults" (229). While there may never be a consensus about the merits of the E. M. Forster adaptations produced by Merchant and Ivory, or of the various Miramax adaptations of Jane Austen and Oscar Wilde, or the numerous Masterpiece Theater retellings of the works of Charles Dickens and Henry James, there has been a general movement towards greater fidelity and dramatic excellence seldom seen in the past.

Also, in these days of multiple film versions of single texts, film-makers making movie adaptations often have to carry less of a burden of responsibility to the source novel than they did before, since the weight of responsibility is shared by other, parallel, literary adaptations. For example, if there were only one film version of *Moby Dick*, then the literate members of the film audience would put extraordinary pressure on the film to be as perfect and as complete an adaptation as possible. Since there are, in actuality, numerous adaptations of *Moby Dick*, literary critics and lay moviegoers have less of a sense of expectation that each individual adaptation will be perfectly faithful and wholly complete. That is to say, even members of the moviegoing lay public are beginning to realize that an individual movie adaptation should not be judged as a complete recreation of the original work, but as a reading of the original work. Anyone who has seen all three of the recent *Emma* adaptations—*Clueless* (1995), Douglas McGrath's *Emma* (1996), and the Diarmuid Lawrence *Emma* (1996)—should understand, at least on an intuitive level, that the differences in the films can be accounted for by the different visions of the original text they represent. Once this realization concerning the nature of adaptation sinks in, there will be less expectation that future film adaptations will present definitive film renderings of novels and more expectation that they will provide intriguing readings and reinterpretations of the source.

Additionally, in watching older film adaptations, contemporary film viewers are provided with an experience akin to reading literary criticism written in previous eras. These films give the contemporary person the opportunity of observing how filmmakers from a different time interpreted a given classic work and presented it as popular entertainment. Basically, the experience of studying past readings of a classic work is a valuable one, whether that window into past readings is provided by a book of post-World War-II-era criticism or by a lush MGM film version from the 1940s. As Italo Calvino observed in "Why Read the Classics?" (1981), "classics are the books that come down to us bearing the traces of readings previous to ours, and bringing in their wake the traces they themselves have left on culture or cultures they passed through (or, more simply, on language and customs)" (128).

Furthermore, the multiplicity of the *Emma* adaptations, new and old, provides certain intriguing possibilities for lovers of the original novel who share a love of film. As Timothy Corrigan, author of *Film and Literature* (Prentice Hall, 1998) writes:

> ...there is another attraction and activity imbedded in the numerous classics offered up on the contemporary screens and monitors and in the numerous versions of the same work of literature that audiences can now watch. Today, literary classics on film are multiple and redundant in two ways. Not only are different versions of a novel or film sometimes produced by different filmmakers within a few years of each other (including several *Emmas* in the nineties or almost simultaneous versions of Laclos's *Dangerous Liaisons* by Stephen Frears [1988] and Milos Foreman [the 1989 *Valmont*]) but home video and computer technologies have made it possible for viewers to watch and compare even more versions of an adaptation from other periods of film history. After seeing those different contemporary versions of Austen's and Laclos's novels audiences today have the option of watching on video Clarence Brown's 1932 *Emma* [sic] or Roger Vadim's 1960 *Dangerous Liaisons*, and these, of course, could be sampled next to the original novels and, in the case of *Dangerous Liaisons*, next to Christopher Hampton's play.[5] Contemporary film culture offers more versions and more opportunities to see and compare the relationships between film and literature as historical practices and textual performances, and one consequence of this redistribution of literature through the media may be that questions of fidelity or authenticity may be less and less a concern for both filmmakers and their audiences. As Scorsese's *Age of Innocence* seems to suggest in its almost fetishistic obsession with the surface of gowns, wall coverings, and dinner table settings, audiences today may be more interested in the different textures of adaptation than in the textual accuracy of any one adaptation. (73–74)

But what might viewers who see all three of the filmic versions of *Emma* that appeared on the scene in 1995 and 1996 make of them? What can one glean from examining their similarities and differences? While all three films were ostensibly from the same source material, they differ drastically from one another in tone, visual style, reading of the original text, and moral message. The differences between the three are stark and help to demonstrate how rich the original novel is and how well it supports such vastly differing interpretations. While almost any work of fiction may be read differently depending on the personality of the reader, or the methodology which provides the critical lens through which the reader studies the source text, *Emma* appears to be a particularly rich text that is both morally and artistically complex enough that it begins to resemble a crystal that, held one way up to the light seems to cast some colors, and held another, projects other colors.

As for the various film adaptations, there are several ways of understanding the differences between the films, but I will begin by suggesting that the basic structural differences between the adaptations may be examined from a film theory perspective by using the writings of Geoffrey Wagner. A film theorist, Wagner identifies three categories of film adaptation in his 1975 work *The Novel and the Cinema*: the *transposition*, "in which a novel is given directly on the screen, with the minimum of apparent interference" (222), the *commentary*, in which the original is "either purposely or inadvertently altered in some respect" causing "a re-emphasis or re-structure" (223) and the *analogy*, in which an original tale is modernized and the action is shifted "forward to the present, and make[s] a duplicate story" (226). Though loosely defined, these are useful categories of distinction, and each one describes a corresponding *Emma* adaptation.

The most philosophically problematic of Wagner's categories is the transposition, which many would argue is an impossible goal to achieve. Certainly, the production team behind the 1972 BBC adaptation of *Emma* intended to make their miniseries a transposition of Jane Austen's novel to the television screen. The stated goal was "total fidelity" (Lauritzen 112). As a general rule, however, most adaptation theorists are skeptical of any claims that individual film adaptations stake to being transpositions. Adjusting Wagner's category slightly, perhaps it would be more accurate to say that a transposition is most likely a film adaptation that brings a traditional, conservative reading of the novel to the screen that does little to clash with the lay public's vision of the work, creating an illusion that it is a complete and wholly faithful retelling. In these projects, radical readings of the work that are popular in university classrooms are often not even consulted by the director/screenwriter, or are willfully ignored.

Of the adaptations that might fairly be deemed successful transpositions are *Jane Eyre* (1997) and the version of *Emma* written and directed by Douglas McGrath and starring Gwyneth Paltrow that was released by Miramax in 1995. Although McGrath claimed in an interview in *Screenwriter* magazine that he did not write the film using any source along with the original novel, his transposition of the book to the screen unfolds much like a reading of the book by Denise Kohn, who interprets the story as a domestic Bildungsroman and a "Lesson On Ladyhood," or by Reginald Farrer, who offers a fair evaluation of Emma's moral worth as well as her moral failings.

Nineteen-ninety-six's *Jane Austen's "Emma"* (produced for British television and A&E by screenwriter Andrew Davies and director Diarmuid Lawrence, and starring Kate Beckinsale as the title character) can be safely categorized as a commentary since the creative team is clearly looking back upon the original text with a modern eye that condemns the class structure of the period and, consequently, judges the title character even more harshly than Austen did. Traditionally, commentary adaptations inspire strong reactions from audience members—often disappointing those who would have preferred a translation while delighting those who find that a fresh and intelligent look at an old work helps to breathe new life into readings of the original. A commentary adaptation, then, is a reading of the novel that consciously eschews any attempt at self-negation and "total fidelity" in favor of a re-envisioning of the original work. Such an adaptation is more likely to draw upon radical or progressive critical literary readings of the text that are often ignored by more politically conservative transposition adaptations.

Finally, *Clueless*, a 1995 Paramount film written and directed by Amy Heckerling and starring Alicia Silverstone, is clearly an analogy of the original novel, since it sets the story in a high school in modern-day Los Angeles.

Three other *Emma* adaptations—from 1948, 1954, and 1960—could also be classified using Wagner's schematic, and each appears to fit most comfortably in the category of transposition discussed earlier.

Of course, other classic novels have produced numerous film and television adaptations that are different enough to be classified using all of Wagner's categories. However, few sources have proven rich and complex enough to inspire interpretive cinematic works as noticeably divergent as those films that are based upon *Emma*. It is precisely because the novel has generated so many vastly different scholarly interpretations over the years that it has proven capable of inspiring so many vastly different films. That is why, before moving on to an examination of each individual adaptation, it will be important to first explore the rich heritage of literary criticism that has been written about the source novel. For only in understanding the various readings of Jane Austen's original text can one hope to understand the films as similar, dramatized readings of the novel.

A discussion of many of these key works of literary criticism will begin in the following chapter.

Emma and Literary Scholarship

Lionel Trilling famously observed in 1957 that "the difficulty of *Emma* is never overcome" (viii), and that no matter how many times the novel is read, we will never be able "to flatter ourselves that we have fully understood what the novel is doing. The effect is extraordinary, perhaps unique" (ix).

In recent years, Austen scholars have come more and more to the conclusion that the "difficulty" that Trilling sees in interpreting *Emma* is not actually a difficulty at all. It is, in fact, the central beauty of the text that it is open to so many divergent and fascinating readings. In the previous chapter, I described the novel as being akin to a crystal held up to the light, able to project different—but equally beautiful—readings. I also observed that this prismatic quality of the novel is the chief reason it was able to inspire so many different filmic adaptations. Hence, it is important to discuss what kind of scholarly readings the novel has supported over the years before proceeding to an analysis of the individual films themselves.

Admittedly, since the scholarly interpretations of the novel are so diversified, they are difficult to categorize and make generalizations about. However, it is possible to suggest that there are two essential ways in which most scholars read the novel—firstly, as a domestic Bildungsroman, and secondly, as a social critique. The domestic Bildungsroman school of *Emma* interpretation includes those scholars who read the novel as if it were a coming-of-age story, or a tale of moral reform. These readings, though themselves often starkly different from one another, tend to emphasize the need for the title character to shed her snobberies, outgrow her overactive imagination, and put an end to her alienation from other women. Notably, such readings may be framed with a charitable eye towards the heroine, in which case her maturation is viewed as empowering and as a normal process for a woman of her age, or they may have a more moralistic and disapproving tone, condemning Emma for her flaws and seeing the exposure of her many errors as a humorous chastening and humiliation of the character.

On the other hand, scholars who regard the novel as a social critique tend to view it as a story of the pressures placed on young women to conform to certain modes of behavior deemed appropriate to class, status, and gender. These readings generally cast Emma's home life with her hypochondriac father as a form of domestic imprisonment, view her marriage to Mr. Knightley as predetermined by societal expectations, and regard the claustrophobic setting of Highbury as a site of boredom and repression. Critics who see Emma as existing in a very confining world are all the more apt to look kindly upon her revolutionary attempts to shake up the status quo with her matchmaking, her sponsorship of Harriet, and her reluctance to marry and befriend those whom society demands that she marry and befriend. In many such readings, several of the personal "faults" that were assigned to Emma above seem to be revealed either as secret virtues or as a natural consequence of the confining society in which she lived. Indeed, Knightley might ultimately come to a similar conclusion himself, since he is inspired to proclaim Emma "faultless in spite of her faults" at the end of the novel.

The word Bildungsroman literally means "formation novel" and defines a storytelling mode that focuses on the maturation and education of a central protagonist. Although the genre traditionally has featured a male hero who comes of age during the course of a long, sometimes picaresque, journey, *Emma* breaks the conventions traditionally attributed to the Bildungsroman by featuring a heroine who essentially stays at home. According to Denise Kohn, author of "Reading *Emma* as a Lesson on 'Ladyhood': A Study in the Domestic Bildungsroman":

> The main problem in recognizing *Emma* as a Bildungsroman is that the genre has always been associated with the theme of journey or quest. And *Emma* is the antithesis of the novel of quest: it is a domestic novel....What seems to be the safety of the world of domesticity—compared to the world of quest—caused both male and female readers to dismiss the domestic setting. But heroines such as Emma do have to overcome obstacles in order to become adult, and these obstacles are often domesticated or different versions of those that heroes face on their quest for independence....It is also crucial to realize that the development of the domestic heroine differs from

the development of the men, because female development is based upon a definition of self within a web of personal relationships. Although the domestic heroine must achieve intellectual independence and self-understanding to become an adult, she does not want to physically and emotionally sever herself from her family and friends. (47–48)

To read the novel as a Bildungsroman is to read it either as the gradual maturation of Emma Woodhouse or, less charitably, as the moral reform of Emma Woodhouse. In either case, Bildungsroman critics tend to view the character as growing less fanciful, less snobbish, and more empathetic to the less fortunate women of Highbury as she learns to better understand her own heart and the world around her.

Of all of these three imperfections—imaginism, snobbery, and coldness towards other women—Emma's tendency to be too much of a fantasist (or imaginist) is the one which readers generally find the most endearing and forgivable. According to a Bildungsroman reading of the novel that focuses on Emma's runaway imagination, Emma has read a few too many romance novels, and does not have enough experience in the real world to truly understand how society works. Hence, Emma is apt to see Frank Churchill as an idealized Byronic figure and thinks too well of him, leaving her vulnerable to his charms and credulous of his lies. She has also concocted a fanciful fiction around the parentless Harriet, whom she believes to be of noble birth simply because orphaned characters in novels are invariably revealed to be the children of counts and barons during the closing chapters. This error causes her to entertain rather lofty aspirations for finding a wealthy, upper-class husband for the lowly Harriet. Other symptoms of Emma's imaginism include her painting an idealized physical portrait of Harriet, whom she makes too tall, and her romantic-fiction-induced assumption that Jane Fairfax fell in love with the married Mr. Dixon when he saved her from a boating accident.

A. Walton Litz is emblematic of critics who interpret the novel in this fashion. In his 1965 book *Jane Austen: A Study of Her Artistic Development*, he wrote that "[t]he basic movement of *Emma* is from delusion to self-recognition, from illusion to reality" (132). According to Litz, the heroine knows neither how to properly view the world around her, nor understands the workings of her own heart, but her perceptions are aligned by Mr. Knightley, a character who is shown to be a realistically noble role model, as opposed to an idealized figure.

A more contemporary critic who reads the novel in a similar fashion is Loraine Fletcher, who writes in "Emma: The Shadow Novelist" (*Critical Survey* 4, 1992), that *Emma* is "[a] novel about Romanticism, balancing the claims of unique disruptive imaginism against the claims of Christian patriarchy, and finding—it's a close-run thing—for the latter." For Fletcher, Emma and Frank Churchill are "fictionalizers and self-fictionalizers" inspired by the romanticized figures from the sentimental fiction of the time, who are in need of correction, but whose whimsical perspectives are missed when they are altered or expelled from the world of the novel (36–44).

Domestic Bildungsroman readings tend to associate Emma's imaginism with a form of childishness that needs to be shed in order for Emma to reach maturity. The novel does indeed seem to support this critical view of Emma's imaginism, especially since her whimsical plan to marry Harriet to a well-off clergyman results in the disruption of Harriet's romance with farmer Robert Martin, causing great emotional pain to all parties involved and nearly condemning Harriet to a life of impoverished spinsterhood. Because of these plot developments, many readers assume that Emma's match-making practices, which are strongly linked to her imaginist worldview, should be condemned by the reader for their destructiveness.

Another domestic Bildungsroman reading of the novel emphasizes Emma's need to shed her snobberies and her elitism on the path to maturity and adulthood. While many critics agree that Emma is an elitist, there is some disagreement over the exact nature of her elitism and its causes. For Beth Fawkes Tobin, Emma's snobbery is a function of her vanity, and of her fear of other, less socially important women than herself, whose real virtues and beauty would outshine hers if they occupied the same privileged position in society.[1] Other critics have viewed Emma's snobberies as a defensiveness born of confusion concerning the sweeping cultural changes that she was seeing in her lifetime. John Mosier has made a strong case in favor of reading Jane Austen as, in the words of Frederick Engels, a chronicler of the "progressive inroads of the rising bourgeoisie on the society of nobles that reconstituted itself after 1815" (241) and the surest sign of this concern in *Emma* itself is the inclusion of characters such as the Coles, Mrs. Elton, and Mr. Weston, all of whom are buying their respectability. Emma's attitude towards this rising middle class seems somewhat inconsistent, as she approves of Mr. Weston's upward mobility but gives little support to the Coles and Mrs. Elton. Since she personally likes Mr. Weston, her snobberies seem chiefly directed against those she is indifferent to, or those she actively dislikes.

As Maaja A. Stewart explains in *Domestic Realities and Imperial Fiction* (1993), "[t]he imperial British culture that brought unprecedented wealth to England also increased the poverty of the underclass and of women in all classes," (137) causing a cultural shift that bewildered Emma:

> Emma's unfulfilled relations with women are determined by her radical confusion about the relation of class to gender, a confusion exacerbated by the shift that the novel registers from a society divided by status to one defined by class. This confusion about class and women becomes especially striking in a heroine who is notorious for spelling out with ruthless genteel snobbery the exact degree of status that can be conferred on men like Mr. Martin, Mr. Elton, and Mr. Cole. In contrast to this clarity, Emma consistently tries to ignore or reinterpret the real class standing of women like Miss Taylor, Harriet Smith, Miss Bates, and Jane Fairfax.

> Emma's confusion and potential anxiety about the asymmetrical relation of class and gender assume two forms. In the first, typified by her interactions with Harriet Smith and Miss Taylor-Mrs. Weston, Emma ignores economic and class differences and attempts to confer her own status on the other women. In the second, dramatized in her interactions with Miss Bates and Jane Fairfax, Emma attempts to avoid any relationship with those whose destiny and "nature" or class status glaringly do not harmonize. In the first place, Emma mimics the role of a man by assuming control over the status of women; in the second, Emma refuses to acknowledge her kinship with women whose destinies have marked them as victims of the class structure. Both responses displace attention from the material condition of women's lives. (153)

While Emma's views on class and status might seem abstract, they assume tremendous importance when one remembers that Emma bases a great many of her actions in the novel on assumptions about what kinds of relationships are appropriate for her to have with the other residents of Highbury. Also, as Stewart explains, these class and status issues cannot be viewed as distinct from gender issues, as the novel is principally concerned with Emma's relationships to other women, all of whom occupy social positions beneath Emma.[2] These thoughts about Emma's snobberies in relation to other women bring us to a discussion of the flaw that critics have most often attributed to

Emma in recent years—she is alienated from members of her own sex. While Stewart attributes this alienation to specific social causes, it is equally possible that the root of the problem is psychological. The early death of Emma's mother and the marriage of Emma's sister might well have left Emma feeling abandoned by the women in her life. Also, the soothing, uncritical attentions of her governess, Miss Taylor, might have accustomed Emma to flattery, causing her to seek out relationships with the same power dynamic and to forgo more equitable and challenging friendships with women.

Janet Todd makes a similar argument in *Women's Friendship in Literature* (1980), suggesting that Jane Austen was skeptical of women's ability to form meaningful, honest relationships with one another as equals. Todd finds evidence of this skepticism in all of Austen's novels, but focuses much of her attention on Emma's unhealthy interactions with the women of Highbury. In her study of *Emma*, Todd observes that Austen places Emma in the company of Harriet and Miss Taylor (both of whom she can manipulate) for most of the novel. Emma's relations with the other women in the novel are no healthier. She is most resentful of Miss Bates, the spinster she fears she may one day become, and of Jane Fairfax because Jane is an intelligent woman of her own age who competes with Emma for the affections of those around her.

It is only at the end of the novel—when Jane's secret engagement is revealed and the two apologize to one another for nurturing ill feelings—that there is a promise of potential friendship. However, Austen rapidly writes Jane out of Highbury, causing Emma to remark that their time together was ending just as they were getting to know one another. For Todd, a friendship between Emma and Jane could have been the most rewarding and intimate female friendship in all of Austen's novels, but Austen refused to portray it. What makes Todd's reading of the novel so intriguing is that it suggests that Emma is never able to fully overcome her alienation from other women, making the text a story of a woman who never completely achieves the maturity and self-fulfillment she should (274–301).

If some of the above readings—which focus on Emma's need to reform her attitudes about imaginism, class, and gender—seem too hard on Emma, and seem to moralize too much about her behavior, then it is important to note that there are some domestic Bildungsroman critics who notably see Emma's personal growth as her empowerment instead of as her chastening or humiliation. For example, Denise Kohn posits that "[o]ne of Austen's greatest achievements in *Emma* is that she writes a novel of education—a Bildungsroman—that instructs her readers to deconstruct the pervasive images of 'Ladyhood' created by her period's conduct-book writers" (45).

Kohn explains that, "[i]n the eighteenth- and nineteenth-century world of a rising middle class and declining upper class, social status and survival depended not only on money but also on manners—those culturally constructed markers that define community membership....During a period of what seemed like class chaos to many Britons, readers increasingly turned to the rising artistic form of the novel to find narrative guidance for their behavior" (46). And what they found in the heroine of *Emma* was not the shy, silly heroine of most conduct books, but a far more complex character who grows during the course of the novel. "So while the character of Emma is a celebration of female individualism and power, Austen also shows how Emma abuses her power by crossing the threshold of propriety and domesticity in her manipulation of Harriet and insensitivity to Miss Bates. By the end of the novel, however, Emma as a character is strengthened by her experience, gaining greater social and self-knowledge. As Austen's portrait of an ideal 'lady,' she is strong and assertive but is also more caring and sensitive to others" (46).

Although domestic Bildungsroman critics may differ about the nature of Emma's personal flaws, they tend to agree that, if Emma's quest to improve herself ultimately succeeds by the end of the novel, it is because she has learned the proper mode of behavior from her interactions with another major character. Critics in recent years, including Sandra Gilbert and Susan Gubar, have emphasized all that Emma learns from the other female characters, particularly Jane Fairfax. In *The Madwoman in the Attic*, Gilbert and Gubar explain that Jane Fairfax and Emma are doubles in their antithetical natures:

> Jane is totally passive and quiet, despite the fact that she is repeatedly humiliated by her lover. Indeed, although Jane Fairfax is eventually driven to a gesture of revolt—the pathetic decision to endure the 'slave-trade' of becoming a governess rather than wait for Frank Churchill to become her husband—she is a paragon of submissive politeness and patience throughout her ordeal (157–158).

...A player of word games, a painter of portraits and a spinner of tales, Emma is clearly an avatar of Austen the artist. And more than all the other playful, lively girls, Emma reminds us that the witty woman is responding to her own confining situation with words that become her weapon, a defense against banality, a way of at least seeming to control her life....Yet Austen could not punish her heroine more than she does....The very brilliant and assertive playfulness that initially marks her as a heroine is finally criticized on the grounds that it is self-deluding....Not only does the female artist fail, her efforts are condemned as tyrannical and coercive. (158–159)

So, for Gilbert and Gubar, what is the nature of the lesson that Emma learns in the novel?

The civil falsehoods that keep society running make each character a riddle to the others, a polite puzzle. With professions of openness Frank Churchill has been keeping a secret that threatens to pain both Emma and Jane Fairfax. Emma discovers the ambiguous nature of discourse that mystifies, withholds, coerces, and lies as much as it reveals....Although Emma is the center of Austen's fiction, what she has to learn is her vulnerability as a female. (158–159)

Although Gilbert and Gubar make an excellent case for Jane Fairfax as the one from whom Emma learns the most about herself and her position in society, there has been a long tradition in literary criticism granting Mr. Knightley the primary role of tutor to Miss Woodhouse. A strong argument can be made to that effect, and many critics who view the novel as a domestic Bildungsroman cast Mr. Knightley in this light. Firstly, Mr. Knightley appears to be more perceptive and more prescient than Emma. He predicts that Emma's involvement with Harriet Smith will lead to trouble, and the novel seems to bear out the validity of his fears. He is also proved correct in his worries that Frank might reveal himself to be more of a Churchill than a Weston at heart. Also, while Emma is the first to determine that Jane nurtures a secret and forbidden love, Knightley is the first to discern that her love is Frank and not Mr. Dixon. As a protector of impoverished gentlewomen, Mr. Knightley also outshines Emma, giving food and attention to Miss Bates and insisting, properly, on making Jane's life in Highbury as comfortable as possible. Perhaps most importantly, it is also Mr. Knightley who is afforded the distinction of chastising Emma following her ill-judged behavior at the Box Hill picnic.

In various ways, Emma offends virtually all gathered during the Box Hill excursion. She humbles Mrs. Elton by assuming the position of the head of the gathering, she flirts openly with Frank Churchill (making both Jane and Mr. Knightley jealous), and she slyly labels the poor Miss Bates a talkative bore in front of the whole assembly. Mr. Knightley disapproves of all of these actions, but he focuses on Emma's insult to Miss Bates, whose poverty should secure Emma's public support and compassion instead of her derision. Since many critics agree that Mr. Knightley is correct to criticize Emma for her ill treatment of Miss Bates, his role in this key segment is central to a reading of Mr. Knightley as the hero of the novel and even, possibly, as the voice of the author herself. The segment in which Mr. Knightley humbles Emma is also critical to the novel because she weeps after hearing Mr. Knightley's words. The tears signify her shame over realizing the error of her ways. They are also a sign of the growing love that she feels for Mr. Knightley, since her tears are partly from disappointment that her actions have garnered such strong disapproval from one she esteems so highly.

For many domestic Bildungsroman critics, such as Nigel Everett, Mr. Knightley's wise example as landowner and first man of Highbury makes him symbolic of society as a whole, and of the idealized value system of the Christian patriarchy. Therefore, as Emma aligns her worldview to match his, she has ended her fruitless rebellion against the dictates of a just system and embraced the Tory values that made England a global superpower. Also, although such readings have fallen out of favor since their post-World-War-II heyday, some Bildungsroman critics have suggested that Knightley's principal task in the novel is to awaken Emma's cold heart with love. These critics (who include Edmund Wilson, Marvin Mudrick, and Mark Schorer) see Knightley as the only man strong enough to domesticate Emma, ending her resistance to marriage and redirecting her affection from an unnatural crush on Harriet to healthy feelings of romance for him. Critics who read the novel as a social critique, however, generally adopt strikingly different views of the character than those presented by domestic Bildungsroman critics, as we shall see later on in this chapter.

Because Emma's love for Knightley increases as she grows in knowledge and sensitivity, many domestic Bildungsroman critics see the romance between Emma and Mr. Knightley as linked directly to the story of Emma's moral improvement. The possible connection between Emma's maturation and her romance with Knightley grants tremendous symbolic weight to the marriage that takes place between the two at the end of the novel. Hence, any interpretation of the ending of the novel and the significance of the marriage bears great weight on an interpretation of the overall themes of the story. For many critics, the marriage between Emma and Mr. Knightley at the end of the novel is problematic because it is unclear how the famously ironic Jane Austen intends her readers to interpret the final line, which describes "the perfect happiness of the union" between the two central characters.[3] However, domestic Bildungsroman critics tend to read the closing lines of the novel literally and anticipate a happy marriage between Emma and Mr. Knightley.[4]

In her 1975 book *Jane Austen and the War of Ideas,* Marilyn Butler describes the plot of *Emma* as "the classic plot of the conservative novel" in which "the heroine's classic task, of choosing a husband, takes her out of any unduly narrow or solipsistic concern with her own happiness" (250). Butler writes that the moral reform of Emma that accompanies this quest is facilitated by Mr. Knightley, whose jealousies and imperfections do not call into question his essential "rightness" throughout the novel. The reform is also qualified by the fact that even at the end of the novel Emma makes mistakes, among them being her assumption that Mr. Knightley is about to proclaim a love of Harriet when he is really trying to propose, and her continuing to harbor sympathies for Frank Churchill.

One key point that distinguishes Butler's analysis from other critics who see the novel as principally about the reform of Emma is that Butler explores the social limitations placed upon the character, and the pressures on Emma to marry:

> Emma is vulnerable, and one reason is that her stake in Highbury is not deep. Her very claim to social precedence is so precarious, while she remains a spinster, that she is superceded by Mrs. Elton. When she marries Mr. Knightley her rank will be secured, and she will become involved in the land by sharing in its ownership....At the end of the novel Emma is about to assume a clearly defined and permanent role in the community, and what is left outside has been touched with the insubstantiality which Burke gives to the people and the ideas that will not belong. (274)

Here Butler appears to recognize the validity of some of the claims of scholars who read the novel as a social critique by acknowledging the external pressures placed upon Emma to marry. However, these observations do not compel her to conclude that the novel is anything other than a traditional, conservative work. There are, of course, other interpretations of the novel that cast the novel as conservative and patriotic, and that see Highbury as idyllic and Donwell Abbey as an impressive imperial seat. For example, in "The View of Donwell Abbey," a chapter in his 1994 book *The Tory View of Landscape*, Nigel Everett described Austen's novels as gradually demonstrating the author's "increasingly unambiguous desire to contrast Old England with the new uniformity of a shallow, urban-inspired sophistication" (183). In the context of this agenda, Austen depicts Donwell Abbey as "the essential idea of England herself" as a seat of freedom, beauty, and virtue (197).

However, there is an undeniable claustrophobia inherent in the small community, and a critic such as Meenakshi Mukherjee, who sees the novel as more of a social critique than a coming-of-age story, seems largely correct in describing Highbury as a "landlocked, static world" (86) and in pointing out that "the entire action [of the novel] except the Box Hill picnic takes place within an area of two square miles" (60–61).

> It is characteristic of Jane Austen that...she portrays a society that closely restricts mental space—particularly of women, who are allowed very little solitude or freedom....The sense of being hedged in, being watched and discussed by the whole community, characterizes most of her novels. Paradoxically, it also forces her characters—at least the central ones—to be very private. What are the areas of life where thoughts, feelings, and information can be shared, and what are the areas where secrecy is desirable, forms one of the implied moral debates of her work. (74)

Mukherjee further describes Highbury as a world in which class divisions are clearly delineated and reinforced by events in the novel, in which annoying outsiders are expelled, and in which a recurring "motif of spatial enclosure...becomes a metaphor for [the] stasis" that constitutes life in Emma's social circle (65). In this community, no action taken by any resident or visitor is too trivial to go uncommented upon, and the smallness of the social circle forces intimacy and civility upon those who would much rather not have to spend time in one another's company. The world of Highbury is so confining and personally invasive, in fact, that Mukherjee concludes that, "[i]n this hothouse atmosphere, unless a person is very determined and strong willed, the pressures of the group, constant interaction, gossip and rumor will predetermine the course of his or her life" (85).

Mukherjee, like other critics who read the novel as a social critique, does not moralize about the personal flaws of the characters in Highbury, but laments that the society is repressive to the point that it forces strict conformity and punishes and expels all those who fail to fit seamlessly into a provincial lifestyle. Despite the fact that he is aware of Jane Austen's moral interest in "true speaking," Tony Tanner also qualifies as a critic who reads the novel as a satire of the confining life of bourgeoisie women in Regency-period England. In his 1986 critical survey *Jane Austen*, he writes:

> Emma often has to have recourse to silence rather than utter her real feelings—her one slip in this matter, her joke at Miss Bates' expense, looms amazingly large and serves to indicate, among other things, what a degree of repression such a community, and its matters, depends upon. And it would be wrong to mentally gloss over the difficulties—the tediums, the longueurs, the "inelegances" of that society. (193)

Tanner is intrigued by Austen's repeated use of the word "evils" when discussing Emma's situation, and meditates on the possibility that the "evils" do not originate from within Emma, but from society itself:

> The real "evil" or terror in Emma is the prospect of having no one properly to talk to, no real community, in fact. Imagine those long evenings Emma has only her father to converse with, which she has to get through with the aid of backgammon. For a person of her "wonderful velocity of thought" they must be nearly intolerable. Hence Emma's dread, near the end, when she foresees the possibility of all the society she knows dispersing for one marital reason or another....We have noted how various and potentially discordant are the discourses within this small society, so that it is a question of who really listens to, or is heard by, whom. But the image of Emma spending long hours with her father and no one else brings home to us the real threat to her and her position. Not that she might not find sexual satisfaction (that question is scarcely raised), but simply—and terribly—that she be condemned for years to have no one to talk to wittily, playfully, rationally, or in any way at all that transcends pork, eggs, muffins and gruel. That would be a doom indeed. (203)

Because of the evils of Emma's situation, Tanner finds her small personal flaws—such as her overactive imagination and her unrealistic expectations for finding Harriet a privileged husband—highly understandable and forgivable. Other cultural critics go even farther in their defense of Emma, to the extent that they chasten scholars who read the novel as a domestic Bildungsroman for being too judgmental about the protagonist's foibles. As Casey Finch and Peter Bowen observe:

> [i]t is Emma's matchmaking, of course, that leads her to the series of blunders over which so many Austen critics are fond of moralizing. But while critics—along with Mr. Knightley—chastise Emma, few remember at the same time that the novel itself is unashamedly in the business of matchmaking. Few remember that at the very moment when Emma attempts to renounce matchmaking Emma has made its most glorious match. (555)

Examining the issue from a slightly different angle, Claudia Johnson suggests that Emma's matchmaking cannot be dismissed as trivial and feminine precisely because so many of the men in Austen's novels use match-making as an important political and economic tool. In her book *Jane Austen: Women, Politics, and the Novel* (1988), Johnson explains that

> [i]n Austen's fiction the making and prohibiting of matches preoccupies country squires like Sir John Middleton and great gentry like Darcy himself just as much as it does well-meaning gossips like Mrs. Jennings...[In *Mansfield Park*,] Sir Thomas's principal activities are much the same as Emma's: he manages his household—with less aplomb—and he oversees the destinies of those around him. This he accomplishes principally by encouraging or discouraging specific marriages. That this is Emma's activity as well, and that this constitutes socially significant activity, are points that merit emphasis. Progressives and reactionaries fought their ideological battles in the arena of family and neighborhood, and the whos, the whys, and the why-nots of matchmaking were not idle concerns of meddlesome women with nothing better to do....[In addition,] far from being above applying his own understanding to other people's business, [Mr. Knightley] oversees the personal affairs of his neighbors more closely than Emma does, and his indignation over Emma's 'interference' with Harriet Smith is due in part to the embarrassment he feels for his own, now futile, interference with Robert Martin. (131)

Indeed, Johnson has emerged as one of Emma's chief defenders, and has put forward strong rebuttals for the most common attacks upon Emma's character, which have come from both conservative and liberal quarters. Johnson most effectively challenged readings of the novel—which were popular shortly after World War II, but which are rarely heard now—that Austen satirizes Emma for her opposition to marrying, and problematizes Emma's frigidity and homoerotic attraction to Harriet.[5] In *Equivocal Beings*, Johnson turns her attention to the homoerotic attraction between Emma and Harriet, and to traditional critical views of Emma as "frigid" or "autoerotic," writing that

> ...quite susceptible to the stirrings of homoerotic pleasure, Emma is enchanted by Harriet's "soft blue eyes"; displaying all the captivating enjoyment of "a mind delighted with its own ideas," Emma is highly autonomous and autoerotic; and, finally, displaying shockingly little reverence for dramas of heterosexual love, Emma's energies and desires are not fully contained within the grid opposed by the courtship plot. (195)

As Johnson has indicated, critics of the post-World War II era had previously noticed Emma's lesbian inclinations, most notably Edmund Wilson in his review essay "A Long Talk About Jane Austen" (1944), Marvin Mudrick in "Irony as Defense and Discovery" (1952), and Mark Schorer in "The Humiliation of Emma Woodhouse" (1959). In fact, these authors exhibited some anxiety about Emma's disinclination towards marriage and heterosexual romance, suggesting that she would never fully shed her "cold" or "lesbian" traits sufficiently enough to have a successful marriage. For Johnson, all of these essays by post-World War II critics are "cheerfully misogynist" and seem to miss the point that Austen's novel does not make an issue of Emma's independence or her reluctance to marry. Instead, it criticizes Emma for not being enough of a democrat while praising her for not mirroring the "conventional femininity" represented by Mrs. Elton, Isabella Knightley, and Harriet Smith. The femininity represented by these characters, who dote far too much on the men in their lives, is "a degradation to which Emma does not submit" (202).

In addition to challenging these conservative critics, Johnson has also refuted a common complaint advanced by some feminist critics that Emma's marriage to Mr. Knightley is a sell-out in which she allows herself to be tamed by a lover-mentor figure, suggesting that the end of the novel has a far more subtle and subversive message. The ending of *Emma*, "which seemed tamely placid and conservative...takes an unexpected turn" when Mr. Knightley chooses to live at Hartfield with Emma and her father. Thus, "the guarantor of order himself cedes a considerable portion of the power which custom has allowed him to expect. In moving to Hartfield, Knightley is sharing *her* home, and in placing himself within her domain, Knightley gives his blessing to her rule" (143). This reading suggests at least a more equitable relationship between Emma and Knightley than the lover-mentor readings would generally allow for.

While some domestic Bildungsroman critics would disagree with this interpretation on the grounds that it undermines Mr. Knightley's authority and grants too much moral clout to Emma, Allison Sulloway goes even father in challenging Mr. Knightley's position as the novel's moral compass in her reading of the novel as a social critique. Sulloway contends that Mr. Knightley cannot be considered the novel's voice of morality because his world-view is too limited. She focuses her attention on the debate between Emma and Mr. Knightley over Frank Churchill's apparent lack of ability to stand up to his surrogate mother and go pay his respects to his father and the new Mrs. Weston. It is a particularly morally ambiguous conversation and one in which I have often suspected that Emma has more of a point than many conservative critics would allow. As Sulloway explains:

> Knightley invariably interrupts Emma with all the cool authority he exercises over Miss Bates and Mr. Weston. On one such occasion, Emma makes an unusually exasperated retort: "You are very fond of bending little minds; but where little minds belong to rich people in authority…they have a knack of swelling out, til they are quite as unmanageable as great ones." Emma's comment itself has "a knack of swelling out" until it encompasses even the kind, complacent Knightley himself, as well as Emma's other target, her gently predatory father. But she hurls this accusation at Knightley during a debate when she is begging him to consider "the difficulties of dependence," the daily frustrations "of having tempers to manage," the impossibility for anyone "who has not been in the interior of a family" to "say what the difficulties of any individual of that family may be." She is ostensibly defending the conduct of Frank Churchill, although it is indefensible, as Knightley insists. But he is too deaf to anything she says, too used to dismissing her articulate speech as the petulant utterances of a spoiled child, and too used to playing the social arbiter in Highbury to hear the personal despair behind Emma's excuses for Frank. She reminds Knightley that he has "no habits of early obedience and long observance to break through," but for dependent people, including herself, "it might not be so easy to burst forth at once into perfect independence," and to "set all…claims…of gratitude and regard at naught…Oh! The difference of situation and habit! I wish you would try to understand!" (Sulloway 165)

In Sulloway's reading of the novel, Knightley's reflections upon the status of women of the time are categorized by "euphemistic" descriptions of their plight, brief expressions of sympathy, and a series of arguments "favoring women's disenfranchisements, without actually admitting that [he] is doing so" (166–167). The narrative style and content of the scenes in which Mr. Knightley makes moral observations, especially those concerning Jane Fairfax and Miss Bates, "offers 'received opinions' in so sensible a way that no realistic person can altogether refute them. And then it undercuts them, before, during, and after Knightley has uttered them, but in such a way that they might easily be ignored, as they have been for almost two centuries" (167). Since Knightley seems to have such a poor grasp of Emma's true feelings and situation here, Sulloway's observations somewhat call into question the notion that he will be an understanding and empathetic husband.

Having canvassed the readings of the novel that could be categorized as domestic Bildungsroman readings and those that could be called social critique readings, what conclusions may be drawn? It would appear that the readings all have insightful comments to make about the most dramatic and most controversial moments in the novel—the Box Hill segment, the marriage of Emma and Mr. Knightley, Emma's failed attempts to find Harriet a husband—but that they tend to view these segments from opposing angles. Generally speaking, the domestic Bildungsroman critics seem to place their sympathies more with the society at large than with Emma, and are most satisfied when Emma's more creative and selfish impulses are stifled or redirected to more socially beneficial ends. These critics may disagree about how Emma must change—either she must change to ally herself more firmly with the patriarchal Christian worldview represented by Mr. Knightley, or she must change to be more sympathetic to the impoverished gentlewomen of Highbury (or do both)—but they agree that Emma must change from within. Social critique critics view the novel with more empathy for Emma, and champion the rights of the individualist and the iconoclast by criticizing society for forcing Emma to fit in and become exactly like what everyone expects her to be. This reading is more tragic and less comic than the Bildungsroman readings tend to be. And social critique critics tend to hope that, at the end of the novel, Emma has retained as much of her old mischievous self as she can, married to the serious Mr. Knightley; they further hope that Emma changes her husband as much, if not more, than he changes her. She has, at least, helped him learn to enjoy dancing.[6]

While it is always possible for any given reader to choose one particular interpretation of the novel as either a domestic Bildungsroman or a social critique and to be convinced of the essential correctness of that decision, it is equally possible to remain perpetually unsure. In a similar manner, many of the film adaptations wrestle with the problem of dramatizing Emma's situation. Some films choose to depict Emma as the chief architect of the conflicts in the story, just as others emphasize the tensions created by her adversaries, or by the restrictive nature of Highbury society itself. And still others strive to achieve a balance in their depiction of both Emma and Highbury, showing the virtues and vices of both in equal measure.

Having examined the issues of adaptation and interpretation that each film version must contend with when accepting the challenge of adapting Jane Austen's *Emma*, we can begin a discussion of each of the first four extant television dramatizations as critical interpretations of the novel put to film.

CHAPTER THREE

The Early Television Versions (1948–1972)

Analyzing the Transposition Adaptations

E mma is a rich novel, not only because of its complex characters and the contentious social and moral issues it tackles, but also because its narrative structure is highly sophisticated, to the point that Ian Watt grants it a place of honor as the groundbreaking text that first realized the true potential of the novelistic medium.[1] In his 1957 work *The Rise of the Novel,* Watt suggests that Jane Austen wrote the first complete novel by merging the psychological, personal storytelling style of Samuel Richardson (a style that would be further developed by Henry James) with the plot-driven, satirical style of Henry Fielding into a "harmonious unity [with] the advantages both of realism of presentation and realism of assessment, of the internal and external approaches to character…" (297). Consequently, "her novels have authenticity without diffuseness or trickery, wisdom of social comment without garrulous essayism, and a sense of the social order which is not achieved at the expense of the individuality and authenticity of the characters" (297). Watt also explains that Austen's writing style:

> is employed with supreme brilliance in *Emma* (1816), a novel which combines Fielding's characteristic strength in conveying the sense of society as a whole, with something of Henry James's capacity for locating the essential structural continuity of the novel in the reader's growing awareness of the full complexity of the personality and the growing situation of the character through whom the story is mainly told: the unfolding of Emma Woodhouse's inner being has much of the same drama

of progressive revelation with which James presents Maisie Farange or Lambert Strether. (297)

Austen's writing style—commonly described in academic circles as a "free-indirect" style—navigates deftly between representing the inner life of the protagonist and the perspective of the narrator, just as it simultaneously relates the stories of Emma the individual and Highbury the society. In the case of *Emma*, this shifting back and forth between Emma's perspective and the narrator's is at the core of the narrative richness of the novel. Much of *Emma*'s irony and humor comes from the disparity between these two perspectives, as the narrator is more critical of Emma, and seems to have a better grasp of the world of Highbury, than Emma herself.[2]

This selfsame innovative narrative voice of Austen's ironically proves to be the most challenging aspect of her novels to bring to the screen—and yet, any filmmaker hoping to evoke the tone of the source text in a film version arguably should at least attempt to do just this. The narrator is most often missing, whereas Emma's perspective is always included, even if it is not assured the dominant dramatic viewpoint. Some adaptations do include bookend narrative voice-overs that place the story in a larger context, but it is arguable that the narrator heard on the audio track is never quite the same as the narrator from the novel. For example, *Clueless* recreates Austen's irony by juxtaposing what the heroine is thinking via voice-over with what is shown visually on-screen, often in a manner that inspires the viewer to laugh with "Emma" and at "Emma."[3] Other adaptations choose to focus on recreating one element of Austen's narrative voice, or "free-indirect" style, giving primacy either to the "inner being" of Emma or to the sense of the society as a whole. In other words, some films emphasize the "Henry Fielding" influences found in *Emma* and other films emphasize the "Samuel Richardson" influences in *Emma*. As we shall see, the American adaptations of *Emma*, with their focus on the lovely heroine, tend to highlight the "Richardson" that Watt sees in Austen—thereby encouraging feelings of intimacy with the heroine, her thoughts, and feelings. The British television adaptations, with their focus on Miss Bates, Jane Fairfax, Robert Martin, and Highbury as a whole, emphasize the "Fielding" that Watt sees in Austen by regarding the heroine from a more clinical distance, and by focusing more on the ensemble cast of characters.

According to Linda Troost and Sayre Greenfield, the reason that the films tend to choose one narrative style over another is that the limitations of the filmic medium demand that such a choice be made. In making this assertion, they seem to infer that no complete adaptation, as such, is possible ("Filming Highbury" 1-3). They are correct, up to a point. Since the running time of most adaptations is not adequate to dramatize all of the events of the novel in their entirety, cuts to the story need to be made, and different adaptations choose different scenes, characters, and storylines to excise. While such cuts are often deemed a necessity by adaptation theorists, they are not dictated solely by the differences between the written and audio-visual mediums, as has often been suggested, but by the vision of the story that the creative team wishes to present to the public.

As discussed in Chapter One, John Wiltshire has posited that, in the case of each individual adaptation, the "scriptwriter and filmmakers be understood as readers" who "make public and manifest what their reading of the precursor text is" (5). Given that the production team members are readers, they are likely to come to certain conclusions about the novel itself—for example, whether it is more of a domestic Bildungsroman or a social critique—and their determinations about the nature of the novel influence how they bring the novel to the screen. And so, for example, if the screenwriter and the director interpret the focus of the novel to be on Emma and her "coming of age," then they will craft an adaptation in the style of a domestic Bildungsroman. Such a reading would highlight Emma's thoughts and feelings and show the world of Highbury primarily through her eyes. As a natural consequence, some of the supporting characters will be given less attention, and they may even be presented to the audience solely through the distorted lens of Emma's personally biased perspective, without the narrator to qualify or correct Emma's judgments.

On the other hand, if the production team thinks the real focus of the story is on social issues, or if the creators prefer characters such as Knightley or Jane Fairfax to Emma, then the narrative focus will shift away from Emma onto Highbury, and the adaptation will take greater care dramatizing the thoughts, feelings, and trials of the supporting characters than it will making manifest Emma's inner life. Either way, once the production team determines whether the novel is a social critique or a domestic Bildungsroman, that determination has a very real and practical effect on how the adaptation will take shape, and will influence the adaptation's plot structure, narrative perspective, and tone.

In terms of plot structure, there are essentially three basic ways in which *Emma* adaptations transform Austen's story: those that highlight Emma's relationship with Harriet Smith, those that focus on Emma's competitive relationship with Jane Fairfax, and those that attempt to grant equal weight to both storylines. Within the framework of these three possible plot structures, the transposition adaptations tend to present five possible narrative viewpoints: Emma's, Mr. Knightley's, an unidentified narrator's, the citizens of Highbury (a multitude of perspectives that unify into a single voice not wholly unlike a Chorus in Classical drama), or any combination of the above.

In each of the Austen adaptations, narrative perspective is assigned to a particular character in a number of ways. The characters who appear in the most scenes, by their nature, stake a claim to the audience's attention and emerge as central to the plot. Of course, a large role for a particular character does not necessarily mean that he or she claims the right to be called the narrator of the story. However, if the camera lingers on a character's face, or if private thoughts are revealed in voiceover, then that character has assumed a place of primacy in the unfolding of the story that is denied to other dramatic players who are kept at a greater distance from the audience. The importance a particular character assumes in a given narration is also determined by the nature and quality of the actor's performance.

Another factor in determining which narrative perspective a given adaptation favors is the inclusion of "invented scenes." Adaptations which desire to tell the story of *Emma* from the perspective of characters such as Mr. Knightley or Jane Fairfax tend to create additional dialogue and even entire scenes for these characters to further cement audience identification with them, often undercutting the empathy that viewers feel with Emma herself in the process. Writing about the Austen film canon in general, and the *Emma* films in particular, critic Sarah R. Morrison observes that the most interesting elements of the adaptations,

> ...are those invented scenes and bits of dialogue not found in the novels....It is in such marked departures from the novels that we can detect filmmakers

struggling with the differences in the two media—and in particular, with the lack of a narrator...(1)

Precisely because they are departures from the novel, "invented scenes" in a film adaptation act as strong indicators of the interpretive gloss that the production team wants to give the source story.

Additionally, the dramatic tone a given adaptation strikes is yet another indicator of the kind of reading it represents. Differences in tone from one transposition adaptation to another may be accounted for by differences in the plot structure and in the narrative voice.[4] However, tone is also influenced by the costumes, which can be historically accurate or fairy-tale like, and by the music, which could evoke jubilant emotions with up-tempo melodies or thoughtfulness with more sober strains (either through Regency-period compositions or an original motion picture score). Stage-bound productions that have little or no location shooting might create feelings of claustrophobia in the viewers, while location shooting could use natural sights to create a lush and verdant Highbury just as easily as it could paint the "Garden of England" in drab and forlorn colors. All of these dramatic elements influence the overall feel of the production, as well as contribute to a given adaptation's reading of the novel.

Those filmic adaptations that grant primacy to the narrative perspective of the citizens of Highbury (and that emphasize the Jane Fairfax subplot) are readings of the *Emma* story as a social critique. Such adaptations usually strike a darker tone, and they consistently realign the emphasis of the story, minimizing the attention paid to Emma's personal journey and focusing instead on the story of Highbury. Those adaptations that center most strongly on Emma's perspective are the domestic Bildungsroman adaptations. These adaptations concern themselves more particularly with Emma's thoughts and feelings, and have deliberately chosen to keep the audience at a distance from Jane Fairfax, who might distract too much from audience sympathy with Emma and the evils of *her* situation.

Based on the criteria outlined above, it is a relatively straightforward task to determine what kind of reading each adaptation of *Emma* represents. Once the reading is identified, it will be compared with comparable, pre-existing interpretations from writings of literary critics about the novel. In matching a reading taken from a film adaptation with a reading from literary criticism, my goal is to demonstrate the value and validity of judging film adaptations as interpretations and envisionings of the novel.

The first four adaptations of *Emma* that will be discussed in detail in this chapter–the 1948, 1954, 1960, and 1970 versions–may be categorized as *transposition* adaptations that represent readings of the novel as a social critique instead of as a domestic Bildungsroman.[5] Although all transposition adaptations share the same goal of dramatizing the events of the novel as faithfully as possible, they often diverge from one another in striking ways because of the different readings of the novel that they represent.

A discussion of the very first filmed adaptation of *Emma*, a 1948 television production written by Judy Campbell, follows.

The Judy Campbell Screenplay

"Emma." May 24, 1948. (BBC, live, B&W, 105 minutes).

Casey Finch and Peter Bowen, authors of "'The Tittle-Tattle of Highbury': Gossip and the Free Indirect Style in *Emma*," contend that Austen portrays gossip ambivalently in the novel, simultaneously trivializing it through scenes in which it is depicted as amusing and validating it by evoking a narrative style that is "gossipy" in nature. According to Finch and Bowen:

> Itself never identifiably authorized—who, after all, is ever the originator of a rumor?—gossip functions as a powerful form of authority because its source is nowhere and everywhere at once. (Finch 545)

The first *Emma* adaptation made for television–a live BBC TV broadcast that aired between 8:30 p.m. and 10:15 p.m. on Sunday, May 23, 1948–dramatizes gossip in action with a similar ambivalence.[6] Screenwriter Judy Campbell, who also starred as Emma, treats gossip seriously as a social phenomenon but also sees the funny (or even the endearing) side of tittle-tattle.[7] Her screenplay captures both the charm of Highbury and its rigid class structure, detailing the light and dark sides of the community through showcasing the gossipy conversations that unfold in Ford's shop. The scenes in which Miss Bates and Mrs. Ford exchange rumors as they conduct their business in the store demonstrate how gossip is used as a source of news, as a means of knitting the community together, and as a manner of influencing the course of people's lives in town.

Since the program's comparatively brief running time and the studio-bound nature of the production demanded that the action of the novel be compressed, significant cuts and alterations to the story were made. Interestingly enough, the changes to the story structure that Campbell made in her screenplay would later become standard alterations for most of the adaptations that would follow. For example, here, as in the majority of versions, Emma's sister Isabella and brother-in-law John Knightley are mentioned but do not appear, and the Box Hill excursion and the strawberry picking at Donwell Abbey are dramatized as taking place during a single afternoon. As Sue Parrill observes, the most notable features of this particular version include a larger-than-usual role for Mr. Perry (who, oddly enough, does not mention any plans for a carriage) and a final scene that shows a post-nuptial kiss between Emma and Mr. Knightley (Parrill 111). The scenes featuring Emma alone are largely excised, and the scenes staged at Ford's, here presented as Miss Bates' home territory, seem to loom larger as a result.

The special attention that Campbell pays to Miss Bates and, by extension, Miss Bates' niece Jane Fairfax, moves the focus of the story away from the title character, and offers a more distant, mediated view of Emma's gradual transformation than the novel does. Part of this special attention appears deliberate, as the screenplay is clearly more interested in portraying, in detail, the financial and emotional crisis that Jane is enduring, and is less interested in Emma's confining situation. The consequence of this significant emphasis is that Campbell's version of *Emma* may be interpreted as reading the novel as a social critique instead of as a domestic Bildungsroman.

Campbell's screenplay simultaneously brings class issues to the forefront and creates a critical distance between the audience and Emma by preserving the narrator, who–speaking as an audio-track voiceover–analyzes Emma's actions and situation, as well as presents important information about the society of Highbury as a whole. It begins with a narrative voiceover reading an abbreviated, and slightly rewritten, version of the opening paragraphs of the novel that introduces the setting as Surrey, 1816, and explains Emma's background and current situation. As the camera focuses on Mr. Woodhouse snoozing by the fire and Emma playing the pianoforte, the narrator relates the circumstances of the death of Mrs. Woodhouse, the departure of Isabella, and the recent marriage of Miss Taylor, leaving the "handsome, clever, and rich" Miss Woodhouse very lonely indeed. As one of the few adaptations to include a narrator—the others being the 1995 *Clueless*, which includes voiceover narration by the heroine, and the 1996 Douglas McGrath *Emma*, which features "bookend" narrations by Greta Scacchi—this first dramatized version helps clarify the history of the central characters and their position within Highbury society with ease and immediacy.[8] Later adaptations, by contrast, tend to bombard viewers with a parade of characters who seem to have a specific position in society, and in relation to Emma herself, that is not readily apparent.[9]

In addition, information about class and social mores that is critical to the development of the central themes of the story, as well as to the advancement of the plot, is conveyed through the depiction of gossip in Highbury society. As mentioned earlier, it is Ford's which serves as a focal point for the initiation and spread of rumor and insinuation, assuming an unparalleled importance as a window into the complexities of Highbury society. It is in Ford's that we find the girls of Miss Goddard's school staring lovingly at the handsome Mr. Elton, and Miss Bates and Mrs. Ford expressing surprise that he didn't marry the woman whom they thought he was going to marry (presumably Emma). In another Ford's scene, Harriet inquires after Elizabeth Martin during a discussion with Mrs. Ford, an inquiry that Mrs. Ford later reports to Robert Martin, encouraging him to believe that he still has hope with Harriet. Finally, and most importantly, Miss Bates keeps groups of Ford's patrons up-to-date on the comings and goings of Frank, Jane, and Mr. Elton, with subtle commentary on the odd discrepancies in their behaviors included free of charge. As these moments can attest, this adaptation emphasizes the feminine community of Highbury and Miss Bates' all-important role as the gossip equivalent of town crier. The result is an adaptation that treats gossip seriously as a legitimate source of news and social pressure, and that appears to lightly mock the practice by giving cute, sly dialogue to the gossips.[10]

Writing about Austen's depiction of gossip in the novel, Finch and Bowen observe:

> ...gossip in Highbury derives its power neither from the opinion of a single individual nor from the dictates of an identifiable institution—the police, the law courts—but from the collectivity of voices that whisper about neighbors in private rooms and across gateways. Just as the free indirect style of the novel functions as a form of narrative surveillance over the novel's characters, so gossip in the novel deploys a mild surveillance over the members of the Highbury community. Through covert insinuation rather than overt pressure, gossip delineates a circle of consensual values. (Finch 549)

As powerful as Emma is in the Highbury community depicted in the novel, she is far from above the social pressures exerted by the gossipers. Indeed, Finch and Bowen suggest that the climax of Austen's work, in which Emma discovers her love for Mr. Knightley during a moment of epiphany, is brought about by the final, and long-delayed, harmonizing of Emma's personal desires with the expectations of gossipy Highbury society. For Finch and Bowen, "Free indirect style has here literally created the space of the unconscious as the natural source of Emma's inner desires, which, naturally enough, now discover themselves perfectly aligned with the overriding social imperative the novel has been at pains to establish from the start: 'Mr. Knightley must marry no one but herself!'" (554).

In the novel, Emma certainly feels social pressure to marry Knightley, partly from the gossip phenomenon that Finch and Bowen discuss, but also from the active competition of Mrs. Elton, which threatens to marginalize Emma's position in society. It is no accident, for example, that Emma's first conscious recognition of Mr. Knightley's attractive bearing follows shortly after the newlywed Eltons lead the first dance at the Crown Inn Ball, taking Emma's rightful place as the star of the party merely because they are married and she is not. To what extent the various social pressures brainwash Emma into *believing* herself to be in love with Mr. Knightley because she *must* be in love with Mr. Knightley is unclear. To what extent those pressures come from local gossip is also unclear—although we do know that the Westons plot to see Emma married to Frank, Elton and Knightley plot to have her for themselves, and the locals as a whole are eagerly watching to see if her new surname with be Churchill, Elton, or Knightley.

As the critics discussed in the previous chapter demonstrate, there is disagreement as to how to read the pressure placed upon Emma to marry. For Wayne Booth, marriage to the excellent Mr. Knightley is exactly what a character as wonderful as Emma deserves. Other critics expressed reservations that Emma was too independent to be married and would be unhappy wedded to Mr. Knightley. Campbell's screenplay, with its kind-natured portrait of the matchmaking gossips who whisper about Emma's love life, seems to take the more positive view and assume that marriage to Mr. Knightley is good for Emma. Therefore, the gossips who encourage the match are acting in Emma's best interest. In a way, Campbell's gossipy characters are not all that different from the readers of the novel themselves, who also tend to eagerly follow Emma's romantic adventures and wonder which eligible bachelor Jane Austen will marry her to in the end. Such readers enjoy "the tensions of the story and the illusions of autonomous self" that delay the romantic union of Emma and Mr. Knightley just as they "enjoy the pleasure of closure, the harmonious reconciliation of self to society" when the lovers finally come together in the end (Finch and Bowen 554-555).

In Campbell's screenplay, gossip is generally shown to be benign and is consistently portrayed as beneficial to the community. Campbell's gossips share the main concerns of Emma and Mr. Knightley; their chief interests are matchmaking and making known the needs of the distressed and disenfranchised. While Emma does not participate in the gossiping that takes place in Ford's, (underscoring her alienation from other women discussed by several critics in the previous chapter,) sensitive *men* lend their ears to the gossips.[11] And so, both Mr. Knightley and Robert Martin learn vital information about the plights of Jane and Harriet through the grapevine at Ford's. In fact, the gossips at Ford's may even be said to work in opposition to Emma as a populist alternative to her queenly influence in Highbury. While Emma wishes to disrupt the marriage between Harriet Smith and Robert Martin, Mrs. Ford works to bring the two separated lovers back together again by hinting to Robert that he is still loved. While Emma declares her wish to remain single, Miss Bates and Mrs. Ford wonder in whispered tones whom she will marry. And while Emma shows indifference to Jane's ill health and financially dire situation, those at Ford's are concerned with little else. Since Mr. Knightley's goals align so perfectly with the goals of the gossips, he is symboli-cally linked with them, although he does not engage in any gossip at Ford's himself.

Although there is much gossiping about developments in Mr. Elton's love life, most of the gossip in this adaptation concerns Jane Fairfax–particularly her health, her love life, her livelihood, her taci-turn nature, and her mysterious trips to the post office. Jane's com-plicated back story from the novel–which includes the death of her parents, her life with Col. Campbell, the marriage of Mr. Dixon to Miss Campbell, her brush with death on a boating excursion, her fears of becoming a governess, and the cancelled trip to Ireland–are difficult to relate on screen, and virtually every adaptation fails to rise to the challenge of presenting this material clearly and with adequate dramatic weight. The highlights are tolerably well presented here, however, and the inclusion of the oft-excised boating accident anec-dote helps validate Emma's fanciful romantic pairing of Mr. Dixon and Jane as tragic lovers. Jane's loaded comparison between the slave trade and the governess trade survives the translation to the screen (when it, too, is often omitted), dramatically emphasizing how hope-less she feels in her situation. Also included is the usually eliminated romantic moment that Jane shares with Frank as he is supposed to be tending to the rivet in Mrs. Bates' spectacles.

In fact, Campbell's screenplay places such dramatic emphasis on Jane that Emma's concerns are considerably muted; this is especially true because Jane features as a central point of debate in virtually every argument between Emma and Mr. Knightley. Mr. Knightley criticizes Emma for not befriending Jane during their argument over her interference with Robert Martin's proposal, and he also spends as much time warning her of the secret connection between Frank and Jane as he does scolding her for insulting Miss Bates.[12] Knightley's constant evocation of Jane Fairfax's name in this version gives great weight to Mrs. Weston's theory that the two are destined for mar-riage. And, when Mrs. Weston voices her suspicions to Emma, the re-action borders on violent:

Emma: Nonsense, he does not care about Jane Fairfax–I'm sure he does not.

Ms. [sic] Weston: All the same I should not wonder if it was to end in his marrying her!

[Emma clenches her fists and shakes them at her.]

Mrs. Weston: Do not beat me! (Campbell 56)

It is hard to imagine how this scene would have "played out" on screen. I cannot visualize Mrs. Weston speaking those lines in genuine terror, but there is a seriousness to the dialogue, and to Emma's still-subconscious fears of losing Mr. Knightley, that makes it equally hard to imagine the scene played purely as two old friends having a jolly laugh at one another's expense. Since the scene ends here, no subsequent interaction between the two characters can provide further context. Despite its abrupt ending, the scene is significant because it hints that Emma's as-yet-undiscovered feelings for Mr. Knightley are passionate and internalized, and that Emma will not ultimately be pushed into marrying someone that she does not love.

Still, Mr. Knightley's attentions to Jane Fairfax are not included in this adaptation solely as a means of making Emma jealous and keeping the viewers at home in suspense. His attentions to Jane in this adaptation do indeed stem from "disinterested benevolence," and he is not the only one in Highbury to fuss over Jane Fairfax in this version. Mr. Perry, the apothecary, is worried about her medical condition, noting that she sports "the pallor of the Metropolis" and assuring her that "Our Highbury airs will soon restore the color to those cheeks." Attention of an even more stifling kind is given Jane by Mrs. Elton, who serves admirably in this version as yet another example of a flawed teacher and mother figure—outpacing Mrs. Weston and Emma as the worst patron in Highbury with her coercive insistence that Jane Fairfax take a position as a governess.

To the extent that the Campbell screenplay emphasizes Jane's story over Emma's, it rewrites the novel and recasts Jane as the central figure of the story. Since Jane is a passive heroine, however, the active protagonists in this version are those who come to her aid, namely Mr. Knightley, Miss Bates, and Mrs. Ford. An intriguing consequence of this realignment of the story is that those who torment Jane emerge as even more villainous here than they do in the book.

As such, the jealous and neglecting Emma seems less sympathetic here, Frank Churchill is simultaneously more childlike and predatory, and Mrs. Elton's attempts to get Jane work as a governess seem wholly sinister and not remotely motivated by a desire to help.

While great attention is given to Jane Fairfax, Campbell gives comparatively little attention to Frank Churchill's motivations. Since the screenplay does not excuse his actions, they seem all the harder to comprehend. If one is inclined to forgive Frank for his lies and for his abuse of Jane, it is because of his fears of being disinherited by a rich, cold-hearted aunt. However, this screenplay emphasizes his duty to Mrs. Churchill as an invalid instead of presenting his fear of falling victim to her excessively class-conscious views. Compounding the problem, this screenplay (like virtually all subsequent adaptations of *Emma*) is remiss in providing full and comprehensible accounts of Mr. Weston's first marriage and his clash with Mrs. Churchill, the inevitable consequence being that Mr. Weston is portrayed as a bland, affable character who (for no apparent reason) lacks the full confidence of a son who (for no apparent reason) does not share his surname. This screenplay has Knightley voice fears that Frank might take after Mrs. Churchill, but he does not explain the cause for his concern. Mr. Weston begins to describe Mrs. Churchill as a constant thorn in his side, but Mrs. Elton interrupts him to discuss the barouche-landau before he explains how and why. Frank gallantly assumes the blame for the salacious rumors of Jane's "relationship" with Mr. Dixon, letting Emma off the hook, but he emerges less as a fully realized character and more as a distillation of Emma's "cattiest" and most immature traits. In the context of this adaptation, Frank symbolizes gossip at its most destructive—as slander that adds misery to Jane's already pitiful situation, nearly driving her out of town.

However, this version's emphasis on Mrs. Elton and Frank as Jane's chief tormentors does not deflect all blame from Emma. In fact, Judy Campbell's script is one of the few screenplays that faults Emma far more for flirting with Frank Churchill at Box Hill than it berates her for insulting Miss Bates. Campbell dramatizes a scene from Jane Fairfax's perspective that is written from Emma's point of view in the novel, in which Jane refuses Emma's gift of arrowroot after the Box Hill excursion and tells Miss Bates, "I am not in need of kindness from Miss Woodhouse." One might argue that one of the reasons that this scene does not appear in the novel, as such, is that Austen was careful to shield readers from scenes that would provoke strongly hateful emotions towards Emma.[13] Of course, readers with active imaginations could well re-envision several key scenes in the novel from Jane's perspective–particularly the Box Hill segment–and feel vicarious pain for Jane and anger on her behalf towards Emma. By including this scene, Campbell's adaptation brings Jane's pain to the forefront.

Campbell's adaptation draws further attention to the destructiveness of Emma's behavior by offering the audience a more intimate look at another character in the novel whom Emma's actions wound, Robert Martin. In the book, Austen cleverly does not allow readers to feel the full force of the consequences of Emma's interference in the relationship between Harriet Smith and Robert Martin. Robert Martin is described physically through bits of Harriet's dialogue and through Emma's biased eyes when she watches him from afar, but he is not described by the narrator, who is a far more reliable source than either Harriet or Emma. Also, he never speaks for himself, but has his dialogue filtered through Knightley, Harriet, and the narrator. We know that he is a good enough letter writer that Emma cannot, in good conscience, allow herself to attribute the authorship of the proposal to his sister, but we are not allowed to read the letter ourselves. We would never be able to forgive Emma for standing in Robert's way if we saw for ourselves the purity of his love and the beautiful way in which he expresses it; consider how much sympathy Austen evokes for Captain Wentworth and Mr. Darcy when she allows readers the opportunity to examine their letters to the heroines of *Persuasion* and *Pride and Prejudice*.

And yet, Campbell's script gives us some inkling of what Robert Martin is like, as she allows us to experience the character with greater immediacy than we are allowed to in the novel. Unlike in the novel, the screenplay dramatizes the scene when Martin asks Mr. Knightley whether he is financially ready to propose to Harriet. Martin is polite, serious, and calls Mr. Knightley "sir" repeatedly, and Mr. Knightley says he is "honored to offer advice," but the brevity of the conversation suggests that their relationship is formal and hardly the equivalent of a friendship. Later on, Robert Martin is seen shopping at Ford's when Frank Churchill bursts in carrying a faint Harriet, fresh from her unsettling encounter with the gypsies. While Austen's prose pokes fun at the romance-novel "heroism" of Frank Churchill in coming to Harriet's rescue, this version includes a new scene in which Robert Martin vows to protect Harriet from further harm at the hands of vagabonds, and it is a segment clearly meant to be taken seriously as a sign of Martin's continued love for Harriet:

> **Martin:** I will see them removed from the parish…they'll be out within the hour. I shall make certain of that—tell Miss Harriet she need have no fear, ma'am—villainous rascals. (Campbell 64)

By centering its attention on gossip in Highbury, Campbell's screenplay presents a reading of the novel not all that different from Finch's and Bowen's. Although essentially a transposition adaptation that does not alter the text as radically as a commentary adaptation or an analogy adaptation, Campbell's version nevertheless presents an imaginative and intelligent dramatization of Austen's narrative that illuminates the role that Highbury gossips play in the story. For Campbell, the Highbury gossips serve a useful purpose in society, despite how trivial they might, at first, appear. Inasmuch as gossips such as Miss Bates and Mrs. Ford subtly push Emma towards a union with Mr. Knightley, they aid in bringing about her ultimate happiness. Since the gossips draw attention to Jane Fairfax's situation, they alert Mr. Knightley to a woman in distress and see to it that she is looked after in her time of need. And Ford's, as a central meeting place for the Highbury community, alerts Robert Martin when he might be of service to the accosted Harriet, just as the gossips of Ford's give him hope that one day he may win her hand. While the portrayal of gossip is at times tongue-in-cheek, and while Frank Churchill is included as an acknowledgment of the potentially destructive side of gossip, the screenplay takes an intriguing and sympathetic view of tittle-tattle. In fact, for Campbell, rumor and gossip serve as a means through which the less fortunate members of Highbury may gather information, aid one another, and advance their own aims, irrespective of whether those aims align with those of a Miss Emma Woodhouse or a Mr. Knightley.

The NBC Kraft Television Theatre *Emma*

"Emma." November 24, 1954. (NBC, B&W, 60 minutes).

"Emma is simply a figure of fun."

Or so Reginald Farrer maintains in a 1917 *Quarterly Review* piece (24). He writes that the goal of Jane Austen's novel *Emma* is to dramatize:

> ...the gradual humiliation of self-conceit, through a long self-wrought succession of disasters, serious in effect, but keyed in Comedy throughout. Emma herself, in fact, is never to be taken seriously. And it is only those who have not realized this who will be put off by her absurdities, her snobberies, her misdirected mischievous ingenuities....To conciliate affection for a character, not because of its charms, but in defiance of its defects, it's the loftiest aim of the comic spirit. (24)

Farrer's view of *Emma* seems to underpin the first American-based television adaptation of the novel, an hour-long live production broadcast on November 24, 1954 as an episode of *NBC Kraft Television Theatre*.[14] Certainly actress Felicia Montealegre plays the title character for laughs. In her pigtails and puffy-sleeved dresses out of a Disney cartoon film, Montealegre emphasizes all that is infantile and ridiculous about Emma, making her twitter with delight at the beauty of Miss Taylor's wedding spread and squeal with joyous mockery at the illiteracy of Harriet's yeoman beau. And Emma is not the only character from the novel that is portrayed as silly in this version of the story. Peter Cookson plays a bi-polar Knightley who, at one moment, is laughing and carefree and, in another moment, seems so furious with Emma that Mrs. Weston (here looking like a chubby Mother Goose figure) fears he will become physically violent.[15] Meanwhile, Sarah Marshall plays Harriet just as inconsistently. Sometimes she appears to be a starry-eyed and dreamy-voiced innocent and other times she seems to be a sly and scheming figure. Her beau, William Larkins (an inexplicably renamed Robert Martin) is also a quaint, earthy farmhand who enjoys waxing poetic about the birth of a litter of pigs ("We got the finest litter of pigs you ever saw...from Polly, your pig, Harriet. Oh, bless her old sow's heart!").[16] He is even chummy with Knightley, shaking his employer's hand firmly during the scene in which he asks Knightley whether or not he should propose to Harriet, proclaiming, "You, Mr. Knightley, to hear me out and counsel me, are the best friend a man ever had."

Assuming that the dialogue is not ad-libbed, the teleplay by Martine Bartlett and Peter Donat (who play Mrs. Elton and Larkins in the production) emphasizes the comic elements of the novel while downplaying the tragic. Their teleplay omits virtually all of the supporting characters, including Miss Bates and Mrs. Bates, Robert Martin, Frank Churchill, Jane Fairfax, Isabella and John Knightley, and the gypsies. In fact, in the fashion of the *Wuthering Heights* movie directed by William Wyler, the Kraft adaptation opts to adapt primarily the first portion of the novel rather than attempting to render the entire novel dramatically in sixty minutes.

In place of many of the more serious elements of the novel that have been eliminated (such as the Jane and Frank subplot), this adaptation presents a series of originally conceived comic interludes that contribute to its broadly farcical tone. These moments include Mr. Woodhouse repeatedly moaning in sorrow at the Weston wedding so that the whole assembly could hear him, Knightley's wincing with pain in front of Serle the butler when he overhears Harriet and Emma's "caterwauling," and—most incredibly—the moment when Harriet rushes into Hartfield, frantic that "Old Jim" the bull has gotten free and that William has had a terrible time catching him, inspiring the following memorable line from Knightley: "If I can't rescue Emma from herself I can rescue William from a bull." When Sue Parill refers to this moment as having "shades of *The Beverly Hillbillies*" in her book *Jane Austen on Film and Television* (113) she is not exaggerating.[17]

Because so many of the darker elements of the story have been lost on the way to the small screen, and because this version includes so many original comic moments, the story becomes a silly romp focused primarily on the love triangle between Harriet, Mr. Elton, and William Larkins, and on Emma's attempts to steer Harriet away from Larkins and towards Elton. While few expect film and television adaptations to scrupulously preserve every single character, scene, and bit of thematic minutiae presented by the author in the source material, this particular adaptation goes so far in its pruning of Austen's novel that it effectively eviscerates the work and would offend the sensibilities of almost any Austen scholar. As Parrill writes:

> The Kraft Television Theatre adaptation can hardly be considered among the best cinematic presentations of Emma....The adaptation gives little indication of the novel's core of ideas. It exploits only the most superficial elements of the novel. (114)

In her review of the adaptation, Parrill makes accurate objections to the massive cuts made to the story, the silliness of the tone, and the lackluster quality of the production as a whole. Also, Parrill observes that the class conflict that is so central to the source novel is misunderstood and misrepresented by the American production team—a complaint that critics such as Carol M. Dole have leveled at more contemporary American Austen adaptations as well. Parrill writes:

> The introduction of William Larkins as a country bumpkin makes for an incongruous kind of low comedy that is typical of American television of that time. A peculiarly American twist to the handling of Larkins' character resides in the emphasis on his cultural and intellectual inferiority, rather than class difference. Larkins, however, reveals no sense of his inferiority or shows any marked deference to either Emma or Mr. Knightley. As for Harriet, there is no reference to her being of low origins. Her inferiority resides in her silliness and her lack of polished manners (Parrill, 114).

While I agree with Parrill's analysis of the adaptation as a whole, I would suggest that certain moments in the production evoke class concerns, but in a less sophisticated and less coherent manner than Austen would. For example, Harriet's social status is unclear, but several large and inconsistent hints as to her background are dropped, leaving viewers confused as to the real state of affairs. Harriet seems to be greatly inferior to Emma in class and social status when she shows awe at Emma's wealth, asks Mrs. Goddard what a footman is, and creeps reluctantly into Hartfield as if she were an intruder expecting to be found out. Yet these clues are undercut by the revelation that—in this version of the story—she and Emma took music lessons together with Mrs. Goddard "around the quadrille" and have been reunited for the first time as young women at the Weston wedding. Several male members of the upper class also observe Harriet at the wedding and express a romantic interest in her by staring, and one even remarks, "Whoever she is she is uncommon pretty," giving weight to Emma's theory that Harriet's looks could land her a wealthy husband after all.[18] Also, whether it was by accident or design, this adaptation presents the Eltons as sympathetic figures. Their opposition to Emma, who is clearly more socially and economically powerful than they are, raises some class issues that might provoke meditations from thoughtful viewers but which are not fully explored by the program itself.

The chief reason that the Kraft adaptation of *Emma* is so difficult to discuss as a reading of the novel is that, while the production team as a whole seems intent on making the story a laugh-riot, several key actors in the broadcast appear to treat the proceedings seriously. Roddy McDowall's interpretation of Mr. Elton is entirely in earnest, adding a dramatic weight to his character that no other character in this version (including Emma and Mr. Knightley) has. Also, while the actresses playing Harriet and Mrs. Elton (Sarah Marshall and Martine Bartlett) usually seem to be striving to make their characters amusing, there are subtle shadings to their performances that make their characters still more serious than the two main characters.

While the Judy Campbell adaptation draws attention away from Emma and towards the other residents of Highbury on the screenplay level, the Kraft adaptation refocuses audience attention away from Emma because of a more intangible factor—the nature and quality of the actors' performances. Although the means are different, the end result is the same: this adaptation, like the Judy Campbell adaptation before it, redefines the protagonist of the story. While the Judy Campbell adaptation offers its sympathy to Jane Fairfax and her allies, (Mr. Knightley, Miss Bates, Mr. Perry, and Mrs. Ford,) this Kraft adaptation aligns its sympathies with the social climbers—Harriet, Mr. Elton, and the new Mrs. Elton (formerly Augusta Hawkins).

Since the Kraft adaptation treats the supporting characters with greater attention and seriousness than it treats Emma, it plays as more of a social critique reading of the novel than as a domestic Bildungsroman. Emma makes mistakes in this adaptation, failing to register that Mr. Elton is in love with her and that Harriet is in love with Mr. Knightley, but she is not shown to grow much emotionally or intellectually during the course of this adaptation. If this Emma learns anything from the wise patriarch Mr. Knightley, it is that she should not be too comfortable associating with members of the lower classes who have powerful social ambitions. Such inappropriately intimate associations at the very least cause pain to the likes of Elton and Harriet, whose hopes of marrying into stewardship of Hartfield and Donwell Abbey Emma first encourages and then dashes.

As observed earlier, one of the reasons Mr. Elton emerges as sympathetic in this version of *Emma* is that Roddy McDowall is so superb in the part. McDowall is the best of the actors to play Mr. Elton on film to date, and he outshines all of the other cast members in the Kraft adaptation with his subtly nuanced performance. McDowall presents an Elton whose love for Emma seems genuine, and his marriage to Augusta Hawkins is presented as a mistake made while he was on the rebound. This is a striking contrast from the Elton of the novel, who bears a far closer resemblance to the Mr. Collins character from *Pride and Prejudice*, in his uncanny ability to substitute one wife for another with little or no emotional cost to himself so long as the dowry is right.[19]

Admittedly, even in the Kraft production Knightley observes that Elton is eager to marry well, and jokes with friends that Elton is a little too eager to please ladies. Also, Elton's snobbish reaction to Miss Smith, the "everyone has their level" speech, is preserved here when it is sometimes cut from other, more serious adaptations. Still, there is a marked difference between the pleasant attentions he offers Harriet (glancing at her as he begins reading aloud Byron's "She Walks in Beauty Like the Night," theatrically proclaiming to those gathered at the Weston wedding that she will make a beautiful bride when she catches Miss Taylor's bouquet) and the longing looks he gives Emma and the tender whispers he slips into when he speaks to her. During the proposal scene, McDowall's Elton seems sincere in his affections throughout, demonstrating lust for Emma and jubilation at the thought of their imminent union, before his emotions turn to surprise, anger, and dejection. Later on, when Emma explains to Mr. Knightley what has transpired, he scolds her for encouraging Mr. Elton by inviting him to so many meals and parties and asks her, "What did you expect but that he'd fall in love with you?", suggesting that the perceptive Mr. Knightley has decided that the clergyman has a heart to wound after all.

Also interesting in this version is Mrs. Elton, who is comically portrayed by co-scriptwriter Martine Bartlett. This Mrs. Elton appears in only one scene, in which Mr. Elton introduces her to Mr. Woodhouse and Emma at Hartfield, and the only reason she appears to have been spared the culling that other secondary characters fell victim to is that she serves the purpose of reassuring viewers that Mr. Elton has found love after all, despite being led on by Emma (and Mrs. Elton is funny, and all funny elements of the story have been scrupulously preserved in the script). Her dialogue is close enough to the dialogue from the novel; she speaks of having a full calendar, having to downgrade from two barouche-landaus to one, the "formidable" nature of country life, and the necessity of music and watercolors.[20]

As with Roddy McDowall's performance, the change in the character comes not from the script but in how the lines are delivered. Here Mrs. Elton seems nervous the entire time she is at Hartfield, and she seems to be talking herself up mainly as a means of fishing for compliments from an audience she partly expects to be hostile. That she keeps asking Mr. Elton to vouch for the truth of each of her statements suggests insecurity, and her nervous laugh hints at greater depths of personality than the shallow-seeming dialogue would attest to. Far from declaring herself an enemy of Emma, she expresses a wish to visit every Tuesday and, when the idea is not greeted with enthusiasm from Emma, she beams, curtsies, and flees from the sitting room, dragging Mr. Elton after her. Again, the scene is presented as broad comedy, but any version of the story that fails to show Mrs. Elton in her darker moments, especially when she bullies Jane Fairfax or encourages her husband to snub Harriet, is a version that leaves viewers feeling sorry for the nervous newcomer.

Interestingly enough, while the Eltons emerge as virtual victims at the hands of Emma, Harriet herself has never seemed so consistently ambitious.[21] In the novel, Harriet is skeptical of Emma's plans to marry her to Elton, believing herself to be unworthy of the match even as she fails to prevent herself from developing feelings for Elton. It is only after the dance at the Crown Inn, when Mr. Knightley rescues her from Elton's rebuff, that she begins to love Mr. Knightley. And it is only after a confused conversation with Emma, with misunderstandings on both sides, that Harriet begins to believe herself capable of capturing Knightley's fancy and becoming mistress of Donwell Abbey. In this version, which does not feature the Crown Inn segment, Harriet appears to fall in love with Mr. Knightley at first sight, seduced by his wealth and upper-class polish, and she refuses William Larkins' (read: Robert Martin's) proposal primarily because she is already head-over-heels for Knightley. Hence, when Emma suggests that she should refuse Larkins' proposal, Harriet takes even less manipulating than usual to come around to Emma's way of thinking. In fact, she talks herself into turning down Larkins as much, if not more so, than Emma does.[22]

The last time viewers see Harriet in this version is the scene in which she informs Emma that she is in love with Mr. Knightley. Instead of seeing Harriet personally after this point, all news of her fate is filtered through Mr. Knightley who, in the final scene, tells Emma of Harriet's engagement to William Larkins before segueing into his own proposal to Emma. The exchange concerning Harriet happens in this fashion:

> **Knightley:** I must admit that I had a hand in bringing them together.
>
> **Emma:** [amused and feeling vindicated that even Knightley can play matchmaker.] You mean you made the match yourself?
>
> **Knightley:** Yes, yes. And it is a good thing, Emma. I believe that Harriet has always loved him and he's never stopped hoping that one day she'd accept him. And he's a good man, Emma.

Based on all that came before this exchange, and considering the fact that Harriet is not the one telling Emma this, I believe that Harriet is actually not in love with Larkins, but chooses to settle for him once she sees that Mr. Knightley was courting her on Larkins' behalf and not on his own. When I think of the Kraft adaptation in purely evaluative terms, I do not object to this departure from the novel on the basis that it is a departure, but I do wish that it was executed more skillfully.

And yet, even this dramatically ineffective presentation of Harriet as a somewhat socially ambitious figure serves my reading of the novel by making me question just how vast a departure it is from Austen's characterization of Harriet after all. Indeed, this Kraft Harriet inspires me to reflect upon Janet Todd's observation that readers

are allowed only a mediated exposure to Harriet and are never afforded the opportunity to get to know the *real* woman behind the
hype. Distrusting the romanticized vision of Harriet offered by
Emma, Janet Todd constructs a particularly disturbing interpretation
of the character that sees her as akin to the monster in Mary Shelley's
novel *Frankenstein* (283). In her *Frankenstein* analogy, Todd charts Harriet's gradual transformation from someone "humble" and "totally
subservient to Emma" into a "smug" and "presumptuous woman
who insists on inappropriate equality," first by trying to "please
Emma by denigrating Jane," and then by "assuming the matchmaking herself" and choosing Mr. Knightley as her future husband (Todd
287-288). Todd cites as the culminating moment of this monstrous
metamorphosis Harriet' s boldest moment, in which she rebukes
Emma for mistaking Frank Churchill as the object of her affection and
physically turns away from Emma for the first time:

> Hopeful of Mr. Knightley's affection, Harriet turns on her Pygmalion, and
> the experience shatters Emma....Like Frankenstein, Emma has created a
> monster she heartily wishes destroyed, but which instead seems about to
> take from her all she values. Unlike Frankenstein, Emma stays somewhat
> responsible for her creation and she learns from her error...Like the
> monster, Harriet is the product of isolation and fear, created to fill the needs
> of her creator alone. She exists against the social order of things as the
> monster had contravened the natural. Inevitably both monsters assert
> themselves and the assertion rebounds on their creators. As a result, the
> monster's self or the creator's selfishness must be destroyed. (Todd 288)

Of course, most readers see Harriet's dreams of becoming Mrs.
Knightley as nigh impossible given her mysterious parentage and
lineage—ultimately revealed to be far humbler than Emma had antici-
pated—so Harriet's disturbing ambition to supplant Emma would appear to be doomed from the outset, given the social realities of the
time.[23]
In effect, the mistake that Emma makes in this social critique adaptation is similar to the mistake that Maaja A. Stewart sees Emma
making in the novel. Stewart writes that Emma, in "her interactions
with Harriet Smith and Miss Taylor-Mrs. Weston...ignores economic
and class differences and attempts to confer her own status on the
other women" thereby mimicking "the role of a man by assuming
control over the status of women" (153). Also, as Beth F. Tobin has
observed, by "assuming the role of match-maker, Emma assumes the

right to tinker with the very delicate social and economic adjustments involved in arranging a marriage in a highly structured world" (480). This adaptation portrays Emma as deluded in thinking that she has the influence to blur class and status distinctions enough to success-fully orchestrate a match between Harriet and Mr. Elton. The end re-sult is that Harriet is disappointed in her desire to marry Mr. Knightley and Mr. Elton's heart is broken when he realizes that Emma never intended to have him for herself. In fact, despite the comic tone of the production, (and its insistence that Mr. Knightley is a more suitable mate for Emma than Mr. Elton,) Mr. Elton in particu-lar emerges as sympathetic in the Kraft version, giving a bittersweet quality to an ending that sees him fail to win Emma.

Because the Kraft *Emma* is not readily available for viewing, I have taken great care in describing it, and I have been honest about its glaring dramatic defects. Indeed, I have stated that I agree with Sue Parrill that it is a poorly mounted production. However, I have also treated seriously the implications of its seemingly unorthodox por-trayals of Harriet and the Eltons, and have found those portrayals to be both fitting and intriguing. In its handling of these characters, the Kraft *Emma* challenges Emma's dominating perspective from the novel, opening up the possibility that the motivations and actions of certain characters—whom Emma is either biased against or in favor of—may be misrepresented by the heroine. In this manner, the Kraft adaptation can offer a rewarding interpretation of the novel to those who are willing to forgive its dramatic shortcomings.

Vincent Tilsley's Screenplay & the "Lost" Adaptation (1960)

"Emma." Feb. 26–April 6, 1960. (BBC, B&W, 180 minutes);
"Emma" August 26, 1960 (CBS, 60 minutes).

Critic Sarah R. Morrison cited "those invented scenes and bits of dia-logue not found in the novels" as the most intriguing elements of an adaptation of *Emma* (1). For her, the ways in which an adaptation de-parts from a source text is more interesting to discuss than they ways in which it faithfully retells the story. Certainly all of the adaptations of *Emma* include invented scenes and dialogue that shape their presentation of Austen's story. As the Judy Campbell and Kraft adaptations have already demonstrated, sometimes these new scenes are more dramatically satisfying and more brilliantly conceived than at other times. One of the most remarkable features of the third consecutive *Emma* adaptation, a live BBC miniseries broadcast in 1960, is that the screenplay creates a number of new scenes that cast Highbury's ruling class in a truly unsympathetic light.[24] While at times melodramatic in style, and hardly up to the standards of Austen's wonderful prose, the new scenes crafted by screenwriter Vincent Tilsley present inventive and entertaining perspectives on the relationships between the central characters in the novel.

The longer running-time of the Tilsley adaptation (it was a six-part miniseries with a total running time of 180 minutes) helped facilitate a more complete rendering of the events of the novel than either the Campbell or the Kraft adaptations that preceded it was able to. And yet, rather than try to fill the running time of the miniseries exclusively with material from the novel, Tilsley's screenplay includes a number of almost entirely original scenes. Focusing on the darker side of Emma and Mr. Knightley, as well as on the villainy of Mrs. Churchill and Mrs. Elton, the new scenes show the privileged characters from the novel neglecting or actively tormenting the members of the Highbury community who depend upon them for support. Those characters who emerge more sympathetically as a result of the "invented scenes" include the often charitably rendered Jane Fairfax, Harriet Smith, Robert Martin, and Miss Bates, but this time even Mr. Weston and Frank Churchill are portrayed sympathetically as victims of a failed patronage system. The Tilsley screenplay naturally suggests that the ruling class is protecting its own sovereignty when it abuses these more dependent figures, but it complicates the issue further by hinting that sexual jealousies and vanities also underpin the main class conflicts.

For example, Tilsley's screenplay expands the segment in which Mrs. Elton makes her first visit to Hartfield to include a new scene in which Harriet has a tense first encounter with the woman to whom she lost Mr. Elton. The conversation between Emma and Mrs. Elton begins much as it does in the novel, with Mrs. Elton's casual comments insulting all aspects of Emma's life, but then it deviates sharply from Austen's prose when Harriet appears unexpectedly at the doorway:

Harriet: I know you didn't expect me, Miss Woodhouse, but I was passing and I wanted to ask you—

(She breaks off, appalled at the sight of the Eltons. She doesn't know what to do with herself. She is too confused even to flee. Emma realizes there is nothing else for it but to introduce her.)

Emma: It's very lucky you came, Harriet. You can make the acquaintance of Mrs. Elton. Mrs. Elton, allow me to introduce my friend, Miss Harriet Smith.

Mrs. Elton: Indeed? I am very pleased to make your acquaintance, Miss—what was the name?

Harriet: Smith.

(Mrs. Elton has obviously heard all about Harriet from the very biased point of view of Elton and is contemptuous of her.)

Mrs. Elton: Smith, yes. No relation to the Smiths of West Hall near Maple Grove?

Harriet: I don't think so. (Desperately to Emma) I really think I'd better go—

Mrs. Elton: Very vulgar people encumbered with low connections, and yet expecting to be on a footing with the established families. Isn't it extraordinary how some people have so little sense of rank?

Harriet: Yes, it is—indeed.

Mrs. Elton: These particular Smiths come from Birmingham, you know, which is not a place of much promise. Have you any connections with Birmingham, Miss Smith?

Harriet: I don't believe so.

Emma: Pray sit down, Harriet.

Mrs. Elton: Very unpleasant people. (4:6-7)

Here Tilsley presents a Mrs. Elton who is already in full possession of the facts of her new husband's previous association with Miss Woodhouse and Miss Smith and is enraged about it. She has already struck out at Emma by belittling Emma and her friends, but her venom is more veiled because she is still assessing Emma's strength as an enemy. Since the socially inferior Harriet constitutes a safer target, Mrs. Elton's veil of amiability can fall away and she can be more overt in her hostility. In the dialogue quoted above, Mrs. Elton appears to be motivated as much by sexual jealousy of Harriet, knowing that Harriet had designs on her husband, as by fears that Harriet will try to marry well, emerging on more equal social footing with herself.

The scene does not appear to contradict anything in the novel itself, and it sets the stage for Mr. Elton's snub of Harriet during the Crown Inn ball scene later on. Most importantly, the scene casts the central concern of the Tilsely adaptation as the abuses of power that authority figures commit in the novel, most especially those abuses committed by women against the women beneath them in the social order. This thematic emphasis on issues of class-based competition and jealousies earmarks the Tilsley adaptation as a social critique rather than as a domestic Bildungsroman. As Paul Delaney writes in "'A Sort of Notch in the Donwell Estate': Intersections of Status and Class in *Emma*," the novel depicts a fierce class struggle in which:

> female aggressors inflict harm on female victims, and are implicitly condemned for it by the narrator's judgment. Both Mrs. Elton and the friend with whom she wants Jane Fairfax to find employment, would enjoy humiliating Jane because she is more genteel than they are....Miss Bates is attacked by Emma and Mrs. Elton, Harriet by Mrs. Elton, Jane Fairfax by Mrs. Elton and indirectly by Mrs. Churchill. None of the victims has any power to hit back. Austen motivates the aggressions of Mrs. Elton and Mrs.

Churchill by revealing that their own origins are suspect: they take advantage of the status they have gained through marriage to become self-appointed guardians of the boundaries they themselves have crossed. They have gained power from their association with men, then use it to oppress women....(518–519)

In the Tilsley adaptation, Emma is less overtly hostile to Harriet than Mrs. Elton is, but the moment Harriet declares her love for Mr. Knightley, Emma becomes fiercely jealous of her young friend. Naturally, Emma experiences similar jealous feelings in the novel, but the Tilsley screenplay complicates the situation further by suggesting that Mr. Knightley's desire is not fixed solely on Emma. Although Mr. Knightley claims to be interested in Emma alone, his dialogue in Tilsley's script is often cryptic and his attentions to both Jane Fairfax and Harriet have romantic overtones that suggest that, if Emma does not shape up in his eyes, he may seek his bride elsewhere.

There are essentially five originally conceived scenes that suggest Mr. Knightley's search for an ideal wife has not yet reached its conclusion, three of which deal with his possible love for Jane and two of which concern his budding romantic relationship with Harriet. In the first romantic-tinged scene between Mr. Knightley and Jane Fairfax, he reveals his suspicions to Jane that she is secretly attached and in pain over how the relationship is progressing. He offers to send William Larkins to and from the post office on her behalf to help her keep her romance secret. Jane is flustered and ends the conversation quickly. In a follow-up scene, Jane admits to having a secret relationship and thanks Mr. Knightley for his concern, but refuses his offer of help. In the third scene in this vein, Mr. Knightley has a quiet moment with Jane on the balcony at the Crown Inn ball. She confesses to her inclination to end her unhappy relationship and begins to cry. Mr. Knightley suggests that they go back inside and dance before the Highbury gossips begin to talk of their growing romance. These scenes, which ostensibly show Knightley trying to help Jane keep her secret relationship healthy, have a subtext which suggests that Mr. Knightley hopes to supplant Frank in Jane's affections.[25]

In a thematically related subplot, Mr. Knightley also appears interested in Harriet. He has at least one tender conversation with her following her trying experience at the Crown Inn ball that might raise suspicions in a viewer that he has designs on her. The possibility that he may well be attracted to her seems even more likely in a scene between Mr. Knightley and Robert Martin. In this scene, Mr. Knightley discourages Robert from renewing his proposal to Harriet since Emma's influence remains too strong and it would be fruitless to try again so soon. Something in Mr. Knightley's tone suggests to Robert that Knightley is not being completely honest. The yeoman begins to suspect that Knightley wants Harriet for himself and he decides to renew his suit as soon as possible, before Mr. Knightley can steal Harriet away from him.

Since Emma is in love with Mr. Knightley, his interest in both Harriet and Jane ultimately brings Emma's friendship with Harriet to an end and delays (or prevents) any connection from forming between Emma and Jane.[26] Once it is revealed that Jane has married Frank, Emma no longer sees Jane as a threat and is able to have kind words with her. On the other hand, Emma's relationship with Harriet comes to a disastrous close when Harriet literally flees from Hartfield into a raging thunderstorm after overhearing the news that Emma and Mr. Knightley will wed. Harriet is later rescued by Robert Martin, who dutifully offers to fetch an umbrella for her, but the breach between herself and Emma appears to be lasting even after she is reunited with her lost love.

While the powerful women in the Tilsley adaptation try to humble the less socially and economically powerful women whom they see as romantic rivals, they also strive to humiliate lower-class men with designs on marrying into a higher class. In these cases, the motivation for the opposition appears to be based more firmly in class bias and in a desire to keep social upstarts from marrying into the family. This theme is not too far removed from Delaney's interpretation of the novel:

> Austen shows that, in the status struggle, female power is often misused. The gender system prevailing among the gentry subordinates women to men, and unmarried to married women, at the same social level; but it gives women the power of their status rather than their gender in relations with subaltern groups. Emma can therefore humiliate Robert Martin, and Mrs. Churchill can do the same to Mr. Weston, without fear of reprisal (518–519).

Thanks to its concern with this theme, Tilsley's screenplay treats Mrs. Churchill as a far more formidable, off-screen threat than other adaptations of *Emma* do, emphasizing her evil influence over the lives of Mr. Weston, Frank, and Jane. While other adaptations rarely fail to mention Mrs. Churchill, they generally do so briefly, and they consistently fail to include a full and comprehensible history of her relationship to Mr. Weston. Since this version takes greater care in fleshing out the characters of Frank Churchill and Mr. Weston than many other adaptations, it makes more manifest the pain that they have felt suffering at the hands of Mrs. Churchill.

Of all of the characters in the novel, it is arguably Mr. Weston who has been the least served by the film and television adaptations of the novel, primarily because not one of them gives enough attention to his background, which Austen herself deemed important enough to include as an opening for the second chapter.[27] Austen generally portrays Weston as an agreeable man who speaks of his own ability to weather personal crisis and disappointment with a Zen-like peace-of-mind, particularly when he has just received yet another letter from his son putting off a visit. Still, he is capable of great anger, especially toward Mrs. Churchill, the arch nemesis who opposed his first marriage, took his son from him following his wife's death, and compelled Frank to change his surname from Weston to Churchill. The novel also has an intriguing subplot involving Mr. John Knightley's intense personal dislike for Mr. Weston that is usually omitted from film versions, but is briefly hinted at in the Davies-Lawrence version with Kate Beckinsale. John darkly reflects on Weston's motivations in allowing a hated sister-in-law to raise his son, and takes every opportunity to complain of Weston's social opportunism.

Although the Tilsley screenplay does not include John as a character, it retains Mrs. Churchill's objections to Weston's attempts to marry well. The screenplay further develops Weston's character by emphasizing his own match-making hobby (Weston and the former Miss Taylor have a noteworthy scene to themselves where they observe Emma and Frank walking together in the garden and express their eagerness to hear of an engagement soon). Additionally, there is a particularly effective moment towards the end when a wrathful Mr. Weston vows to Emma that he will punish his son for wronging them all, suggesting that he has a temper to set off after all. By making Weston a more fully developed character, and by emphasizing the pain that Mrs. Churchill has caused him, the screenplay seems more concerned with the rights of wronged men than the two previous adaptations.

To the same end, Tilsley's screenplay takes great strides in giving Frank more life than he usually has on screen, primarily by emphasizing how beholden he is to his aunt's whims—something other adaptations fail to do because the characters spend so little time explaining *who* Mrs. Churchill is and *why* her influence is felt so strongly in the lives of those close to Emma.[28] The first sign in the screenplay that still waters run deep and that Frank is not as frivolous as he appears is in the following exchange between him and his father in episode three:

> **Frank:** What would you think of my marrying, Sir? Do you think I am too young?

> **Weston:** Of course not. If you had your future to make, it would be different, but a young man of your expectations—

> **Frank:** If my aunt and uncle disapproved of my choice, I would have very few expectations left, Sir. (3:26)

Frank is more honest and direct here than he tends to be in the novel, but the scene demonstrates effectively how much power authority figures have to ruin the lives of those dependent upon them—even the lives of their own male heirs. This exchange lays the groundwork for Frank's later defense that he had to keep his engagement secret or risk his aunt's wrath. Whereas the novel grants Frank the courtesy of defending his actions throughout the story by presenting his long letter of apology/apologia, the films tend to excise the letter, with filmmakers seeing it as just one more example of an unnecessarily long epilogue that inexplicably drags out the final act of the novel.[29] The letter is usually replaced by a brief talk between Frank and Emma that occurs off to the side during a larger party celebrating the three marriage unions at the end of the novel.[30] In this case, Frank's quiet moment with Emma includes this apology:

> **Frank:** You must consider exactly what position I was in. I had fallen in love with her at Weymouth—and yet I did not dare to address her openly. Had my poor aunt discovered the truth I should have been forced to renounce either Miss Fairfax or my inheri-

tance. The latter I would have done gladly—By doing so I should have deprived the woman I loved of future wealth and position. What could I do but induce her to stoop to a secret engagement?

Although his motives remain suspect, and although Mr. Weston does have words with his son about the transgression, Frank Churchill emerges as more complicated and more sympathetic in this screenplay than he does in any other filmed adaptation set in Regency England, partly because this speech is better than the ones written for him in the other versions.

This adaptation's emphasis on unjust female authority figures who discriminate against both men and women leave it potentially vulnerable to the criticism that it is slightly masculinist and antifeminist in its concerns. Tilsley's script is especially likely to evoke this reaction from readers who agree with Claudia Johnson's view that "Austen is not embarrassed by power" and portrayed Emma supportively as a "woman who possesses and enjoys power" (*Women, Politics, and the Novel* 125). To the extent that the adaptation could be defended from claims of sexism, it is important to note that Tilsley casts Mr. Knightley as something of a fair-weather friend to his charges. Since Tilsley's Knightley is flawed, then perhaps the screenplay's criticism of female authority figures is softened somewhat, if not completely cleansed of tinges of sexism.

Although Knightley begins as a good friend to Robert Martin, their amicable relationship deteriorates as Martin suspects that Mr. Knightley loves Harriet. Like the Kraft adaptation, Tilsley's screenplay dramatizes the conversation in which Robert Martin seeks Mr. Knightley's advice on how to approach Harriet. This Robert Martin is articulate, polite, and well-aware of the class distinction between himself and Mr. Knightley, and he broaches the subject with dialogue of this flavor: "If you'd be good enough to spare a few moments, Sir, I've a very particular problem I'd like to talk to you about." There are subsequent scenes between Martin and Knightley in which Knightley warns Martin against making further proposals to Harriet so long as Emma's influence remains a constant. Martin is a stalwart figure throughout the miniseries, despite the fears and suspicions which Mr. Knightley develops in the final installments of the story. Since this incarnation of Robert Martin is less clownish than his equivalent character (William Larkins) in the Kraft adaptation, it reflects badly on Mr. Knightley when Robert loses faith in him.

Time and again in the script, this Mr. Knightley's actions tend to create suspicions in others that his motives are not inspired by "disinterested benevolence." Although some of these suspicions are based on assumptions that cannot be verified, there is one scene in the script in which his behavior is notably rude and hostile. The scene occurs shortly after Frank arrives in town and it is the first encounter between the two men. In this "invented scene" Mr. Knightley, in a rare moment of indecorousness, drops all pretense of amiability towards Frank the moment that Emma and Mr. Weston leave them alone to talk amongst themselves:

Frank: I'm very glad to know you, sir.

Knightley: And I you. I remember you well as a little boy.

(Emma and Weston drift a short way off)

Frank: I must confess, Mr. Knightley, I am so entranced by everything I find at Highbury that I am sorry I ever had to leave.

Knightley: Perhaps you will visit more frequently, now you find it agrees with you.

Frank: As frequently as I can, sir, though it is not always in my power. My aunt puts many difficulties in the way.

Knightley: (Dryly) So I understand.

Frank: Well, what do you think of the situation, Mr. Knightley? I read in the papers that the government is expected to fall within the week. Do you expect it to?

Knightley: I am not interested in politics, Mr. Churchill. They seem to be conducted by men generally too dishonest to lead a life of crime.

Frank: (Amused) I agree with you heartily. A gentleman has better pursuits. I passed Donwell Abbey on the way here and saw a very fine herd of cattle in your meadow. Do you use the new methods of breeding?

Knightley: I have always found the old methods to work very well. Excuse me, sir. I must speak to Mrs. Weston. (2: 23)

Certainly, there is no shortage of reasons for Mr. Knightley to dislike Frank. From Mr. Knightley's perspective, Frank is impulsive, trivial, a liar, a slanderer, a flirt, and a dandy. In short, Frank is a "politician." These objections to Frank's supposed moral relativism constitute less selfish reasons for Mr. Knightley to dislike Frank than jealousy alone. However, the theme of jealousy is so central to Tilsley's script that it grants the greatest weight to envy as the chief reason Mr. Knightley hates Frank, the fop who has courted both of Mr. Knightley's favorites. Of course, as the most important man in Highbury, Mr. Knightley might be in a position to offer some guidance and assistance to Frank, who is younger and less secure in his economic and social status, but the natural consequence of Knightley's fierce jealousy of Frank is that he refuses to assume a mentor role of any kind in relation to the young man.

It would be difficult to argue that either Emma or Mr. Knightley grow in maturity or social awareness during the course of the Tilsley adaptation. Although both characters are capable of great kindness, even here, they are motivated primarily by jealousy and a desire to protect their land and position against any and all threats. The end of the miniseries is happy because they have defeated all of their rivals in love, not because they have grown as people. At the beginning and at the end of the miniseries, they are perfectly willing to embrace and assist members of the lower classes who do not constitute a threat to their sovereignty, such as Miss Bates. However, in Tilsley's screenplay, when it comes to protecting their own interests, they are more similar to Mrs. Churchill and Mrs. Elton than they are dissimilar.

As a reading of the novel, this transposition adaptation dovetails nicely with critical writings by Paul Delaney, presenting a darker view of the protagonists without altering the tone and storyline enough to qualify it as an outright deconstructionist dramatization. In choosing to spotlight the concerns of the less fortunate members of the Highbury community, the Tilsley adaptation shares a kinship with the Judy Campbell and Kraft versions that preceded it. However, Tilsley's script is more concerned with representing the problems faced by the men of Highbury than Campbell's is, and it treats issues of class with a less broadly comic tone than the Kraft version.

Nineteen-sixty saw one further television production of *Emma*, this time airing on American television as an hour-long broadcast that was part of the CBS drama series *Camera Three* on August 26. Soap star Nancy Wickwire, of *As The World Turns* and *Days of Our Lives* fame, played the title character in an adaptation written by Claire Roskam, produced by John McGiffert, and directed by John Desmond. Outside of these scant few facts about the creative team behind the special, no significant information is available for study since both the screenplay and the original footage are "lost."

The Glenister-Constanduros Version (1972)

"Emma." 1972. (BBC2, color, 5-parts, 257 minutes)

The fifth adaptation of *Emma* is a miniseries that was first broadcast on BBC2 in 1972, written by Denis Constanduros and directed by John Glenister.[31] At 257-minutes, this miniseries (commonly referred to by critics as the "Glenister-Constanduros version") is the longest adaptation of *Emma* and comes "closest to the novel in its inclusiveness of the scenes and characters described in the novel" (Parrill 123).

Interviewed in Monica Lauritzen's book-length examination of the production, *Jane Austen's* Emma *on Television* (1981), director Glenister explained that:

> I judged my responsibility was to those who had never read the book. My responsibility was to have them so engrossed in the story and its development that they would rush to read the other Jane Austen novels. I'm not concerned with those who'd already found Jane Austen—it may be pleasant to see somebody else's interpretation of a character they knew/.../but the direct responsibility of doing *Classic Serials* at all are to those who don't know them at all, and who might be frightened off them by bad English teaching at school—there's enough of that/.../I was frightened by much English literature because it all seemed so grand, and eloquent and

unreachable. And it seems to me that one of the main purposes of the *Classic Serials* is to say to people: look these are cracking good stories. (Lauritzen 53–54)

That Glenister was true to his word is evidenced by the production itself, which many might argue is scrupulously faithful to Austen's novel. Essentially all of the key scenes in the development of the plot survive the transition from book to screen. Even elements of the novel that are often excised entirely by film adaptations survive the transition to the screen in this version. Certainly this is the only adaptation to include Mrs. Weston's pregnancy and to feature John and Isabella Knightley in anything beyond a cameo appearance (although John is possibly too jovial here). Of course, the "verbal content" of the scenes "is very much abridged; so much so, in fact, that the manuscript has the appearance of a distillate of the original" (Lauritzen 127). In places in the script where original dialogue is written that has no corollary in the novel, Constanduros strove to "preserve as much as possible the 'flavour' of Jane Austen's language. 'What you've got to do,' he said, 'is to give the impression of it sounding like Jane Austen, without it being really, literally Jane Austen's dialogue' (Lauritzen 127).

Since some scenes were cut and others were combined, the natural consequence is that some characters have more scenes in the miniseries than they do in the novel (at least percentage-wise) and others appear in fewer. Largely to emphasize the romantic element of the storyline, Knightley's role is emphasized, while Mrs. Weston's role is reduced (Lauritzen 80). There are also more scenes of Emma and Harriet alone, probably to make their relationship seem more intimate. Perhaps the most unusual departure from the novel is that the miniseries includes more scenes without Emma than the novel does. These scenes, most of which are invented, are not vital to the plot, but they do help develop the characters that they feature (there is an interesting moment when Mrs. Elton appeals to Jane Fairfax as a fellow foe of Emma's and another which takes place after the Crown Inn ball when we see Harriet beaming to herself, obviously smitten with Mr. Knightley) and, as Lauritzen indicates, gives a sense of the Highbury community as a whole while breaking us free of Emma's perspective in the way the narrator (absent in the miniseries) did in the novel. "Through this deviation Constanduros also departs from a general tendency in mass media entertainment to over-emphasize a few main characters in order to give the audience an opportunity for close identification" (Lauritzen 79–80).

Aside from the thoroughness of the retelling, one of the central reasons a modern person would be most interested in consulting this particular adaptation is its anti-romantic quality, which some might argue is in keeping with Austen's tone. The most obvious example of the anti-romantic sentiment behind the film is the director's choice to cast Hammer-film alumnus John Carson as Mr. Knightley, an actor whom Sue Parrill describes as "paunchy and graying" and one who "exudes solidity and complacency" as he "emphasizes the age difference between Emma and Mr. Knightley" (124). The love he demonstrates for Emma is sweet rather than passionate, and the pricklier side of his persona in the novel is perhaps not as emphasized as it should be, but Carson is, nevertheless, excellent at channeling a version of the Knightley character who "with his sidewhiskers, is genial and avuncular. His criticism of Emma is kind and instructive" (Palmer 3). The casting of Carson as an "anti-romantic" Knightley probably also helped prepare some viewers for the ending of the miniseries, which does not feature a climactic kiss between Emma and Knightley accompanied by a swell in the music score. In fact, Carson's Knightley is the only cinematic incarnation of the character who does not kiss Emma on screen.[32]

Ironically, rather than be praised for coming close to achieving "total fidelity" to the source material–the stated goal of the production team (Lauritzen 112)–this adaptation has often been criticized by Austen scholars for being too bland and conservative in its staging and too inept at dramatizing the richness of Emma's emotional and intellectual life.[33] The complaints certainly have some merit, although one might well argue that the "no frills" quality to the miniseries is a strength and not a defect. The staginess of the adaptation arguably causes the viewer to focus on the actors and the dialogue rather than on the historically accurate set design, thereby recreating the novel's emphasis on dialogue over poetic description of setting. As Sue Parrill observes, "if what the viewer wants is a literal translation, unencumbered by superior acting, imaginative staging, or on-location shooting, the 1972 BBC version is the way to go" (Parrill 123) since it "has its appealing qualities" even if it "suffers from a certain claustrophobia" (Parrill 147).

Far more troubling is the fact that this adaptation leaves most of Emma's thoughts and feelings a mystery when they should be laid bare. Since Emma's inner life is so compelling in the novel, her thoughts and feelings are some of the strongest arguments in her favor. Without exposure to her psyche, viewers of the television adaptation may wonder at her motivation and judge her more harshly on the basis of her mannerisms and actions alone.[34]

As weighty as these objections might be, I would argue that the Glenister-Constanduros version succeeds in advancing an intriguing reading of the source novel, even if its deficiencies prevent it from succeeding in duplicating exactly, and in entirety, its artistic effect. Even though Emma does grow and change as a character during the course of the Glenister-Constanduros version, one might argue that the adaptation doesn't play as a domestic Bildungsroman reading because of its failure to appropriately emphasize the workings of Emma's mind. It does, though, succeed admirably as a reading of the novel as a social critique, evoking some of the same issues discussed in academic writings by Tony Tanner, Allison Sulloway, and Sandra Gilbert & Susan Gubar. The stage-bound, claustrophobic feel to the miniseries that Parrill describes creates an effect which reinforces this version's view of Highbury as a static and oppressive environment. Emma seems to have little power over her own life here, and the simple sets seem to close in on her in key scenes, especially when she is shown gazing longingly out of the window at the outside world that her sickly father has denied her access to. This, indeed, is an Emma that is "seldom ever two hours from Hartfield" (Austen 252), and who complains to Mr. John Knightley that attending two dinner parties and making plans for a ball that is cancelled hardly constitutes a mass of "visiting-engagements" (Austen 251) or a great call on her time. Doran Godwin is good at playing up Emma's frustration at her limited social circle, often delivering her dialogue through a fake smile and clenched teeth. She exudes nervousness and restlessness, and pushes the character as far as it can be reasonably pushed in a transposition adaptation to resemble the imprisoned heroine of "The Yellow Wallpaper." According to Lauritzen, Doran Godwin's portrayal of Emma in this version arises from Glenister's vision of the character:

> After reading the novel and various critical studies, [Glenister] had come to the conclusion that "everything that Emma did, her whole behavior pattern, seemed to fit the classic case of the psychoneurotic". He did not see her as a "mischievous, pretty, wicked lady" but as somebody who was "disturbed/ .../slightly unstable/.../with certain repressions and frustrations and certain activities which were sublimations of her own fears and desires". This interesting and quite original conception of Emma was to be his key throughout the production, and in looking for an actress he wanted to find "somebody who would appear slightly high-strung", with a "slightly neurotic tension". This is a quality that is found in very few young leading actresses, he said, and he remembered leafing through the directory "till a face lept out at me which seemed to say what I wanted it to say". And when Doran Godwin eventually appeared for a hearing she seemed just right for the part. "She walked through the door and it was Emma," said Glenister. "Slightly neurotic, a beautiful voice, and a natural grace/.../Doran has 70 per cent of Emma built into her" (Lauritzen 117).

Since the miniseries fails to give the audience a truly intimate connection with Emma by revealing her thoughts in voice-over, it only gradually becomes apparent just how unhappy Emma is, and that her fidgety movements and forced smile are manifestations of her depression. However, the miniseries is most successful in explaining Emma's fidgety nature, and in her feelings of being trapped, when it emphasizes the socially awkward moments in her life. These dramatic moments include those in which Emma is repeatedly interrupted in her conversation by Miss Bates (Constance Chapman); when Mrs. Elton (Fiona Walker) obviously takes precedence over her during the Crown Inn ball, and when Emma is compelled to defuse potential arguments between her father and John Knightley, thereby soothing their nerves and fraying her own.

Emma's social discomfort is reflected in the figure of Jane Fairfax, who is the very picture of tension and repression throughout the miniseries. "Stiff in movements and halting in speech. She appears to be speaking through clenched teeth. These qualities make her convincing since they suggest that she is holding something back" (Parrill 127). During her introductory scene in the miniseries, Jane even yells at Miss Bates in front of Emma and Harriet for talking too much about her possible future as a governess, a melodramatic moment that seems a great public sin against Miss Bates. As jarring as this moment is for those who think of Jane as more reserved and as more indulgent of Miss Bates, it is dramatically effective and draws the viewer's attention to Jane's desperation and secretiveness far more rapidly and effectively than many other adaptations. The similarity between the performances of Godwin as Emma and Ania Marson as Jane also underscores the parallel nature of the characters explored by Sandra Gilbert and Susan Gubar in *The Madwoman in the Attic*:

> Like…antithetical sisters we have discussed, Jane Fairfax and Emma are doubles. Since they are the most accomplished girls in Highbury, exactly the same age, suitable companions, the fact that they are not friends is in itself quite significant. Emma even believes at times that her dislike for Jane is caused by her seeing in Jane "the really accomplished young woman which she wanted to be thought herself" (II, chap. 2). In fact, she has to succumb to Jane's fate, to become her double through the realization that she too has been manipulated as a pawn in Frank Churchill's game. The seriousness of Emma's assertive playfulness is made clear when she talks indiscreetly, unwittingly encourages the advances of Mr. Elton, and when she allows her imagination to indulge in rather lewd suppositions about the possible sexual intrigues of Jane Fairfax and a married man. In other words, Emma's imagination has led her to the sin of being unladylike, and her complete mortification is a prelude to submission as she becomes a friend of Jane Fairfax, at one with her too in her realization of her own powerlessness. (159–160)

Like Gilbert and Gubar's interpretation of the novel, the Glenister-Constanduros miniseries seems to assert that, "Although Emma is the center of Austen's fiction, what she has to learn is her vulnerability as a female" (158-159). The central difference between the Glenister-Constanduros miniseries and the writings of Gilbert and Gubar is that, at the start of the miniseries, Emma already seems acutely aware of her limitations and frustrations, but has not yet learned to see similar pain in other women, especially Jane Fairfax. As the miniseries progresses, Emma begins to see echoes of her situation in Jane's and gradually feels greater empathy for Jane. That empathy is portrayed as liberating, as Godwin's Emma grows less nervous and mannered as the miniseries progresses and as she feels more of a kinship to Jane.

In this version of the story, Emma's fears of Mr. Knightley's being in love with Jane Fairfax are lifted very firmly and quickly by Knightley himself, leaving Emma free to entertain good feelings towards Jane without having to suppress jealous and possessive feelings concerning Knightley. This alteration allows Emma to grow to like Jane some time before the Box Hill segment and the revelation of the secret engagement. In fact, Emma's sympathy for, and liking for, Jane becomes quite apparent in a dramatic moment when Emma comes to Jane's rescue. During a large indoor gathering, Mrs. Elton and others accost Jane about her mysteriously regular walks to the post office. Their questions are relentless and insinuating, even more uncomfortably framed than the questions put to Jane in the novel on the same subject, and Jane is obviously feeling desperate and trapped. It is Emma who interrupts the questioning by artfully changing the subject and leading the assemblage away from Jane. The screenwriter, director, and actors all put such dramatic weight on this moment that it assumes a great importance as the moment in which Emma has chosen to ally herself with Jane as a friend and fellow woman in trouble. Although the two characters do not speak frankly as friends until after the engagement is revealed, their bond of sympathy is formed in this scene.

But perhaps the greatest dramatic success the miniseries has to offer is its unique and suspenseful handling of the novel's extended epilogue, in which a striking parallel is drawn between Mr. Knightley and Frank, and in which the duality between Emma and Jane becomes even more apparent. Most filmed versions of the tale end rapidly after Mr. Knightley's proposal, taking time only for a final scene between Emma and Harriet and a disgusted look from Mrs. Elton before the closing credits roll. This version, however, casts Emma and Knightley as reluctant to break the news of their engagement to Mr. Woodhouse and places them in a position where they are forced to act almost as indifferent to one another as Frank Churchill and Jane Fairfax had to. It is particularly striking seeing John Carson's Mr. Knightley skulking about sheepishly when he is in the same room with both Emma and Mr. Woodhouse, showing that even the rich and powerful Mr. Knightley, who prizes honesty above all and who was once so unsympathetic of Frank's fear of Mrs. Churchill's disapproval, is capable of resorting to subterfuge to protect his future happiness. His actions prove the validity of many of Emma's defenses of Frank. In a similar fashion, when Emma adopts a reserved manner and dodges pointed questions put to her by a confused Mr. and Mrs. Elton about why Knightley has been acting so distracted lately, she begins to look a lot like Jane Fairfax did when she was asked what Frank Churchill was like when they met at Weymouth. (This scene is very funny, by the way. Doran Godwin is particularly good here, as are Timothy Peters and Fiona Walker as the Eltons.)

Many of these scenes are in the novel, although the narrator leaves much of the symbolic doubling between the future Knightleys and the future Churchills uncommented upon. Austen does offer readers a glimpse into Emma's thoughts shortly after Harriet leaves for London and the John Knightleys. In these thoughts, Emma considers the wisdom of withholding the announcement of her engagement until Mrs. Weston has safely given birth to her child and completed her recovery. "There was a communication before her, one which she only could be competent to make—the confession of her engagement to her father; but she would have nothing to do with it at present.—She had resolved to defer the disclosure till Mrs. Weston was safe and well" (Austen 356). Emma was as good as her word and did, indeed, tell her father "as soon as Mrs. Weston was sufficiently recovered" (Austen 367), but the implication in the miniseries is that Emma and Knightley keep the secret for a while, probably more than the fortnight suggested in the novel, until Emma begins to bristle at the dishonesty of their situation. "Poor father," she says in the final installment of the miniseries. "We must tell him. Not to do so puts us exactly on the level with Frank Churchill."

When she does tell her father in the novel "it was at first a considerable shock to him, and he tried earnestly to dissuade her from it....But it would not do. Emma hung about him affectionately, and smiled, and said it must be so....Mr. Woodhouse could not be soon reconciled; but the worst was overcome, the idea was given; time and continual repetition must do the rest" (Austen 367-368). This conversation, related primarily by the narrator but punctuated by dialogue from both parties quoted by the narrator, plays out as even more aggressive in the miniseries. While in the book Mr. Woodhouse is indeed disapproving and distressed, he never forbids the marriage, but in the miniseries Mr. Woodhouse briefly does just that. Emma tries to ease her way into the subject by mentioning to her father that "Harriet is not the only one who is contemplating marriage." Mr. Woodhouse looks distressed and hopes that it is not his friend Miss Bates. His response when he realizes that Emma speaks of herself is, "What?

No. You cannot mean!" She tries to reassure him that John and Isabel will live in Donwell and that she and Knightley will live at Hartfield:

Emma: So you will be getting two daughters instead of one and more of Mr. Knightley's company for good measure. Oh, there father. Can you not see what a happy arrangement it will be for all of us?

Mr. Woodhouse: I do not care for arrangements. I am too old for such things.

Emma: But father—

Mr. Woodhouse: No! [he resumes reading, signifying that the conversation is over, leaving Emma in miserable silence.]

The director manages to sustain the silence between them for a long, suspenseful moment before it dawns on Emma that the chicken thieves might be the key to breaking the stalemate. But in that moment, the whole of Emma and Knightley's future hangs in the balance, and it is a moment that has no real correlation in the novel. In that moment, viewers will recall an earlier scene when Emma is trapped indoors with her father during a thunderstorm, fearful that she has lost her love to Harriet, and listening to her father mutter how tiresome life is when one lives from one bowl of gruel to the next. The old and frail looking Donald Eccles plays Mr. Woodhouse as a very sickly, fearful man whose pains happen to be darkly comic, as opposed to other screen incarnations of the character, all of which seem too robust to be anything other than hypochondriacs. The seriousness of the physical condition depicted by Donald Eccles, and the loneliness and sadness of the prospect of Emma living out the rest of her youth tending to him is all summoned in that one moment, and it is brilliantly effective. Some of the humorous tone of the ending of the novel is recaptured by the humorous toast offered by Mr. Woodhouse in the final scene. It emphasizes that the old man will be a lot for the newlyweds to put up with, but he will not be deliberately adversarial in his dealings with them. Such a dramatization of the end of the novel is interesting in that it emphasizes the limits of the power that both Emma and Knightley have over their own destinies, but it has the disadvantage (from a feminist perspective) of placing Mr. Woodhouse firmly in charge of his own house, undercutting the brilliant, subversive reading that Claudia Johnson finds in the novel's ending that "in moving to Hartfield, Knightley is sharing her home, and in placing himself within her domain, Knightley gives his blessing to her rule" (Johnson 143).

The central goal of the Glenister-Constanduros adaptation is to make manifest the claustrophobia of Emma's life, the limits of her power, and the scarring psychological effect that it has on her. In this version, Mr. Knightley is wise and gentle, and yet does not fully grasp the extent to which either Emma or Frank suffer at the hands of ill-tempered and mercurial guardians for most of the story. Still, Knightley eventually learns to empathize with them once he has first-hand experience keeping secret his engagement to Emma from the irrational Mr. Woodhouse. In a similar manner, by the end of the mini-series, Emma learns to see that Jane, in many ways, shares her vulnerability, trapped in a small home with a dull-witted aunt. The discovery of kinship with Jane, and the blossoming of her love for Knightley, eventually offer Emma an escape from her neurosis and help her come to terms with her life in Highbury.

The Glenister-Constanduros version is the first *Emma* adaptation to seriously address the evils of Emma's circumscribed life instead of subordinating them in importance to the sufferings felt by the supporting characters. The Kraft adaptation's comic treatment of Emma made her secret pains seem trivial compared to the pain that she caused Mr. Elton. The Campbell and Tilsley adaptations possibly placed too much emphasis on Jane's storyline, and Emma's stature diminished as a natural consequence...to the point that she was *almost* supplanted as the heroine of the story. Here, in the Glenister-Constanduros miniseries, we have an Emma who has assumed center stage, and has not retained her position as protagonist at the expense of Jane, whose storyline remains largely intact. The central problem with this incarnation of Emma is that, aside from one or two sentences included in voice-over, her thoughts are kept from the viewer, so she is not as accessible as the heroine from the novel. (But this is also true of the stagey adaptations that preceded it.)

The adaptations covered in this chapter were all variations of the transposition adaptation, and most of them emphasized the importance of social critique over the story of Emma's personal development, especially since moments in which Emma's thoughts were revealed to the audience in voiceover were few and far between. Also, with the exception of the Kraft adaptation, each early television adaptation granted great significance to the Jane Fairfax storyline, often to the point that it threatened to eclipse both Emma's and Harriet's.

As we will see in the following chapter, the 1990s adaptations reverse virtually all of these trends, offering audience members a more intimate presentation of Emma, meatier roles for Harriet, and (in two of the versions) a far smaller presence to Jane Fairfax. Also, instead of being exclusively social critique transposition adaptations, one film is a domestic Bildungsroman transposition adaptation, another is a commentary adaptation, and the third is an analogy adaptation.

EMMA A.D. 1996

The Two Recent "Period Piece" Adaptations

In 1960, two different television adaptations of *Emma*, one British and one American, were produced and broadcast roughly four months apart. The phenomenon of virtually simultaneous adaptations in both nations recurred in 1996, only this time the American version was released theatrically by Miramax pictures and achieved a somewhat higher profile than its more modestly marketed British competitor overseas. Since the release of the two 1996 adaptations, literary critics and adaptation theorists have often examined the two versions together, as if they were a unit, or cinematic cousins of one another. Such comparisons have yielded intriguing results, primarily because the two films contrast nicely with one another by offering starkly different interpretations of Austen's novel. Linda Troost and Sayre Greenfield suggest one way of understanding the differences between the two 1996 *Emma* films in "Filming Highbury: Reducing the Community in *Emma* to the Screen":

> One could argue that *Emma* is simultaneously the most individual and most social of Austen's six major novels. It is the only one named after its heroine and the only one that sticks entirely to one community—Highbury....
>
> The two recent films unbalance the novel into two different directions, which is all right since a two-hour adaptation cannot and should not try to do everything....One may suspect the different emphases derive from the greater American influence on the Miramax film as opposed to the Meridian/Arts and Entertainment production. The feature film promotes a rising star, Gwyneth Paltrow, whereas the telefilm sits more comfortably within the British tradition of ensemble work. Beyond this, however, the two versions of *Emma* represent two different and legitimate versions of the novel: one more concerned with what happens in the society, the other more

in tune with what happens to the individual. Austen's novel has the luxury
of presenting both visions simultaneously; a film, however, must limit its
scope.

In making this observation, Troost and Greenfield have essentially
identified the American film starring Paltrow as a domestic Bildings-
roman adaptation and the Meridian/A&E "telefilm" as a retelling of
the story as a social critique. The distinction is a useful one. It is certainly true that the American film is interested primarily in Emma
herself, especially in dramatizing her rich inner life and her romance
with Knightley, while the British film focuses more on broader social
issues of class and gender. However, there is a danger in pushing this
distinction too far. Although the American film does make Emma
herself its prime focus, it grants more importance to class and social
issues than has often been suggested. In a similar fashion, while the
British television film seems most interested in representing the perspective of Highbury's more economically vulnerable community
members, especially the servant class, it presents an intriguing vision
of Emma as an "imaginist" that is usually found in more purely
Emma-centric interpretations of the story.

Another key difference between the two films is that they are different enough from one another to occupy two distinct categories of
adaptation delineated by Geoffrey Wagner. The American cinematic
release is a transposition adaptation, which means that it brings to the
screen a traditional, conservative reading of the novel that does little
to clash with the lay public's vision of the work, and avoids including
any elements that might be inspired by more liberal scholarly interpretations that are popular in university classrooms. On the other
hand, the British telefilm is a *commentary* adaptation in which the
creative team is clearly looking back upon the original text with a
modern eye that condemns the class structure of the period. Furthermore, as a commentary adaptation, the telefilm draws upon radical or
progressive critical literary readings of the text that are often ignored
by more politically conservative transposition adaptations. It is also
important to point out that each of the 1996 *Emma* films is unique in
the canon of Austen adaptations: the American film is the only *transposition* adaptation that presents a domestic Bildungsroman reading
of the story, while the British telefilm is the only *commentary* adaptation inspired by this particular text.

Since the two 1996 films have been examined so frequently along-side one another, often with the American production suffering in light of the comparison, I would like to spend the next two sections of this chapter examining each one in its own right. In doing so, and in keeping comparisons between the two at a minimum, I hope to finally afford the two films the opportunity to stand alone.

Douglas McGrath's *Emma*, starring Gwyneth Paltrow

Emma.   Released August 2 (US), September 13, 1996 (UK). (Columbia/Miramax motion picture, Color, 120 minutes)

In *From Reverence to Rape: The Treatment of Women in the Movies* (1973), feminist film critic Molly Haskell writes that the ideal heterosexual romantic union is one based on equality and mutual respect. How-ever, she observes that:

> [t]he love of equals is no more frequently to be found in films than in life. In both, one point of view—generally the man's—usually predominates, seeing the "other" as a creature of his own fantasies, as someone deprived, precisely, of otherness, who then comes to inherit the burden of his neuroses as well....The best of the classical couples—Bacall-Bogey in *To Have and Have Not*, Hepburn-Tracy in *Adam's Rib*—bring to the screen the kind of morally and socially beneficial "pedagogic" relationship that Lionell Trilling finds in Jane Austen's characters, the "intelligent love" in which the two partners instruct, inform, educate, and influence each other in a continuous college of love. In the confidence of mutuality, individuals grow, expand, exchange sexual characteristics. Bacall initiates the affair, Bogey is passive. Hepburn defeats Tracy, Tracy only half-playfully cries. The beauty of the marriage of true minds is that it allows the man to expose the feminine side of his nature and the woman to act on the masculine side of hers (25–26).

Although Haskell is discussing classic screen couples here, her thoughts on marriage, and on Jane Austen, have intriguing bearing on a discussion of the novel *Emma* and the Douglas McGrath film ad-aptation it inspired in 1996. In "Emma: A Woman for All Seasons," Haskell suggests that an ideal representation of the healthy, balanced romantic relationship that she often fails to see rendered in film can be found successfully depicted in classic literature by Jane Austen in *Emma.* Acknowledging that many critics read the relationship be-

tween Emma and Mr. George Knightley as being balanced in his favor, Haskell nevertheless argues that the union is far more equitable
than some claim. She begins her discussion of the romance as it is depicted in the novel by considering Emma's privileged birth and initial
opposition to marrying:

> The irony of Emma's advantaged position is that while it frees her from the
> oppressive alternatives of either marrying ("it is not my way or my nature")
> or becoming a "poor old maid" ("it is poverty only which makes celibacy
> contemptible to a generous public"), it also removes the pressure, born of
> financial necessity, to develop her talents—to practice her playing, to read
> books from that impressive list she has drawn up for Mr. Knightley—so that
> she might be truly independent, i.e., intellectually self-sustaining. By fortune
> and habit of mind, Emma is freed from the necessity of marrying and from
> the romantically indentured mentality of most of her sex (174).

Although the novel ends as Emma's marriage begins, and readers
are left to imagine what married life will be like for her and Knightley, Haskell believes that the closing description of "the perfect happiness of the union" is meant to be taken seriously, and not
interpreted as a tongue-in-cheek rendering of the requisite happy
ending dictated by novelistic form:

> Unlike her continental namesake, the romantically deluded Emma Bovary,
> Emma Woodhouse expects nothing from marriage—does not look to it for
> her fulfillment—and therefore stands to gain everything from it....She is
> very much the type of independent woman who goes for the slightly older
> man, the Katherine Hepburn (or Audrey Hepburn) of literary heroines....
>
> But perhaps Emma's is the most romantic solution of all, the smart woman's
> ultimate fantasy: a man who sees her beauty but responds to her intellect.
> Feminists have taken to complaining that their relationship is not the perfect
> match that Austen seems to think it, that their marriage, far from being a
> delicious duet of mutual edification, is likely to be a grim series of home
> lessons, with the stuffy Knightley (he doesn't dance) scolding and molding a
> passive and pliant Emma. I don't think so. Knightley can dance (he has
> already taken his first step in that direction), he will unbend; while Emma
> will bend with more application to books and studies and discover in her
> mate a worthy adversary and conversationalist. They will draw each other
> out emotionally, expressing the warmth each had previously held in check.
> And perhaps what Emma found in Knightley is not too different from the
> emotional sustenance the celibate Austen found in her family, particularly in
> her sister Cassandra. To my way of thinking, these are no mere
> accommodations. They are as close to the sublime as two human beings get
> (176–177).

Molly Haskell's praise of the quality of the romantic union between Emma and Knightley is for their relationship as it is depicted in
Jane Austen's novel.[1] Although the early television adaptations do
not interpret the relationship in the same way that Haskell does, instead granting Knightley authority over Emma, the 1996 Douglas
McGrath adaptation differs from those that came before by portraying the ultimate union between the two as an ideal marriage of
equals. The result is highly romantic. Writing about the 120-minute
film, which stars Gwyneth Paltrow as Emma and Jeremy Northam as
Knightley, Linda Troost observes that the film is very much a romance, but that is not necessarily a bad thing, since it rewarding to
watch Emma grow as a character as well as win her handsome true
love. ("Filming Highbury" 6).

As a transposition adaptation, as well as a reading of the novel as
a domestic Bildungsroman, the McGrath film has the option of depicting Emma's coming of age story sympathetically, or as a form of
moral parable. Although the film chastises Emma strongly for insulting Miss Bates at Box Hill, and celebrates her eventual shedding of
her snobbish attitudes, it evokes enough sympathy for the character,
and spends enough time making her rich inner life known to the audience through voiceover and telling close-up, that Emma emerges as
more sympathetic in this film than she does in any of the early television adaptations.

In addition to granting Emma more subjectivity than the preceding television versions did, the McGrath film is possibly unique in its
portrayal of Emma as a physical figure who counts archery as one of
her hobbies and who drives herself from place to place in a carriage
without James to accompany her. While these are certainly liberties
taken with the text, Suzanne Ferriss writes that Emma's physicality in
the McGrath film does:

> ...however, capture Emma's daring and reflect the emerging feminism of
> the era. McGrath has done his homework. Archery, for instance, was a
> newly popular sport among the upper classes, with women competing
> directly against men...The image of Emma engaging simultaneously in
> athletic and verbal competition with Knightley has particular resonance for
> contemporary women, who are exhorted regularly to 'just do it' like their
> male counterparts. McGrath's version thus offers an active, competitive
> heroine, whose physical daring mirrors her outspokenness and verbal self-
> confidence. In the film, Emma accuses men of 'preferring superficial

qualities' such as physical beauty, a charge that clearly invokes
contemporary feminist objections to the over-emphasis on the female body
characteristics of consumer culture. (127)

Admittedly, McGrath's script sometimes pokes fun at Emma and
privileges male characters such as Mr. Knightley. As Sue Parrill indicates in "Metaphors of Control: Physicality in *Emma* and *Clueless*,"
Emma's moral inferiority to Knightley is reflected by her inferior skill
as an archer.[2] Emma also proves too headstrong when she drives her
carriage into a large pool of water and gets stuck. When she is rescued from the middle of the small pond by the horseback-riding
Frank Churchill, one might feel that the implication is that Emma
needs to stop being so independent and let the men take over or, con-
versely, that Emma is striving for a self-sufficiency and self-
awareness that she has not yet attained. The imagery of these moments in the film is so striking that it is no surprise that the symbolic
meaning attributed to them is under strong debate.

Just as its portrayal of Emma herself is somewhat unusual for a
period piece adaptation, the McGrath film emphasizes Mr. Knightley's good humor and sensitivity far more than previous adaptations.

Although Jeremy Northam…, Mr. Knightley in the Miramax film, is a
smaller man than [John Carson and Mark Strong, who play the part in other
versions] and does not exude the authority of the others, he seems more
sensitive and vulnerable.…His acting style is understated, and he is good at
sly irony. There are more witty lines for Mr. Knightley in the Miramax film
than in the other versions. For instance, in the scene in which he and Emma
compete at shooting arrows at a target, when Emma's aim deteriorates so
that she misses the target entirely, he quips, "Please don't kill my dogs." In
another scene, in which he is standing with the massive Donwell Abbey
behind him, he tells Emma he would rather not go to the ball but would
prefer to stay at home, "Where it's cozy." Of the three actors, he comes
across as the most tender in the proposal scene (Parrill 125).

McGrath's script allows Mr. Knightley to make jokes at Emma's
expense, but it also pokes fun at Knightley himself for his stodginess,
and Emma's teasing has a welcome deflating effect on the sometimes
overbearing character. In an amusing rewriting of the scene in which
Mrs. Weston and Emma interrogate Mr. Knightley as to the nature of
his true feelings for Jane Fairfax, this Mr. Knightley practically flees
the scene rather than continue the conversation past a certain point
[see Endnote 25 on page 164 for an excerpt of this scene in the novel].

So, while Emma is ridiculous in her inability to drive a carriage and in her poor marksmanship, Knightley is absurd in his stodginess and in his fear of romantic-themed conversation. Although he arguably demonstrates even more "sweetness" than the original Knightley, Northam's interpretation of the character is neither as comic as Peter Cookson's in the Kraft adaptation nor as pseudo-Victorian in his manner as Carson's in the Glenister-Constanduros version, but it strikes a balance between the two. Like the Knightley in the novel, Northam's Knightley is complex and difficult to describe in broad terms.[3] As two flawed-but-sympathetic characters, Northam's Knightley and Paltrow's Emma grow during the course of the film and prove themselves worthy of one another's love by acknowledging their shortcomings and by working to amend their flaws. When, during his proposal, Mr. Knightley says, "Perhaps it is our imperfections that make us so perfect for one another," McGrath has given him a line of dialogue not found in the book that makes the lesson to be drawn from the romance clear.

By exploring Emma's psyche more thoroughly and more sympathetically than any of the other period piece adaptations, and by dramatizing one of the most idealized interpretations of Emma's romance with Mr. Knightley, the McGrath film stands out as a unique and dramatically satisfying reading of the novel. However, its very strengths, its sympathy for Emma and its romantic leanings, have left it vulnerable to certain criticisms which undermine its claim to greatness, both as a film and as a literary adaptation.

Possibly the best remembered of the adaptations set in Regency England, McGrath's film won some popular acclaim as *The New York Post*'s pick for the best film of 1996, and garnered an Oscar for Rachel Portman's music score. However, despite strong performances by an ensemble cast of British character actors, the film has been largely criticized by literary critics as deviating too strongly from the original text to be considered a serious adaptation. This is primarily because, as much as the film is faithful to the novel, its reading is also shaped by the dictates of film convention and of contemporary consumer culture. Although a literary adaptation, the Miramax film is clearly a product of the 1990s, a time in which Hollywood strove to fashion romance films that could please both modern-day feminists and alpha males by presenting the perspectives of both partners with equal respect and attention. The years preceding the McGrath *Emma* saw the release of *When Harry Met Sally* (1989), *Beauty and the Beast* (1991), *Before Sunrise* (1995), and several other films that attempted to recreate the magic of the Bogey-Bacall and Tracy-Hepburn romances, with varying degrees of success. Certain critics have argued that the McGrath *Emma* is a part of the same project, and have objected to its similarities to other romance films of the 1990s.

Thanks to its perceived commercialism and "Americanness," the McGrath *Emma* is widely seen as a romanticized version of the novel with a tone sweetened to make it more palatable for a mass audience. Signs of the film's *"Disney*izing" of the novel include the primacy of the Emma-Knightley romance, the virtual disappearance of Jane Fairfax from the story, the sweeping music score, and the idealized portrait of Highbury—with its verdant green outdoors and opulent houses that are too exquisite for the Westons and the Coles, despite their comfortable fortune and rising status in the community. Its "American" qualities could be said to include an American movie-star lead in Gwyneth Paltrow (whose lack of British birth has irked some native English critics), a smattering of Americanisms in the script written by McGrath, and a lack of attention paid to spelling out the class-standings of supporting characters such as Mr. Weston and Mrs. Elton.[4]

Perhaps the greatest point of contention is the presence of a glamorous American movie star as Emma, which many critics view as a distracting miscasting. On the issue of Gwyneth Paltrow's American background, Lisa Hopkins observes that the loss of a clearly defined accent, based in a specific British region and class, has a detrimental effect on theme and characterization in the McGrath film:

> ...it is difficult for any film that is aimed at audiences on both sides of the Atlantic to convey class by means of that favourite British indicator, accent. In Ang Lee's film of *Sense and Sensibility*, there are, unusually for a major movie, no American actors at all...[therefore] both class positions and indeed character can be indicated by intonation....Similarly, in the ITV [Lawrence-Davies] version of *Emma*, Mrs. Elton has a giveaway West Country accent which significantly undermines her pretensions to gentility, while Miss Bates' extremely upper-class pronunciation, coupled with the preservation of Mr. Knightley's comment that her notice was once an honor, reminds us of the perilously fragile and contingent nature of class position....

The Douglas McGrath film, however, which stars Gwyneth Paltrow, is a very different proposition. That accents were felt to be a sensitive issue is clearly evidenced by the immaculate English tones carefully studied and adopted by Paltrow; but these function primarily to indicate Englishness *per se*, rather than any particular inflection of it. Though, as with Meryl Streep, one cannot but marvel at Paltrow's ability so to disguise her natural pronunciation...it is, nevertheless, a thinner one than that provided by the rich texture of subtly different Englishes being played against each other that we hear in *Sense and Sensibility*" (Hopkins 2).

From the perspective of a contemporary British audience, the substitution of an "American" Emma for a *bona fide* "British" Emma robbed native Englanders of an opportunity to reexamine one of their classic texts in a modern light. This lost opportunity was keenly felt in the 1990s, a time that was filled with uncertainty as to what constituted essential "Britishness" since the very notion of "Britishness" seemed to be challenged by the breakup of the United Kingdom and the creation of the European Union.[5]

Paltrow's status as a movie star has also evoked criticism from American Austen scholars, who argue that her fame is a distraction, and that a less widely known actress would be easier to accept as Emma. Also, Paltrow's association with a specific style of American glamour and "classy" good looks has polarized her audience, making some adore her for her "old world" charms, and others resent her for representing an idealized standard of female beauty that some men love but that few women could live up to even if they wanted to.[6]

Douglas McGrath, who wrote and directed the 1996 *Emma* for Columbia/Miramax, is obviously a male, and one might argue that his photographing of Gwyneth Paltrow got a little too romantic at times during the course of the film, particularly in one obviously posed shot in which he frames her on a Grecian couch between two plants reading the invitation to the Coles' dinner party. Sue Parrill, on the other hand, defends the casting of Paltrow and, to an extent, her romanticized presentation:

Since Emma is a character who is easy to dislike, having an appealing actress like Paltrow play the role is an advantage. She makes Emma a sympathetic figure, even when she is at her most wrong-headed, and she is easy to forgive when she admits being wrong....[Kate] Beckinsale, on the other hand, seems querulous and cold; [Doran] Godwin stiff and superior....The big difference is a matter of charisma, and Paltrow has it. (*Jane Austen on Film and Television* 123–124)

A similar argument can also be made that Paltrow's performance is superb—as engaging as it is nuanced—and that speaks well of her ability to bring a complex character to life. Writing a review at the time, film critic Jamie Peck said that Paltrow "deserves Oscar consideration." "One of the few Americans in the film, it is to her credit she blends right into the smooth talents of the mostly English cast. This is a magical, star-making performance that's perfect every way you look at it."[7]

Whether or not one agrees that Paltrow's performance is "magical," her presence in the film is far from the only point of contention. McGrath's depiction of Highbury as a lush, almost fairy-tale setting in which most everyone is young and beautiful and the weather is always perfect has evoked concerns from certain quarters that the film is relentlessly "white" and takes nostalgia and upper-class worship to a dangerously racist point. The general argument places *Emma* within the context of the whole 1990s popular revival of interest in Austen, and suggests that the interest was generated by a backlash against cultural pluralism and multiculturalism, and part of a nostalgic effort to reclaim whiteness. That line of argument was probably most reasonably presented by James Thompson, who claimed that, during the 1990s, critics often praised Austen films at the expense of other, crasser examples of contemporary popular culture, such as the ultra-violent, curse-filled films of Quentin Tarantino (*Pulp Fiction, Reservoir Dogs*), or the NC-17, full-frontal-nudity extravaganzas of Joe Eszterhas (*Showgirls, Basic Instinct*). For Thompson, such critics and Austen fans often spoke in highly nostalgic terms, mourning the passing of a bygone age (that never actually existed, even in Austen's time/novels) in which politeness, intelligence, and generosity of spirit were the order of the day, not the rudeness, ignorance, and self-interest of today. For such filmgoers and literature lovers, the Austen movies represent a reminder of the greatness of the traditional canon of Western literature, which has been called into question by canon revisionists and a new generation of college English professors who study and teach multicultural literature, cultural criticism, and New Media. The films also act as a reminder of what is great about "white Englishness," the legacy of British imperialism notwithstanding (22-23).

While nostalgia may be the main reason why some readers and moviegoers gravitated towards Jane Austen in the last decade—Roger

Rosenblatt, for one, was inspired by a viewing of the *Sense and Sensibility* film to write an essay in *Modern Maturity* magazine in favor of the classic canon of literature—it would be unfair to suggest that all of the appeal of Austen (and the Austen-inspired movies) is nostalgic in nature. Indeed, the very lushness and glamour of the McGrath film might not have the same moralistic and political connotations for everyone who experiences it. In fact, the film is far from stodgy, and its occasionally hip qualities help prevent it from being regarded as a purely elitist or reactionary work of art. On the other hand, those same "hip" qualities have also harmed the film's reception among those who seek to defend Austen's work from being appropriated (and made "cool") by modern filmmakers who don't have a proper reverence for the restraint and sobriety Austen shows in her writing.

However, in "Clueless: About History," Deidre Lynch defended the candy-colored Austen films, which she felt were being too easily dismissed as serious adaptations because they were pretty to look at: "It is not evident to me…that Austen would dislike even the glitz (even the flounces and furbelows) that inevitably distinguish the period adaptations of her novels…." Although it isn't clear which films Lynch is discussing *per se* (perhaps the more soberly produced *Persuasian* with Amanda Root and the Kate Beckinsale *Emma*?), she criticizes the Austen adaptations that pride themselves on visual sobriety and "historical accuracy" as often being unaccountably depressing. She writes, "Certainly the thickness of texture that results when 'quality' is a byword has on occasion made these films seem claustrophobic—lush but leaden. It is as if a movie can be weighed down by too much re-creation" (85).

Additionally, it might be argued that McGrath's portrayal of Highbury as a beautiful and safe haven for Emma is in keeping with Denise Kohn's image of Emma's home in her interpretation of the novel as a domestic Bildungsroman. Kohn observes that Austen's depiction of nature which, though sometimes surprising, "is always the safe, domesticated nature of the English village, never the violent, raging nature of the Gothic English moors" (51). The environment of Highbury is presented as safe to assure the reader that Emma will indeed be happy there at the end of the novel, Kohn explains. In this view of the novel, Highbury is not a prison for Emma, nor is Hartfield. "And as nature is domesticated in *Emma*, so is the archetypal role of the greenworld lover, who often plays a prominent role in the novel of female development....Knightley, who is associated with farming and orchards, plays the role of Emma's greenworld lover, yet he is a domesticated version of the mythological Pan or Eros who usually endangers the female heroine....Knightley's domesticated ties to nature make Emma's sexual growth safe within the novel" (52).

Ironically, even though the film has been criticized for idealizing a white, imperialist culture of the past, it has also been cited for misrepresenting that culture as egalitarian by blurring the class and status divisions in Highbury. While I would suggest that the egalitarian subtext of the movie, if there, is an outgrowth of the portrayal of Emma and Knightley's match as a union of equals, Carol M. Dole argues that Hollywood wants to encourage the "American myth of classlessness" by making everyone in the story as well-dressed, pretty, and landed as everyone else. She writes:

> The film's mis-en-scene also undercuts hierarchies. Pairs of characters, regardless of their rank or relationships, are routinely positioned within the frame in a lateral configuration so that neither figure is dominant. Harriet and Emma are repeatedly shown seated on opposite sides of a fireplace, or walking side-by-side toward the camera; Knightley and Emma, or Elton and Emma, are often captured in two-shots. Since Harriet bows her head into Emma's lap in one scene, Emma must make a similar gesture in another. Doorways, window seats, and other symmetrical backdrops further emphasize the symmetry of the characters' positioning. This relentlessly symmetrical composition visually reinforces the film's egalitarian views. (69)

In "The Social Constructions of Douglas McGrath's *Emma*: Earning a Place on Miss Woodhouse's Globe" Christine Colon proposes an alternative way of understanding the film, suggesting that it does, indeed, preserve class differences from the novel and confront class issues, but in a more filmic manner than the novel. For Colon, the most telling and striking treatment of class issues in the film comes from the narrative framing device of Emma's artistic renderings of the globe, and of the narrative voiceover that accompanies its display during the opening and closing credits. In the first case, Emma presented a painted, papier-mâché globe with images of the citizens of Highbury painted all around its equator as a wedding present to the new Mrs. Weston. In the second instance, the closing credits, it is implied that Emma has made a second globe for herself on the occasion of her own wedding to Mr. Knightley, again with portraits of Highbury residents painted prominently over the vast seas and landmasses. Colon has suggested that the globes are loaded symbols, partly because they conflate the images of Highbury and the entire planet, and partly because of which portraits are included, and in which arrangement.

Speaking over the opening credits image of Emma's spinning, papier-mâché globe, the narrator of the McGrath *Emma* seems to come more from our present than from the "present" of the story because the words she uses to introduce the film suggest the opening of a fairy tale set in the distant past. These opening words, which do not appear in the novel, are: "In a time when one's town was one's world and the actions at a dance excited greater interest than the movement of armies, there lived a young woman who knew how this world should be run." The voice sounds like Greta Scacchi, who plays Mrs. Weston in the film, but she is not credited as being the narrator, so the identity of the voice actor cannot be confirmed.[8] However, according to Colon, this narrator, like Mrs. Weston, seems "more calmly approving" of Emma than the novel's narrator.

Colon notes that the opening and closing voice-over narration is juxtaposed with images of two of Emma's artistic projects. For Colon, the images of the globes complicate the view of the story presented by the approving narrator because they draw ironic attention to Emma's restricted worldview. For Emma, Highbury *is* the world. Both globes hold portraits of people close to Emma. The first globe, which includes only the Bateses, Mr. Elton, the Westons, Mr. Knightley, Mr. Woodhouse, and Emma herself, "reveals that the beautiful world we are about to enter may actually be only a projection of Emma's own perceptions. We are not going to receive an objective view of Highbury but rather Emma's construction of her own world…The rest of the film continues to emphasize the differences between Emma's perceptions and the realities of the world around her" (3).

The globe that accompanies the closing credits of the film adds Frank and Jane, Robert Martin and Harriet Smith, and Mrs. Elton to the world of Highbury, suggesting that "Emma's circle has widened, and she grants worth to some regardless of class" (5). Still, for Colon,

> The final image of the globe…allows this film to reaffirm the doubleness of the novel even without the decisive rejection of Harriet. By comparing the

two globes, we can see that while Emma has learned several important lessons about snobbery and class, she is still fixed within a world where class distinctions remain important. While friendship may obscure the fact that Mrs. Weston was a governess, Mr. Weston made his fortune in trade, Mr. Martin is a farmer, and Harriet is illegitimate, it cannot completely overcome these distinctions; for ultimately, Miss Woodhouse still remains the center of this tiny world and she decides who may inhabit it (6).

But what of the other residents of Highbury? How are they portrayed in this film and what level of subjectivity are they afforded? These are important questions given the fact that the film focuses so closely on Emma herself, and sometimes at the expense of the other characters.

The character who emerges as the least sympathetic in the film, and as the most broadly comic, is most likely Mrs. Elton (played with great flair by Juliet Stevenson). In constantly praising herself, and attributing the praise to her unnamed "friends," she is amusingly vain, and in boasting of her possessions, she appears greedy and materialistic. In most adaptations, as in the novel, Mr. Elton's presence in the story shrinks to virtual nothingness once Mrs. Elton appears on the scene, but the McGrath film suggests that Mrs. Elton has a habit of cutting off her husband and overshadowing him, suggesting even more forcefully than the Box Hill picnic scene in the novel that the marriage is not all that Mr. Elton had hoped for.[9]

Aside from Mrs. Elton, and a perpetually cheerful Mr. Weston, all the other characters in the film are more complex than they at first appear. Frank Churchill, for example, seems more mischievous from the outset than he does in the novel because it is he and not Emma who invents the slander about Jane loving Mr. Dixon, so the blame for the gossip is shifted more strongly to him. However, it is even more obvious in the film than in the novel that Frank (here played by Ewan McGregor) eagerly awaits Jane's arrival at social gatherings and he spends more time with her in public. Additionally, Frank is allowed to redeem himself for his early ill treatment of his fiancé by not flirting with Emma at Box Hill in this version of the story. In fact, it is he who subtly comes to Jane's rescue by continually interrupting Mrs. Elton's intrusive and persistent prodding to procure employment, and by turning people's attention away from Mrs. Elton and towards Emma. So, a character who begins seeming even more immature and mean-spirited in this film than he does in the novel finishes by proving himself more worthy of Jane than he does in the pages of Austen's text. The effect is to reassure the audience that the couple will be happy and loyal to one another, and that they are marrying for love. The romantic interpretation of the relationship can be justified within the text itself, dovetailing with William Galperin's view that Frank and Jane are revolutionary lover figures in the novel.[10]

This romantic view of the characters also fits well within the confines of a film adaptation that emphasizes the romance plots from the novel over the social commentary elements of the novel. However, anyone who views the Frank and Jane romance from the novel in the same manner that Sandra Gilbert and Susan Gubar do is bound to be disappointed by the film's depiction of their relationship. Gilbert and Gubar interpret Frank as a figure who imposes upon both Emma and Jane, making apparent their vulnerability as women. In making Frank nice, and in de-emphasizing Jane's poverty and poor health, the McGrath film does not grant any significant attention to Jane's vulnerability as a woman. Therefore, an important theme from the novel is glossed over, and any reader who sees the themes of female friendship and poverty as the primary themes of the novel is bound to see the film as skewed at best, and is still more likely to regard it as a hollow and fluffy romanticizing of the source text. Still, such a view does not invalidate the film's portrayal of Frank and Jane as a romantic couple, because such a portrayal is justifiable if compared to Galperin's view of the characters.

It is also important to observe that, as a domestic Bildungsroman adaptation, McGrath's *Emma* is more interested in Jane Fairfax's effect on Emma's emotional and intellectual state than on the problems of Jane Fairfax *per se*, which would receive greater attention in a social critique adaptation. Hence the reason that Jane is presented more as a competitor of Emma's than as a suffering figure. It is often observed that Jane Fairfax (Polly Walker) has little to do in this film, and that is quite true. She is allowed a scene when she refuses to gossip with Emma at Miss Bates' home, and she is shown several times suffering from the loud-volumed attentions of Mrs. Elton, but that is about the extent of her role in the film. Her most significant screen time comes during the Coles' party, when she is presented essentially as Emma's most formidable romantic and social competitor. It is suggested, but not said directly, that Jane is the superior piano player, although Mr. Knightley reassures a slightly humbled Emma that her "playing was lovely." When Mr. Knightley shows some attention to Jane, Emma glares jealously at her from the shadows. In turn, when Frank shows attention to Emma by joining her in song at the piano, the camera cuts to Jane's perspective, and she is seen glowering at Emma. Given the role that Jane is supposed to play in the film—chiefly as a prod for Emma to improve herself and to cling to Knightley before he is taken from her—Jane should probably have at least one more scene to give her more presence and make her a more formidable adversary.

Although the McGrath *Emma* minimizes Jane Fairfax's role in the story, it does not eliminate her from the story altogether, as the Kraft *Emma* and *Clueless* essentially do. Like the two adaptations that strike Jane from the text, the McGrath film uses other characters, specifically Robert Martin, Miss Bates, and Harriet to illustrate Emma's ill-treatment and manipulation of the less politically and economically powerful Highbury denizens. As with the character of Frank, the McGrath film presents all of the above characters as initially trivial, but with deeper wells of feelings and thoughts than Emma (and viewers) might at first perceive.

The Robert Martin of the McGrath film, Edward Woodall, has a sweet round face, and a loveable child-man quality about him. His first on-screen footage depicts him walking uncertainly past a flock of waddling ducks, the accompanying cute clarinet music earmarking him as a "clownish" figure. And yet, as the film unfolds, Robert demonstrates gentlemanly qualities and a consideration for Harriet that marks him as a good man and a worthy suitor for her. In a similar fashion, Harriet (in the person of Toni Collette) spends the early parts of the movie looking particularly foolish and easily influenced. Parrill writes:

> In the Miramax film, Toni Collette is good at looking and acting stupid, but she is so very unprepossessing that it is difficult to imagine that Emma would be interested in her as a friend. The term 'bovine' may even creep into the viewer's mind....Her portrayal of Harriet reveals few gradations of development or nuances of feeling. She holds nothing back, she gushes with happiness—over puppies, Mr. Elton's pencil, Mr. Martin's letter—or weeps copiously at disappointments. In her tendency to excess, Collette is, perhaps, a more pathetic figure than the other Harriets. (125)

However, Collette has two excellent scenes as Harriet, both of which are genuinely moving despite some humorous undercurrents, and these scenes effectively evoke viewer sympathy for Harriet without casting her as secretly brilliant or deep. The first is the one in which she sits and listens as Emma begs forgiveness for encouraging her to pursue Mr. Elton and the second involves her ceremonial disposal of her mementoes of the failed romance with Elton. The burning ceremony should be either funny and absurd or touching and sweet, but somehow it manages to evoke all of these conflicting feelings from the viewer, and the solid acting from Collette is what makes this possible.

Perhaps the supporting character who is most effectively portrayed is Miss Bates who, despite being a little younger than one might expect her to be, is almost as significant a character in this film as she is in Judy Campbell's screenplay. On the subject of Miss Bates, Parrill writes in "The Cassandra of Highbury: Miss Bates on Film":

> Sophie Thompson's Miss Bates is by far the most memorable rendering of the character. Thompson brings the character to life by blending the comic and the pathetic. Her mannerisms are comic—the constant smile, the myopic peering, the hesitations in speech, the nervous giggle. Yet, her delight at the thought of food, her concern for her niece and her mother, and her pain at Emma's jest are rendered with feeling (3).

Although her perspective on events is not granted the same weight as it is in Campbell's screenplay, Miss Bates is of central importance to the McGrath film because she represents, with her sweetness and tiresomeness taken as a whole, all that is wonderful and all that is trying about Emma's life in Highbury. McGrath gives Miss Bates several long monologues in imitation of her extended speeches from the novel, which Thompson delivers with great comedic flair, allowing viewers to feel with full force why Mr. Knightley would like her and why Emma would *not*. This version sets up the Box Hill scene quite well, increasing its ultimate dramatic impact. When Emma finally insults Miss Bates, all conversation ceases and Mr. Knightley and Mrs. Weston (not absent from the picnic in this film, and not pregnant) look upon Emma with disapproval. As John Wiltshire observes, "This is a moment to make readers of the novel shiver, its sudden interruption into the supposedly convivial scene well caught in the Douglas McGrath film of *Emma*, as the camera is allowed to dwell upon Miss Bates's face, her nervous words spelling out the full significance of the jibe, only implied in the novel" (125–126).

In interviews, McGrath has called this scene the "emotional centerpiece of the film," and one might well say that he succeeded in granting the Box Hill picnic a place of prominence as the most important scene in the film. The Box Hill segment in general is filled with superb acting, from Sophie Thompson's moving performance as the wounded Miss Bates to Jeremy Northam's powerful speech criticizing Emma for her infraction against the poor woman, but one must not forget how moving a moment it is when Paltrow's Emma sheds tears of shame at the scene's end.

Readings of the novel as a domestic Bildungsroman have constantly grappled with the issue of Emma's infraction on Box Hill and of the lesson that she must learn by the end of the story. The McGrath film manages to succeed in maintaining audience sympathy for Emma without minimizing the significance of her harmful jest at Miss Bates' expense. It also takes great care in dramatizing Emma's thought processes and emotional development. In this emphasis, it evokes Denise Kohn's interpretation of the novel as a coming-of-age story, and portrays Emma's growth in a similar vein:

> In the beginning of the novel, Emma takes pride in the fact that she had helped to make a match between Miss Taylor and Mr. Weston. Although Knightley discredits her role, Emma explains that she has taken an appropriate middle-ground as a matchmaker, "something between the do-nothing and the do-all" (7). Her explanation of her role seems reasonable: she "promoted Mr. Weston's visits," gave many "little encouragements," and "smoothed many little matters" (7). Emma's success as a matchmaker, however, leads her to abuse her power as she exchanges her role as social facilitator to become a social manipulator. She tries to realign Harriet's affections and soon believes she can judge everyone's true emotions. When she tries to be the "do all" and force others to follow her plans, Emma crosses the threshold of Austen's depiction of the ideal "lady" (13). Her "kind designs" for Harriet lead her to the grossest unkindness—the belief that she can recreate Harriet on and off the canvas. Emma's desire for social control also causes her snobbery to the Martins and her rudeness to Miss Bates. Her snobbery to the Martins is morally reprehensible to the modern reader, but it was also reprehensible to nineteenth century readers. Trilling writes that the yeoman class had always held a strong position in English class feeling, and at this time especially, only stupid or ignorant people "felt privileged to look down upon them" (37). And Emma's treatment of Miss Bates at the picnic is made to seem doubly heartless by Miss Bates' quiet acquiescence.

But Kohn, unlike many World War II era critics who celebrated Emma's humbling, is able to acknowledge Emma's flaws without judging her too harshly:

> [T]hough Emma sometimes acts in an unconscionable manner, the reader is well aware that she is not without a conscience. It pricks her throughout. For instance, after Harriet meets Robert Martin at Ford's, Emma realizes that she was "not thoroughly comfortable" with her own actions. At the end, though, Emma has changed enough to think it "would be a great pleasure to know Robert Martin" and happily attends the wedding (328). She apologizes to Miss Bates and befriends Jane Fairfax. She learns to treat others with tenderness and to respect their personal privacy and autonomy. She learns to reject both the roles of a "do-nothing" and a "do-all." At the end she considers a future match between Mrs. Weston's daughter and one of Isabella's sons, but her matchmaking is no longer dangerous because she now realizes the problems caused by the abuse of power. She has leaned a lesson: a lady is not a bully. But Emma also learns an equally important lesson: a lady is not a weakling. Unlike so many nineteenth-century heroines, she does not confuse kindness to others with fear of others and subjection of self. At the end of the novel, she is still able to say to Knightley, "I always deserve the best treatment, because I never put up with any other" (327).
>
> Emma's awareness of her own "unpardonable arrogance" allows readers to continue their empathetic construction of her character. Emma has learned to balance power and propriety, reflecting Austen's ideal of a lady as a woman who is strong but not manipulative. (Kohn 51)

In the film, when Emma goes to visit Miss Bates to apologize, her overtures are spurned as Miss Bates races from the room. Although the apology is neither heard nor accepted on screen, the attempt marks the beginning of Emma's reform in the film. Shortly thereafter, when she comes to realize her love for Mr. Knightley, her journey towards self-knowledge and sensitivity to others is well underway. Hence, by the time Mr. Knightley proposes to Emma, there is a feeling that Emma is ready for, and deserving of, marriage to Mr. Knightley. But what makes the proposal scene even more intriguing for readers of the novel is that it emphasizes Mr. Knightley's moral and emotional journey as well, demonstrating that he needed to learn and grow as much as she did in order to be ready to take on the role of ideal husband.

As Hilary Schor explains, McGrath writes original dialogue for Emma that is appropriate for the character, in which she emphasizes how little she deserves Knightley's love. However, in crafting Knightley's proposal, McGrath draws upon material that appears in the book *after* the proposal scene, in which Knightley apologizes to Emma for lecturing her in a paternalistic fashion while confessing that he was unsure of the accuracy of his own perceptions of the events that occurred during the course of the novel.

> In the novel, this speech comes after his declaration of love and is given not directly in his voice, but in a version of free indirect discourse. It is an important speech, to be sure, but it has much less dramatic weight than if it had come before Emma was certain of his love; in a sense, it comes after the suspense, in a slight let-down of reader attention, which is no doubt why it has gone unnoticed in most Austen criticism.

> However, in the film the speech *is* Knightley's proposal. His proposal is nothing other than the confession that he has been as blind and jealous and confused as the supposedly much-mistaken Emma all along; that he, too, has been blind in the affairs of the heart. (168)

Because both characters grow and change before the end of the film, and since each seems to love and respect the other, the film works to convince the audience that its representation of the romance is as balanced and romantic as Kohn sees it in Austen's novel.

Since the adaptation of *Emma* written and directed by Douglas McGrath bears a close resemblance to readings of the novel written by literary critic Denise Kohn and film critic Molly Haskell, it seems fair to say that the film represents a legitimate interpretation and dramatization. In emphasizing the growing love between Emma and Mr. Knightley, and the ways in which both characters mature emotionally and socially during the course of the text, the McGrath film places some of the larger social and class issues from the novel into the background without eliminating them altogether. Since, to my mind, no other adaptation presents the romance in as satisfying a manner, or (*Clueless* aside) foregrounds Emma's inner life and emotional development so effectively, this adaptation stands out as one of the best made from Austen's novel. However, for those who object to the romanticism of the film, and to the harsh cuts made to the Jane Fairfax storyline, the adaptation which follows, a British telefilm starring Kate Beckinsale, offers a far more satisfying and thorough treatment of issues of class and gender than the Douglas McGrath film.

The Lawrence-Davies *Emma*, starring Kate Beckinsale

Jane Austen's Emma. 1996 (UK) February 16, 1997 (US).

(Meridian-ITV/A&E "telemovie," Color, 107 minutes)

Jane Austen's "Emma" starring Kate Beckinsale is noteworthy as being both the most recent of the period piece adaptations of the novel and one of the most innovative.[11] As the only commentary adaptation of *Emma*, this Meridian-ITV/A&E television movie is the one that draws most noticeably upon radical or progressive critical literary readings of the text that a more traditional adaptation such as McGrath's seems to ignore completely. In doing so, this version of *Emma* uses recent psychoanalytic theory to deconstruct the motivations of its protagonists; and it has also been inspired by recent Marxist-historicist writings to dramatize in unusual detail the lives and perspectives of the servant class of Highbury, characters whom Austen chose not to represent directly. Additionally, director Diarmuid Lawrence and screenwriter Andrew Davies appear to be consciously looking back on the Regency period and evaluating it, criticizing the more rigid class structure of the time while praising the powerful, wealthy Mr. Knightley for having a greater sense of civic responsibility and fairness than contemporary globalist corporations have. In telling the story of *Emma* primarily as a social critique, *Jane Austen's "Emma"* has been applauded by many feminist and new historicist critics for granting primacy to issues of class and gender instead of casting the story as a sort of Regency period Harlequin romance, while other critics have taken exception to the emphasis that the production places on servants who have no discernable role in Austen's text.

As supporters of the adaptation, William Phillips and Louise Heal, authors of "Extensive Grounds and Classic Columns: *Emma* on Film," credit Davies for making most of the innovations in the story:

> He claims that 'there's...always some hidden scenes in the book that Austen didn't get around to writing herself, and it's nice to fill in some of those little gaps.' ...Davies's vision of what is between the lines gives this film some of its visually better moments, such as several scenes which elaborate Austen's characterization of Emma as an 'imagist' (6).

Consequently, Phillips and Heal suggest that the Lawrence-Davies film "is perhaps the most important of the period adaptations" despite its tendency to violate "the spirit of *Emma*," because it "raises questions about the lives of characters who rarely, if ever, appear in the pages of Austen—the servants (6)."

While the McGrath *Emma* embraces a reading of the novel that portrays the romance between Emma and Mr. Knightley as healthy and fulfilling, the Lawrence-Davies film suggests that Mr. Knightley is clearly the more dominant personality, as well as the more morally righteous. The implication is that their marriage will involve Emma submitting herself to Mr. Knightley's wiser, paternalistic judgment and curbing her will to his. This depiction of the relationship is far from unusual as, aside from the McGrath film and the Glenister-Constanduros film, all of the other period piece adaptations suggest much the same thing, only in this version, Mr. Knightley has far more of a temper, making one fear he might have occasion to treat Emma too harshly once they are married. Consequently, the relationship between Emma and Mr. Knightley in this adaptation bears a close resemblance to the one described by Frances L. Restuccia in her psychoanalytic reading of the novel "A Black Morning: Kristevan Melancholia in Jane Austen's *Emma*."

Restuccia argues that Emma's unresolved feelings of grief over her mother's premature death caused her to seek out a parental replacement as an inappropriate and almost incestuous love-match, forever preventing her from recovering fully from her mother's death. Restuccia employs Julia Kristeva's theory from *Black Sun* to view *Emma* as a melancholic/masochistic text, whose addiction to the 'maternal Thing' operates both at the level of the story (the *fabula*) and at the level of the functioning of the narrative itself (the *sjuzet*)" (451). The article, which first appeared in *American Imago: Studies in Psychoanalysis and Culture* in 1994, explains that, "[t]o Kristeva, matricide is the first step toward autonomy' one must 'kill' the mother to become individuated. And daughters are especially prone to dodge this murderous act by enclosing within themselves, by consuming, 'the lost object' (or, in Kristeva's lexicon, 'the mother-Thing,' the 'maternal Thing.'), which is then 'not so fully lost'" (452). Notably, the novel *Emma*

...commences with a double maternal loss—the latter [the marriage and departure of Emma's governess Miss Taylor] so traumatic, effecting a "melancholy change"...because founded on the former [the death of Emma's biological mother, Mrs. Woodhouse]. Emma begins by offering a glimpse into the abyss—sustained throughout the novel by the accumulation of lost, dead, and dying mothers—for which it attempts to provide compensation.

In Restuccia's view of the novel, Emma's matchmaking enterprises become an outlet through which Emma can "vicariously pursue an 'other' who can liquefy the mother inhabiting her" but it is a half-measure that "also conveniently exempts her from participating in desiring bonds that would threaten her primary allegiance" (453). Since Emma's ultimate love object is old enough to be her parent and is fond of referring to her as "a spoiled child" or as "little Emma," Restuccia views Mr. Knightley as a substitute mother figure. Indeed, "[j]ust as the loss of Miss Taylor revives Emma's sadness over the loss of her mother, the potential loss of Mr. Knightley seems instantaneously to trigger panic that is a function of Emma's history of loss" (460). According to Restuccia, the unhealthy ramifications of Emma's mental association of her husband with her dead mother are far-reaching. "It might be tempting to ignore Knightley's linkage with Emma's mother and to conceive" of the marriage at the end of the novel as a triumph in which "all traces of the mother [are] wiped out, her loss negated" but such a reading is undercut by Emma's altered behavior on becoming engaged to Mr. Knightley. "In the last chapters, we find Emma parroting Mr. Knightley's views (especially on Harriet) and failing to speak, as if in rehearsal for what promises to be a silencing marriage celebrated at the very end. The Emma we knew, sparkling with wit, is reduced to insipid remarks of gratitude to Knightley" (463) who, for his part, will likely make Emma a "distant, punishing husband" (468).

In matching Restuccia's diagnosis of the novel's leading characters, the British telefilm directed by Lawrence and written by Davies brings a more radical interpretation of the original text to the screen than has been seen before, even in the previous adaptation that wrestled with the issue of Emma's mental health, the Glenister-Constanduros miniseries. The Lawrence-Davies film makes manifest Emma's thought-processes by allowing the audience to see the world as she sees it during key moments in the story. The scenes that result evoke strong emotions from viewers that at once applaud Emma for her colorful and vivid imagination and fear that she is living too much in a fantasy world of her own creation to see the world as it truly is. Seemingly paradoxically, at the same time that the film works to present an unfiltered view of Emma's perceptions of reality, it radically realigns the overarching perspective through which the story is told by relating the narrative primarily from the perspective of the servant class of Highbury. There is an interesting incongruity to splitting the perspective of the film between Emma herself and the servants. There is little rhyme or reason to when and how this shift in narrative perspective will occur, but that is, perhaps, one of the best possible ways for a film to recreate the free-indirect style of Austen's narrative, which breaks similar narrative conventions with equal offhandedness.

The experiment should not work as well as it does but, somehow, Lawrence and Davies manage to tell the story through two radically different narrative lenses—presenting Emma's own fanciful outlook on events and contrasting it sharply with the perspectives of the less financially and socially powerful members of Highbury. Consequently, the film demonstrates that Emma's chief problem is that her imagination clouds her perceptions of reality to the point that she is blind to the very real suffering of Harriet (who would be happier marrying a yeoman farmer than Emma is willing to admit to herself), Jane Fairfax (whose love life is far less romantic and far more troubled than Emma can understand), and the servants (who go to great lengths setting up a lot of heavy furniture on Box Hill so that an assembly of well-off Highbury natives can experience a socially awkward and upsetting afternoon outdoors). In this manner, the Davies-Lawrence film makes Emma a misguided figure with a slight snobbish streak and a very vivid imagination who needs to observe with greater clarity and empathy the people who populate the community of Highbury.

While Emma is primarily kept at a solid critical distance from the viewer to encourage a more objective view of her actions than the McGrath film offers, there are key moments in the Lawrence-Davies film in which the viewer is allowed to share her perspective. During these moments, Emma has amusing and highly romanticized daydreams that are dramatized for the viewers though a combination of vignettes and special effects shots. These daydreams of Emma's, which are easily the most engaging segments in the movie, underscore an element of Emma's character that is rarely evoked by the film and television adaptations of the novel. To some extent, the Emma from the source novel shares some of the qualities of Jane Austen's earlier creation, Catherine Morland of *Northanger Abbey*, and of Charlotte Lennox's heroine from *The Female Quixote*. Principal among these qualities are an overactive imagination, a tendency to read too many romance novels instead of histories and more serious works of literature, and an inability to completely discern the difference between a novelistic convention in a book and an objective representation of reality. In the novel, one of the largest clues to Emma's skewed perception of reality is her expectation that Harriet's birth parents will be revealed to be royalty. In the popular fiction of the time, whenever an adopted character or an orphaned character was part of the story, by the novel's end it was usually revealed that the character's real parents were rich beyond the reader's wildest dreams. Since Emma expects a similar, novelistic development to occur in real life and validate her patronage of Harriet, she is not being realistic. Austen's presentation of Emma's misreading of the real world is partly at Emma's expense, but also partly a critique of the novels of the time, which gave an incomplete education to the women whose primary source of enlightenment were those cliché-ridden novels.[12]

Unfortunately, many of the film adaptations have found it difficult portraying Emma's fanciful side and this makes some of Emma's decisions difficult to fathom—especially her short-lived and amazingly unlikely project of trying to marry Harriet to Frank, or her assumption that Jane is in love with a married man. In most versions, particularly the Glenister-Constanduros version and the McGrath version, it is unclear why Emma jumps to the conclusion that Jane Fairfax has fallen for Mr. Dixon. In contrast, the ITV film makes it perfectly clear when she visualizes a disastrous sea voyage in which Jane is nearly washed overboard, only to be rescued by the chivalrous husband of her best friend. The moment is overblown, funny, and instantly graspable by an audience member unfamiliar with the original text. In a similar fashion, the issue of Harriet's mysterious birth is brought into sharp focus by another dream-image of Emma's, which also offers a clue as to one of the reasons why Emma has taken up matchmaking: she anticipates the warm thanks that she'll get for a match well made. She imagines a wedding between Mr. Elton and Harriet in which the two are standing together outside of the church, beaming at Emma. Mr. Elton says, "How can I ever thank you enough, Miss Woodhouse, for showing me where true joy was to be found? Mrs. Elton and I are eternally indebted to you!" And Harriet adds: "And to think that I should turn out to be the daughter of a baronet!" This is a really funny moment that works beautifully.

In establishing Emma so firmly as an imagist, Davies lays the proper groundwork for his adapting of the gypsy attack on Harriet, a segment from the novel which forms yet another part of Austen's satire of romantic fiction. Emma is not present for the scene, in which the hungry, pathetic gypsies seem to be looking primarily for food and do not constitute much of a threat to Harriet's safety. Later, when Emma hears of the encounter, and of Frank Churchill's prompt intervention on Harriet's behalf, she makes the observation that "It does seem like Providence—or something in a romance, full of brigands and outlaws...but for this to happen in Highbury..." This time the viewers are not let into Emma's thoughts, but if they were, one can wager that Emma's imagined recreation of Harriet's traumatic clash with the gypsies would look far more like a scene from adventure fiction of the time than what actually occurred. It is actually good of Davies to trust the audience to have reached enough affinity with the character to do Emma's imagining for her.[13]

In one of the most successful dramatic explorations of 'Emma the imagist,' the Davies-Lawrence film actually improves upon the source material by providing Harriet with a memorable introductory scene.[14] While attending church, Emma imagines which member of the congregation would make Reverend Elton a suitable bride. As if on cue, a seemingly divine light shines down from heaven onto Harriet. The scene is funny, provides an excellent character moment for Emma, and helps get the story started smoothly. David Monaghan, author of "*Emma* and the Art of Adaptation," has a particularly noteworthy interpretation of this moment in the film and its significance to the overall themes of the Davies adaptation as a whole. He argues that Emma's fanciful imagination prevents her from recognizing just how socially vulnerable Harriet is. After all, should Harriet fail to marry successfully, she will become a spinster who, like Miss Bates, "will serve as a daily reminder of how flawed the patriarchal hierarchy is when it comes to accommodating women who fail in the marriage market." Therefore, instead of exercising her social responsibility to "mitigate Harriet's situation" by encouraging her to marry the "eminently worthy but romantically uninteresting Robert Martin," Emma "puts the naïve young woman into great peril by persuading her to" think of Elton as an attainable mate. "The scene in the church is therefore significant not only because it gives visual expression to the seductive effect of fantasy on Emma, but also because it immediately points up the negative impact that Emma's preference for personal indulgence over responsible social involvement can have on the established order" (208).

While it is certainly true that Emma does neglect many of the duties of her station that she finds unpleasant, it is important to note that, in Austen's novel in particular, there is more to Emma than her fantasies. For all of her much-discussed daydreaming and snobberies, Emma is connected enough to the people of Highbury to perform charity work in the community, tend to her sick father, and agree to look after the Knightley children while John and Isabella are otherwise engaged. The Beckinsale film is very good at using the fantasy segments to demonstrate Emma's good intentions but the film, on balance, still seems hard on Emma, leaving out many of the novel's arguments in Emma's favor while preserving some of her gravest infractions. For example, the screenplay scrupulously preserves the scene in which Emma brings Harriet to the Martin farm for a painfully brief visit (a quarter of an hour) but does not preserve the qualifier that exists in the novel—that she spent that fifteen minutes visiting a former servant who had retired to Donwell Abbey. In the novel, Emma has donated food to Miss Bates just as Mr. Knightley has donated food, but in this version only Knightley is congratulated for feeding the Bates family. Emma also knows quite a lot about her own servants' lives and their families in the novel, but here Knightley seems to know her servants far better than she does. Also, Knightley is shown playing with his brother's children, but Emma is not. At every point, Davies chooses to credit Knightley alone for a virtue that he and Emma share in the novel. However, these changes are all in the service of this adaptation's reading, which suggests that, despite the charity work that Emma has been doing regularly, she is not enough in touch with the needs of the poor and is too caught up in her own rose-colored perceptions of the world.

However, it is possible to interpret the dream motifs from the Lawrence-Davies adaptation as more than just attempts to make Emma seem foolish and irresponsible. At the risk of sounding condescending, the film's dream-images are charming, and Kate Beckinsale's performance as Emma is so captivating during these segments that she wins back viewer sympathy for her character that helps alleviate the dark feelings viewers develop contemplating the plight of Highbury's disenfranchised. These imaginings also, arguably, give her the power to mentally rebel against an oppressive, patriarchal world.

On the other hand, in "Emma and the Servants," Lisa Hopkins ponders the possibility that the dream sequences may be read more as involuntary hallucinations than as active creations of a gifted mind. They may suggest the power of Emma the artist and they may suggest the possibility that Emma is mentally ill. It is debatable to what extent Emma is presented as mentally unbalanced thanks to these hallucinations. I am inclined to think that Hopkins is closer to the mark when she assumes that Emma is in control of the fantasies than when she suggests that the fantasies control Emma. After all, Emma could be a mentally healthy person with a vivid fantasy life who, nevertheless, needs to learn how to see people as they truly are instead of as how she wants to see them.[15]

Hopkins also observes that the Mr. Knightley of the Davies film has a borderline incestuous attraction to Emma and argues that his bad temper is a sign of inner turmoil. Some of the behind-the-scenes literature written to accompany the broadcasting of the telefilm validates Hopkins' views, and has revealed that the production team intended to present Mr. Knightley as a conflicted character. In the book *The Making of Jane Austen's "Emma,"* written by Sue Birtwistle (the telefilm's producer) and Susie Conklin, Mark Strong revealed that he did not wish to play Mr. Knightley purely as a moral exemplar, but instead strove to emphasize Knightley's flaws. Essentially, Strong felt that the most meaningful and rewarding way to portray Mr. Knightley was as a man terrified that he is on the verge of losing his true love to a foppish rival. He says:

...a friend I spoke to who had read Emma at university said, 'Oh, you're playing boring old Knightley.' And I knew what he meant, reading it as a teenager you feel like this man is set up as 'Mr. Goody' or 'Mr. Establishment.' So I had to go back and find out who this man really was.

Jane Austen didn't give that many clues in the book as to his character. Other characters in the book say a lot about him and it's all good. What I found underneath, however, was a man desperately struggling with his emotions. For example, there's a scene where he gets really annoyed because Frank Churchill has gone all the way to London to get his hair cut. It's a witty scene, and you put Knightley's behavior down to his being an older guy who sees that as foppishness. But it suddenly came to life for me when I realized it is his jealousy of Frank that is motivating him. This is something I just didn't glean from the book the first time I read it (Birtwistle 20–21).

Strong's view of Mr. Knightley is a perfectly valid and interesting one, but it is possible that he plays Mr. Knightley as somewhat too jealous and a bit too angry, especially given the fact that he is supposed to act, in this version of the story, as a socially conscious, highly noble figure. In fact, Strong himself feared that he played the scene at Box Hill (when Mr. Knightley berates Emma) a little *too* fiercely. As he said, "At one point I worried that, because I was having a go at Emma, the audience might not see the love behind it" (Birtwistle 21). However, many critics have argued convincingly that Strong's performance as Knightley is far more interesting and complicated than performances given by actors such as Carson and Northam, who make Mr. Knightley too affable.

For Sarah R. Morrison, one of the reasons that Mr. Knightley emerges as a brusque and sullen character in *Jane Austens's "Emma"* is that Andrew Davies did not pay enough attention to the dictates of decorum that were scrupulously adhered to by the protagonists of the novel. In *"Emma* Minus its Narrator: Decorum and Class Consciousness in Film Versions of the Novel," Morrison argues that screenwriters often feel the void left by the absence of the narrator when they adapt Austen's novels into screenplays, and they try to make up for it by placing lines attributed to the narrator into the mouths of the characters. (For example, in film adaptations of *Pride and Prejudice*, the famous opening lines of the novel spoken by the narrator are usually delivered by the actress playing Elizabeth Bennet, such as Jennifer Ehle in the A&E miniseries or Aishwarya Rai in *Bride & Prejudice*.) Screenwriters also have characters speak aloud sentiments that were thought, and publicly proclaim statements that were shared in private in the novel. As Morrison explains, these alterations to the original story usually have broader implications for the screen version than one might first think, especially when Mr. Knightley's reservations about Frank Churchill are not spoken privately to her but expressed publicly and angrily at dinner, for a large assemblage to hear. "These seemingly slight alterations," Morrison writes, "make this Mr. Knightley less courteous and less sensitive to others' feelings than he appears in the novel..." (3).

Essentially, the most disorienting, and possibly frustrating, element of the Lawrence-Davies adaptation is that it seems to want to simultaneously evoke two starkly different images of Mr. Knightley. On the one hand, Strong's Mr. Knightley is a fiercely jealous, abrasive figure who seems to have planned since the day of Emma's birth to mold her into his wife. On the other hand, he is meant to be seen as a wise and just landlord, a champion of the people, and the true hero of the story meant to set Emma straight on her outmoded social worldview. Both images of Mr. Knightley have some basis in the novel, and it may even be possible to imagine a portrayal of the character that could comfortably contain all these traits, but the effect is, perhaps, too jarring here. Mr. Knightley does, in key moments, champion the rights of the servant class of Highbury, and of characters such as Harriet and Jane, but the Lawrence-Davies film works best when these characters are allowed to tell their own stories directly to the audience, and not have their interests represented by a problematic figure such as Strong's Knightley.

Regarding the servant class of Highbury, Lisa Hopkins catalogues virtually all of the major moments in the film that highlight the presence of the lower classes in "Emma and the Servants," making a case for the fact that the servants have much more of a presence and a voice in the film than they do in the novel. She cite moments where the camera lingers on the servants as they provide candlelight to illuminate meal times, open doors for wealthier characters as they enter and leave rooms, chase chicken thieves away from Hartfield, and carry heavy furniture uphill to offer seating during the Box Hill picnic. One servant even has dialogue and converses with Mr. Knightley.

In comparison, none of the servants in the novel have speaking parts and their actions are given cursory attention by the narrator, so their existence is most keenly felt when one of them is mentioned by name and discussed by one of the central characters. William Larkins appears to be an important personal aide to Mr. Knightley, although the nature of his job, the extent of his responsibilities, and his degree of familiarity with Mr. Knightley is not clear. Other characters in the novel mention their servants by their Christian names, often to praise the household cooking. Miss Bates enthusiastically explains that "Patty makes an excellent apple-dumpling" (195) and Mrs. Elton explains that she "should be extremely displeased if Wright were to send us up such a dinner, as could make me regret having asked more than Jane Fairfax to partake of it" (229). After Mr. Woodhouse, Mrs. Elton is the character in the novel most concerned with her servants and their relative merit. She is particularly proud of her coaches and horsemen, who "drive faster than anybody" (258), but she seems to have more reservations about her housekeeper, whom she has been known to spend "a half hour shut up with" (225) giving directions. Still, she reserves most of her criticism for Knightley's servants at Donwell Abbey, on whom she repeatedly casts aspersions (361, 284).

Essentially, since the servants are never afforded the opportunity to speak for themselves, one can only grant the testimony of their employers as to their general state-of-being so much credence, especially since most employers consider themselves benevolent authority figures whether or not that is the case in reality. However, it does not necessarily follow that the Woodhouses make unreasonable demands of their servants, as they appear to in the Davies adaptation. In fact, enough scraps of evidence are presented early on in the novel that it would be just as reasonable to assume the opposite. While Mr. Woodhouse distrusts servants attached to other households— especially strange coachmen driving him through inclement weather (120)—he remains fiercely proud of his own servants, including his cook Serle, who "understands boiling an egg better than anybody" (38) and the unnamed butler, to whom he entrusts the security at Hartfield, and Emma's maid, whom he trusts to look after his daughter's health and comfort (176). Above all, Mr. Woodhouse seems to trust his coachman James with his own safety and with Emma's. Although the valetudinarian feared for Emma's going to the Coles' party alone, some of Mr. Woodhouse's concerns were alleviated when he contemplated Emma making the journey in James' carriage: "I have no fears for you with him. We have never been there above once since the new approach was made; but still I have no doubt that James will take you safely" (175).

Amusingly, if Mr. Woodhouse is not praising James' reliability, he is speaking aloud fears of putting James to too much trouble. And if he has made too much of sparing James, Mr. Woodhouse is apt to transfer his concern to the horses themselves, as on one occasion when he observes, "not that James ever complains, but it is right to spare the horses when we can" (206).[16] While this concern for James seems to speak well of Mr. Woodhouse's empathy with the lower classes, it is most likely a selfish sympathy, as Austen establishes from early on in the novel, especially through Mr. Woodhouse's relationship with Mr. Perry, that Emma's father is prone to project his own feelings onto others. Therefore, his concern for James is little more than a projection of his own hermit-like tendencies onto the coachman.

Mr. Woodhouse's seeming fixation upon James is the funniest running joke of the novel, primarily because James lacks subjectivity and is never granted the opportunity to speak for himself. However, we learn in the very first chapter that Mr. Woodhouse recommended James' daughter to the Westons for a servant position at their home, Randalls, when no one else thought of her. Emma informs her father that "James is so obliged to you!" a sentiment that she would not pass on if it were not true, suggesting that she has condescended to speak to James on this subject. Mr. Woodhouse said it was lucky he thought of Hannah for he "would not have James slighted on any account; and I am sure she will make a very good servant; she is a civil, pretty spoken girl; I have a great opinion of her. When I see her, she always curtseys and asks me how I do, in a very pretty manner; and when you have had her here to do the needlework, I observe she always turns the lock of the door and never bangs it. I am sure she will be an excellent servant; and it will be a real comfort to poor Miss Taylor to have somebody around who she is used to see. Whenever James goes over to see his daughter, you know, she will be hearing of us…he will be able to tell her how we all are" (26).

Based on these passages, it might be reasonable to assume that the Emma from Austen's novel cares more for her servants and their families, and knows more of their lives, than Kate Beckinsale's Emma does.

In recent years, scholars such as Raymond Williams have criticized Austen for not granting enough attention to the lower classes in her novels. In *The Country and the City* (1973), Williams examined Jane Austen's depictions of English country life alongside the writings of populist journalist William Cobbett and found Austen's writing lacking awareness of broader social issues or of true class distinctions. According to Williams "for all the intricacy of her social description...[a]ll her discrimination is, understandably, internal and exclusive. She is concerned with the conduct of people who, in the complications of improvement, are repeatedly trying to make themselves into a class. But where only one class is seen, no classes are seen" (113).

By foregrounding the servants in their adaptation of *Emma*, Lawrence and Davies seem to be implicitly agreeing with Williams that Austen was remiss in not granting greater attention to the servants. It is noteworthy that, while previous screenwriters and directors granted even more attention to characters such as Jane Fairfax and Robert Martin than the novel does, Davies and Lawrence are the first to grant such dramatic emphasis to the servant class.[17] In fact, one might argue that the servants are not only featured players in the Lawrence-Davies version, but that they are granted the prime narrative perspective and serve as the lens through which the story is told.

This adaptation begins and ends with poultry thieves stealing from the wealthier residents of Highbury and being chased off by rifle-toting household servants. That violent action seems an odd way to begin an Austen adaptation, but the opening gun shots are meant to shake out of complacency an audience that might think they already know everything there is to know about Jane Austen and to surprise them with just how much they don't know. For critic Sally Palmer, this bookend image is just part of the way that screenwriter Andrew Davies and director Diarmuid Lawrence give shape to their adaptation's unique narrative orientation. Unlike Phillips and Heal, who find this adaptation's employment of the servants innovative, Palmer objects to the politically liberal slant that it gives to a story that she had always interpreted as socially conservative. Although her overall review of the production is perhaps too unforgiving, Palmer does make an important observation concerning the effect that the use of servant-narrators has on the tone of the production and, by extension, on the audience: the sight of the servants toiling to arrange frivolous parties for Emma makes the contemporary viewer appalled at the exploitation of the lower-classes and less sympathetic to Emma and her peers.

One might argue that the films' emphasis on the servant class acts as the same kind of rebuke of Austen that Williams leveled when he accused her of class-blindness. The filmmakers seem to be implicitly asking the question: If we had to rewrite Austen to get the servants into the story, why did she leave them out in the first place? However, one might just as easily respond to such a query with a counter-question: Why do modern readers feel that Austen *needed* to include the servants in the first place? Why is that, necessarily, a flaw in her artistry? In response to Williams, and to a similar criticism voiced by post-colonial critic Edward Said concerning Austen's reticence to challenge British imperialism, Paul A. Cantor writes that:

> Few authors have suffered as much at the hands of contemporary critics as has Jane Austen. She was just not made for a world of deconstructionism, new historicism, and race/class/gender criticism. She is subtle where contemporary critics are heavy-handed; she uses a tuning-fork where they swing away with sledgehammers. Many critics simply charge her with being blind to the important economic, social, and political developments of her day....Said's essay is typical of much contemporary criticism—he is more concerned with what Austen did not write than what she did....I want to offer a defense of Jane Austen on two grounds: first, that she was in fact more acute in her understanding of social and political questions than contemporary critics give her credit for, perhaps more acute than they themselves; second, that the ways in which she differs from contemporary critics have something to do with the fact that she was after all a novelist and not a political theorist (127–128).)

Whatever viewers may think of the filmmaker's technique in including innovative and provocative footage of the servants, the Lawrence-Davies telefims's overall sympathy for the less powerful citizens of Highbury is actually in keeping with the general social critique bent of previous British television adaptations. The key difference is that, while Judy Campbell and Vincent Tilsley grant significant dramatic importance to the trials of Jane Fairfax and Robert Martin, they do not push the narrative far enough into the realm of populism and deconstructionism to qualify their adaptations as commentary adaptations instead of transposition adaptations. The Lawrence-Davies version does. However, the Lawrence-Davies film is the natural descendant of the previous adaptations in its interest in portraying Jane Fairfax, Harriet Smith, and Robert Martin as positively as possible.

Unlike the Robert Martins from the previous adaptations, who tended to come off as either sweet buffoons or quietly deferential figures, the Robert Martin played by Alistair Petrie in the Davies-Lawrence version seethes with rage that his wife-to-be was stolen from him by this prissy female rival. He quietly glares at Emma repeatedly during the course of the film, and the audience is encouraged to glare with him. He is not presented as a pleasant character, but his righteous indignation is expected to be shared.

As in the Glenister-Constanduros version, the camera often cuts to Jane Fairfax and Harriet Smith during moments when Emma is talking or when her attention is distracted, encouraging audience interest in these women and offering viewers insight into their psyches that the self-absorbed Emma lacks. Given the attention that this adaptation centers on these supporting characters, and given that the actresses who play both characters are so adept, it is not surprising that this version boasts two of the most interesting onscreen incarnations of Jane and Harriet. Sue Parrill in particular has praised the performances of Olivia Williams as Jane and Samantha Morton as Harriet:

> Samantha Morton delivers the best portrayal of Harriet Smith [on film thus far], largely because she is such a good actress...We see Harriet develop from a fearful worshipper of Emma, to confident companion, to assured recipient of Mr. Knightley's attentions. Her Harriet never appears stupid... only slightly dense. (125–126)

Although Parrill does not assert that Williams is the best screen Jane Fairfax, she does observe that, "The director frequently shows Williams' face in closeup, enabling the viewer to see her expressive eyes. Although she rarely smiles and has little dialogue, Williams conveys a wide range of feelings with her eyes" (127).[18]

Critics William Phillips and Louise Heal see the emphasis on Jane Fairfax as one of the chief arguments in favor of the Lawrence-Davies adaptation.

> Lawrence and Davies have clearly decided that Jane is an interesting character who deserves to be strongly featured....Lawrence /Davies's Jane is a tough character, and the viewer sees the trouble and pain she is forced

to endure in her unfortunate situation. This is a memorable Jane Fairfax, not
the shadow of a character....

On the same subject, Linda Troost and Sayre Greenfield observe
that the Davies film takes care to show how much Emma's actions
have emotionally wounded both Robert Martin and Jane Fairfax,
while the McGrath film seems to skirt such issues. They cite as a
compelling example the brief scene in the Davies film when Robert
sees Jane weeping alone and gives her a look of great empathy.

With its interest in the servant classes of Highbury, and in characters such as Jane, Harriet, and Robert, this social critique adaptation
seems to present a bleak picture of a world divided by stark class
lines that cannot be blurred. And yet, with its presentation of Mr.
Knightley as a form of egalitarian figure, the Lawrence-Davies version works to undercut the insurmountable class differences that it
took such pains to represent. Throughout the film, Mark Strong's Mr.
Knightley champions the rights of the poorer residents of Highbury,
speaking kindly but seriously to the servants and arguing fiercely
with Emma over her treatment of Harriet and Jane. The screenplay
appears to encourage the audience to view him favorably for his
populism, despite his somewhat dark persona.

By the end of the story, when it appears that Emma has embraced
Knightley's more democratic (if not borderline socialistic) worldview
and agreed to be his wife, much of his rage melts away and he seems
to uncoil somewhat. He is still serious, but more at peace when he
celebrates his union with Emma alongside the community at large at
a climactic harvest supper, an invented scene that is one of this adaptation's most striking innovations.

Rather than crafting an ending to the adaptation that emphasizes
the wedding between Emma and Mr. Knightley, or that underscores
the romantic nature of the story, Davies wrote a scene in which Mr.
Knightly invited all of his tenants to an egalitarian harvest festival
supper at Donwell Abbey. This harvest scene, which was specifically
conceived for the film as a means of compressing an ending segment
that Davies felt was unnecessarily drawn out in the novel, has inspired a host of commentaries by literary critics eager to tackle its
thematic significance to the adaptation.

For Sally Palmer, the moment when Emma introduces herself to
Robert Martin and invites him to Hartfield is the one in which she has

symbolically transformed into the socialist that Knightley has always wanted her to become; and the accompanying scenes of lower- and upper-class individuals dancing together suggests that society as a whole has become less stratified and more utopian. Notably, Mrs. Elton is the only character who objects to the social leveling that is achieved during the harvest supper in the final scene. She, therefore, emerges as more snobbish than she should for reacting to the socialist scene in a manner perfectly in keeping with the Tory sentiments of her time.[19]

According to Linda Troost and Sayre Greenfield, the ending of the novel sees the Highbury community return to the state it was at the beginning of the narrative, as Harriet, Frank, and Jane are all removed from Emma's circle. Since the unpleasant Mrs. Elton remains as the only lasting addition to the social scene, the Highbury community does not contribute to Emma's happiness, argue Troost and Greenfield. However, in the Davies version, the new couples Frank and Jane Churchill and Robert and Harriet Martin remain in Emma's sphere, and Mrs. Elton's presence in the community appears diminished by her refusal to mingle in the newly egalitarian, idyllic community. Therefore, as Troost and Greenfield observe, the Davies film's happy ending is made complete by the joy the Knightley's take in the reinvigorated community. This ending seems happier than the ending of the novel, which raises the issue of the "necessity" that Emma and Harriet will grow apart after they are married.

Commenting on the controversial passage from the end of the novel, concerning the "necessity" that Emma and Harriet's friendship "must sink," Morrison says:

> This "necessity" will not be apparent to a modern reader. Yet Austen not only makes it clear that Emma and Harriet will not continue to move in the same circle but expects her readers to see the divergence of their paths as inevitable....It is a "truth" presented as tacitly recognized by all, including the heroine (6).

If this is, indeed, Austen's original intention, then the films diverge rather sharply from the source material in ending with Emma and Harriet still friends.

What motivated the filmmakers to make such a striking change in the end of the story, and what are the implications of the alterations? In an interview for *The Making of "Jane Austen's 'Emma,'"* Andrew Davies offers his rationale for his crafting of the egalitarian finale. He cites as his inspiration for the harvest supper itself the scenes in Hardy's and Tolstoy's novels, the scenes of "bringing the harvest home and the haymakers and the good gentleman farmer," but his thoughts behind the symbolic meaning of the harvest in his screenplay have a slightly different bent.

> Though England didn't have a revolution, I think it must have been quite a narrow thing. The Georgians depended quite a lot on the Knightleys of this world, though few were probably as enlightened as he was. These landowners weren't decadent aristocrats who lived millions of miles away from their tenants and just withdrew the profits. They were actually there managing their estates. It's like old-fashioned conservatism, really....
>   I think in a historical period like the one we're living through there's a nostalgia—an "angry" nostalgia even—for any time where you had some sense of fairness—where you might not have had much money but you could believe that you would be treated fairly (58).

While critics such as Philips and Heal have found Davies' approach to crafting the finale intelligent and intriguing (and while I find it to be in keeping with the sensibilities of a commentary adaptation), Palmer voices objections to Davies' entire project. Sounding something like Paul A. Cantor, Palmer feels that the film encourages viewers to be thankful that they live in the "superior" 20th-century by

> foregrounding the inequities and unrest Austen passes over in her own century. In an attempt to highlight the need for today's socialist Labour government, the filmmakers have annexed Austen's socially conservative novel, but invented for it additional scenes and dialogue to make a democratic rhetorical point of their own....*Emma*'s plot underscores the need for proper conduct and noblesse oblige, not abolition of the ruling class or widespread social reform." (1–2)

Palmer's poor review of this adaptation seems to stem primarily from the fact that she disagrees philosophically with the principle of making a commentary adaptation of a novel instead of a transposition adaptation. Based on published interviews with the members of the production and on the way the film plays on screen, it seems clear that the intent was to make a film that consciously commented on the novel, and even used Austen's story to make observations about contemporary society in the process, instead of merely working to translate the text, unchanged, to the screen. As someone who appears to be against the principle of commentary adaptation, Palmer frames the argument against the aims of the Lawrence-Davies version well. However, while less seen than the American cinematic versions, this adaptation has emerged as a critical favorite of academics who, despite a leaning towards viewing *Clueless* as the best adaptation of *Emma* thus far, have a tendency to praise the Davies-Lawrence version at the expense of the McGrath version. Far from being a flaw, the experimental nature of this adaptation, and the liberties it takes with the source text, arguably work in its favor as both a fresh look at the novel and as a form of entertainment.

Clueless: Emma Woodhouse Becomes Cher Horowitz

Clueless. Released July 19, (US), October 20, 1995 (UK). (Paramount motion picture, Color, 113 minutes)

In an interview for the *Orange County Register*, writer-director Amy Heckerling describes how she was inspired to make the 1995 film *Clueless*:

> I wanted to do a happy movie about a very optimistic young girl...I really had her attitude in my head, and what I thought I needed was a strong structure in the style of comedy of manners. (20 July 1995, 30 March 2002.)

Remembering that she loved reading *Emma* in college, Heckerling decided that the Jane Austen novel was an ideal choice to use as a template for *Clueless* because "[t]he plot is perfect for any time" (*Rolling Stone*. August 22, 1996). In writing *Clueless*, Heckerling drew upon Austen's "sense of class and social dynamic" for inspiration and used *Emma* as the "structural tree" for *Clueless*, making a modern-day coming-of-age story from a domestic Bildungsroman narrative from 1816.[1]

By lifting Austen's story out of the Regency period in which it was conceived and setting it in (what was then) present-day California, Heckerling crafted *Clueless* as an analogy adaptation of *Emma* that modernized the tale, shifting the action "forward to the present...mak[ing] a duplicate story" (226).[2] In the process of updating the narrative, Heckerling recast the British, 21-year-old Emma Woodhouse as American high school student Cher Horowitz, and turned most members of the novel's supporting cast into Cher's classmates, giving them California-style names and more racially and ethnically diverse backgrounds.[3] Consequently, the film's Mr. Knightley remains older and wiser than Emma/Cher, but by a narrower margin since he is a college undergraduate.[4]

Writing in *Jane Austen on Film and Television*, Sue Parrill observes that:

> [a] significant difference which Heckerling has made in updating the novel to the last decade of the twentieth century is the changing of the main character's age from twenty-one to sixteen. She probably felt that an American high school student is more likely to experience the kind of idleness that Emma experienced as an unmarried female than an American woman at any other stage of her existence. At the age of twenty-one, a young woman of the upper middle class in the United States is likely to be preparing to graduate from college and to embark on a career. Also, a college is a more egalitarian environment than a high school. (121)

All of the film's events take place in Los Angeles, an environment that, despite its vast size and urbane sophistication, seems like a world unto itself that mirrors Highbury's provincialism. Additionally, since most of the action of the story takes place at Cher's high school or in her father's impressive home, the scale of the narrative is ultimately more domestic and intimate than a Los Angeles locale might initially suggest.

For readers of Austen, a lot of the film's humor comes from the peculiar effect created by the placement of Austen characters and themes in a context as alien as modern-day L.A. David Monaghan, for example, writes that "The novel...provides Heckerling with the opportunity for some intertextual jokes based on the incongruities between scenes set in contemporary Beverly Hills and parallels from Austen's depiction of Regency England. The substitution of a rowdy teenage party held in a suburban bungalow in balmy Los Angeles for the snowy evening when the Woodhouses and Knightleys visit Randalls for a grand Christmas Eve dinner is a particularly effective example of Heckerling's comic method" (214). And yet, despite the possibly jarring juxtaposition created by considering the original settings of scenes from the novel alongside the contemporary settings in *Clueless*, Austen scholars such as Gabrielle Finnane, Lesley Stern, and Suzanne Ferriss have praised the film for so effectively transplanting the story in time. Finnane even goes as far as to say that, like the *Mansfield-Park*-inspired *Metropolitan*, *Clueless* successfully demonstrates that "any small affluent universe of taste and opinion can be anatomized as a series of Jane Austen characters" (Carroll 174).

Of course, not all critics agree that *Clueless* is as successful in modernizing the story of *Emma* as Finnane maintains. Those who view *Clueless* as a failed adaptation of *Emma* tend to focus on the youth and callowness of its heroine, and on the array of pop culture references that place the narrative squarely in the present. For example, John Mosier, who likes the film, nevertheless complains of the elimination of Jane Fairfax from the story, the loss of the sizable age difference between Mr. Knightley and Emma, and the transformation of Emma's father from a sickly figure that fosters Emma's complacency into a lovably grouchy parent who criticizes his daughter for lacking "direction." Critic David Monaghan calls into question the excessive rudeness of the characters in the world of *Clueless*, a trait which bears little resemblance to Austen's polite world. Also, despite its critique of the seemingly rigid class structure of the public high school, the film seems to strive to create a utopian, multicultural society where class and race differences are dissolved into a harmonious whole, and this goal seems too egalitarian for Jane Austen. These observations are all valid and intelligently framed, but most of the changes cited seem as if they arose as a natural consequence of making an analogy adaptation of *Emma*, and none of them appear thoughtless or gratuitous if one considers the demands of the contemporary setting. Also, it seems fair to say that, on balance, more Austen scholars appear to like the film, and view it as a successful adaptation of *Emma*, than dislike the film and question its relationship to the source novel.

Despite the obvious differences between the two time periods, perhaps the chief benefit of setting the story of *Emma* in a modern-day context is that it recaptures the immediacy and the relevance of the novel in a manner that has not been felt since its publication in 1816, when it was a brand new text and not yet a classic, canonical work of British literature. After all, as several critics have pointed out, *Emma* was not a "period piece" when it was written, but became one over time. To that extent, film adaptations that strive scrupulously to recreate the setting of Regency England (a.k.a. "the olden days") are susceptible to making the story seem more conservative and nostalgic than it was ever meant to be. "Heritage" film adaptations also risk paying too much attention to issues of period detail and not enough to giving primacy to the core themes of the text, such as education, female community, civic responsibility, provincialism, courtship rituals, and the woman artist. Therefore, by setting Austen's story of the maturation of a young, gifted woman in the present, Heckerling is able to engage the core ideas of the novel without getting lost during a trip down nostalgia lane. Addressing this issue, John Wiltshire observes that *Clueless* stands apart from other films that "modernize" Jane Austen texts, (such as *Metropolitan* and *Jane Austen in Manhattan,*) which:

> have an undercurrent of anxiety: how do you reconcile loyalty to Jane Austen with contemporaneity, how do you manage the transition between a writer thought to be genteel and elitist with the modernity you seek necessarily to embrace?...Such anxiety has been overcome in *Clueless*: it simply takes Austen for granted. But for this film the Austen taken for granted is not an image or model of high culture and gentility, but of creative zest and brilliance, not 'Jane Austen' the cultural image, but Jane Austen. (56–57)

Inevitably, as a contemporary American film, *Clueless* reflects the social mores of its time and addresses the issues which Austen explores in a very contemporary and American manner. For example, the gulf between 1816 England and 1995 America is readily apparent in the way in which the film deals, overtly and symbolically, with issues of sexuality, drugs, AIDS, and multiculturalism, but *Clueless* demonstrates that, as much as society may change, the essential path that a young woman must follow into maturity and adulthood remains, in many ways, constant. Indeed, despite the change in setting, and despite even some of the substantive alterations to the story that were indicated above, *Clueless* provides an intriguing reading of the *Emma* narrative as a domestic Bildungsroman.

At the start of the film, Cher seems to demonstrate great potential that she is not reaching because she, as her father puts it, lacks "direction." She has possession of a rich vocabulary, is capable of negotiating better grades from her professors, knows a lot about fashion, and has had some striking success as a matchmaker. However, she seems markedly less intelligent than the character that inspired her, and she appears to have a much longer road to travel to maturity at the start of *Clueless* than Emma does at the start of Austen's novel. Cher has some knowledge of literature, but not enough, and she seems to have a compassionate view of Third World refugees without having enough of a grasp of the realities of international politics and global poverty. She also begins the film emotionally unready to commit to a romantic relationship and seems unable to fully understand the sex lives that her fellow students have embraced while she has chosen to remain single. By the end of the film, however, Cher has grown considerably—intellectually, emotionally, and morally—by attaining greater understanding of herself and the world around her, and by finding someone to love.

Like Douglas McGrath's *Emma*, another American adaptation of Jane Austen's novel that followed *Clueless* into movie theaters a few months later, *Clueless* dramatizes the moral, emotional, and intellectual development of the heroine by allowing the audience frequent glimpses into the heroine's mind. Both films achieve this effect primarily through employing the visual technique of the close-up and the audio technique of the voiceover. In *Clueless*, Cher's face is frequently captured in close-up, allowing lead actress Alicia Silverstone the opportunity to demonstrate, through subtle shades of expression, what Cher is thinking, and not saying. A similar effect is created using the frequent close-ups in McGrath's *Emma*. Additionally, both films relate the heroine's thoughts directly to the audience through voice-over during key moments in the story. Consequently, the films forge an intimate connection between audience and heroine which makes the heroine endearing even as it demonstrates the limits of her knowledge and her need for personal growth.[5]

The principal difference between *Clueless* and McGrath's *Emma* is that the narrator of the McGrath film is a woman whose identity remains a mystery while the narrator of *Clueless* is Cher herself. The Cher who is narrating the story in voiceover is a slightly older Cher than the Cher on screen, so she is wiser and more reflective about the actions of her younger counterpart, thereby demonstrating how much she ultimately learns from her experiences.[6] In "'As If!' Translating Austen's Ironic Narrator to Film," Nora Nachumi writes:

> Cher's moral growth and her genuinely likeable nature pose a challenge to those of us who harbor stereotypes about spoiled teenagers who live in Beverly Hills. More seriously, the film goes to great lengths to reinforce an image of Cher that it eventually dismantles. The first-person narration is extremely important to this endeavor because it makes Cher immensely appealing. It lets us know that a good heart beats within the shell of self-

involved ignorance. The fact that Cher finally understands her own heart is—importantly—signaled by a newfound harmony between what she says and what we see on the screen....Cher's new perspective is more than a realization about her feelings for Josh. She sees her old behavior as shallow, and this gives her the power to alter her world....(137).

Notably, aside from the Judy Campbell adaptation, *Clueless* is the only *Emma* adaptation that retains the discussion of the heroine's reading habits, and the quality of the books she chooses. The discussion of reading in both the Campbell adaptation and *Clueless* signals the fact that both films are interested in the moral and intellectual development of their respective heroines. By including the theme of education, both adaptations suggest that there is more at stake in the story than whether or not the heroine finds true love: the heroine's knowledge, self-awareness, and inner life are all at stake as well.

Amusingly enough, Heckerling also allows Cher a better memory of *Hamlet* via a Mel Gibson film than a serious student of literature can claim through direct exposure to the text.[7] When Cher overhears Josh's haughty college girlfriend Heather quote Hamlet as saying, "To thine own self be true," Cher corrects her. Heather looks dismissive of Cher and says, "I think I remember *Hamlet* accurately." But she doesn't. Cher is right when she maintains "That Polonius guy said it." It is a striking moment in the film, especially since it represents one of the first times that Josh smiles in approval at Cher's upstaging of another. Later on, however, Josh teases Cher for not having a direct relationship with works of fine art and literature, but one mediated by popular culture and film adaptations. These two contrasting scenes with Josh, taken together, evoke Mr. Knightley's monologue from Chapter Five in the novel, in which he expresses disapproval with Emma's lack of drive to read more:

"Emma has been meaning to read more ever since she was twelve years old. I have seen a great many lists of her drawing up at various times of books that she meant to read regularly through—and very good lists they were— very well chosen, and very neatly arranged—sometimes alphabetically, and sometimes by some other rule. The list she drew up when only fourteen—I remember thinking it did her judgment so much credit, that I preserved it some time; and I dare say she may have made out a very good list now. But I have done with expecting any course of steady reading from Emma. She will never submit to any thing requiring industry and patience, and a subjection of the fancy to the understanding..." (Austen 47).

While Emma seems aware that she and Harriet should ideally be reading and discussing more significant literary works than the Gothic novels of the time, she does not appear to do much more serious reading for the rest of the book. In *Clueless*, Heckerling pokes fun at Cher for choosing to read diet and exercise books, and encourages laughter at Tai for reading *Men are From Mars, Women are From Venus*, so the theme of reading is retained in the film, even if the Emma character seems less aware that she should be reading more substantive works than *Fit or Fat?* Although the film does not, ultimately, show Cher reading *Hamlet* in its original play format, or even show her actually reading *Fit or Fat?*, the trajectory of the narrative and the tone of the final reel of the film both imply that Cher has grasped the importance of education and will begin doing her English homework more thoroughly and conscientiously because she has leaned the importance of watching the news and listening to advice from her teachers. Therefore, by the end of the movie, Cher may still have more growing and more learning left to do, but she can no longer fairly be called "Clueless."

That having been said, many critics have debated the exact meaning of the mock-condemnatory title, and the exact way in which Cher might be considered "clueless" at the start of the picture. The title is, at least, a striking declaration that the film's dramatic focus will be on the personality of the heroine and her need to "get a clue," earmarking it as a domestic Bildungsroman reading of the novel rather than as a social critique. But how might she be considered clueless? One possibility is that she is clueless because she doesn't see how foolish her attempts at matchmaking are. Certainly many post-World-War-II domestic Bildungsroman critics make similar claims about the need for Emma to shed her matchmaking endeavors, both for her own good and for the good of those whose lives she meddles with. However, Claudia Johnson has presented a compelling case that Emma's matchmaking efforts are not trivial, but potentially very beneficial to the lower-class women whose social status Emma seeks to elevate. Indeed, rather than chasten Cher for her attempts at matchmaking, *Clueless* appears to be in sympathy with them (and, by extension, with Claudia Johnson's reading of the novel).

Although *Clueless* treats humorously Cher's failed attempts to match up Tai (read: Harriet) with Elton, it dramatically demonstrates the concrete good that arises from Cher's matchmaking as well. For readers of the novel, one of the most intriguing segments of *Clueless* comes at the beginning of the film, when it depicts Cher successfully orchestrating a love-match between Miss Geist, an activist-minded social studies teacher, and Mr. Hall, a lovably grumpy debate teacher. Since Geist and Hall are characters inspired by the Westons, the film argues, by extension, that the Emma in the novel may have had more of a role in bringing Miss Taylor and Mr. Weston together than Mr. Knightley would allow.

In the opening scene of the novel, Emma claims that she facilitated the Weston-Taylor romance and observes that, if not for her interference, there might not have been a wedding. The debate from Chapter One is essentially dropped and left unresolved and unaddressed until several hundred pages later when, in a moment of controlled anger directed at Jane Fairfax, Frank Churchill asks Emma to find him the perfect wife since she did so superb a job matching his father with Miss Taylor. The compliment seems to grant Emma the lion's share of the responsibility for the match, or at least as much credit as Emma at first grants herself. Did Frank deduce this himself, or did he get this notion from his father or the former Miss Taylor? Although Frank is a deceiver and a gossip, his line rings true as an opinion genuinely held by the Weston family and appears to be a brief moment of forthrightness on Frank's part.[8]

In *Clueless*, Cher's efforts to bring her two lonely teachers together are motivated, at least initially, by a selfish desire to make them "blissfully happy" enough to give their students higher grades. However, she soon surprises herself by how good it makes her feel to bring happiness to others, and the success inspires her to continue doing good deeds. The "selfish" motivation aside, the film seems largely approving of Cher's matchmaking efforts and presents her as well-intentioned. In fact, while Josh is essentially a likeable character who makes many accurate criticisms of Cher's matchmaking, he is *just* superior enough in his manner that many viewers might well want Cher to continue to challenge his authority by ignoring his advice. Consequently, the film presents a sympathetic view of Cher's matchmaking endeavors that is not unlike William Galperin's view of Emma's matchmaking in the novel:

> Like Marianne Dashwood in *Sense and Sensibility*, Emma is engaged in what may be described as an insurrection. Seeking to wrest power from those men, including her...father, who exercise it most strenuously and capriciously in the world of Highbury, Emma contrives, through the lives she either arranges or hopes to arrange, to effect change in an otherwise stratified society. That these "revolutionary" efforts, specifically the wedding of less advantaged women to more advantaged men, are simultaneously contradicted by Emma's own sense of entitlement and, later, by the appeals made to it by Mr. Knightley (with whose encouragement Emma eventually assumes her rightful place), is less surprising than it is inevitable. (67)

On the other hand, Emma's efforts to elevate Harriet's social position through marriage to Rev. Elton doubly wound Harriet, first by preventing Harriet from marrying her true love, Robert Martin, and, secondly, by raising false hopes that Harriet will be accepted by someone who is uninterested in wedding her. Her actions also wound Mr. Martin, whose feelings she is less mindful of since he is a member of the yeomanry, a class with which she does not associate. Therefore, Emma's earlier, successful effort to promote the Weston-Taylor union led her into a kind of *hubris*, an elevated opinion of her own ability to uncover the secrets of the human heart. In this regard, Cher makes the same mistake as Emma, and needs to learn the limits of her own knowledge.

While it is possible that Cher's cluelessness has to do with her matchmaking efforts, it is equally possible that her real cluelessness is an insensitivity to white Americans from a lower class than herself, such as Travis Birkenstock (a.k.a. Robert Martin), and to immigrant domestic workers such as Lucy, the Horowitz-family maid (who is ever-so-loosely inspired by Miss Bates). Like previous adaptations of *Emma* that cut down the size of Jane Fairfax's role (or eliminate it altogether), *Clueless* makes up for the loss of Jane by granting greater dramatic attention to the scenes in which Cher mistreats the Robert Martin character (Travis) and the Miss Bates character (Lucy). Cher claims to dislike Travis primarily because he smokes too much marijuana, although it is possible that he also proves himself unworthy of her good graces by eating at McDonald's, riding public transportation, and accidentally ruining her good shoes. However, Cher grows to accept him by the end of the film after he goes cold turkey and proves himself "motivated" by winning a skateboarding competition.

Since Travis emerges as less of a "loser" than Cher first thought, she does not regret her failure to keep him and Tai apart.

Meanwhile, in the film's closest equivalent to the moment in which Emma publicly slights Miss Bates on Box Hill, Cher insults Lucy, the family maid from El Salvador, by mistakenly calling her a Mexican in front of Josh. Cher's *faux pas* demonstrates that Cher's "cluelessness" might not only constitute a lack of sympathy for members of "the lower classes," such as Travis, but a lack of proper understanding of other countries and cultures, and of the political dynamic between the First and the Third World. Post-colonial literary critic Gayle Wald writes:

> As this remark about Lucy implies...the film's narrative of a 'multicultural' and class-transcendent American nation (a narrative that co-exists with its portrayal of distinctions in wealth and status) is repeatedly undermined by references to 'Third World' subjects or locales that are not easily assimilable to it....For example, Cher's reference to Lucy, an immigrant domestic worker, not only complicates the film's narrative of the United States as a welcoming 'domestic' space for all those who seek to establish themselves within its borders, but it is also instrumental in situating Cher as a gendered subject who occupies a position of national, racial and class privilege relative to other gendered subjects within the patriarchal 'private sphere.' Even as her remark displays her ignorance and a national obtuseness that viewers can laugh at, it also points to the fact that, within the confines of her home, she enjoys a comfort and freedom that are contingent on Lucy's labour...(227–228).

Wald seems correct in asserting that Cher's ignorance of international politics is central to her "cluelessness." However, it is possible that Cher has more sympathy for the downtrodden and a greater understanding of civic responsibility and global politics than her insensitive remark to Lucy might suggest. The film presents Cher early on as someone who feels abstract sympathy for the plight of Third World peoples, even if she does not have much of an understanding of international politics or foreign cultures, as she argues in favor of the United States granting asylum to Haitian refugees.

Given Cher's confused feelings about the poor and civic responsibility, (which seem to speak as much in her favor as against her,) it is not immediately clear to what extent Cher needs to cultivate more liberal and sophisticated political views under the tutelage of Josh and her social studies teachers or to what extent her heart is already in the right place. For some critics, several of Cher's domestic metaphors for large scale conflict, and even some of her "girlish" means of "finding order in a world filled with chaos," are not fundamentally worthless; rather they are legitimate and are undervalued by the same dominant masculine culture that underestimated Catherine Morland's "feminine" perceptions of the world in *Northanger Abbey*. After all, as silly as Cher can be in the film, Josh's criticisms can be a *little* too frequent and a *little* too sarcastic.

For Deidre Lynch, who discusses the film in "Clueless: About History," Cher does not get quite enough credit from Mr. Hall for her Haiti debate. In her opening statement, Cher opines that the U.S. could afford to make room for Haitian refugees by hurriedly redistributing some of its abundant resources, thereby living up to the symbolic promise made by the Statue of Liberty that America is the land of opportunity for the downtrodden. Cher uses as an example a dinner party she organized for her father's birthday in which guests arrived who did not RSVP. While they were difficult to accommodate at first, Cher managed to provide for both the expected and the unexpected guests. As Lynch observes, despite the fact that the dinner party analogy is "trivializing," it would, nevertheless, "be churlish to deny that the political message it delivers reframes the responsibilities of the state in ways that appeal" (78).

Certainly Cher begins the film with her heart in the right place, expressing liberal sentiments without boasting any real knowledge of social and political issues. She does, however, learn the importance of supporting sentiment with knowledge, and surprises Josh by taking up watching the nightly news to fill the gaps in her understanding.

As a coming-of-age story that emphasizes the importance of the heroine's intellectual and emotional development, the film certainly lauds Cher's decision to learn more about contemporary political issues. It is also clear from early in the film that Cher does not know as much about men, and romance, as she thinks she does, and the movie humorously sets up an audience expectation that her pledge never to date would be broken by the end of the film. Therefore, the awakening of Cher's romantic feelings and sexual desires are also important themes in the story of her emotional journey. In fact, for John Mosier, Cher's ignorance of her own sexuality is at the core of her "cluelessness" and is the central concern of the film.

According to Mosier, Cher is "clueless" in the same way that Emma is, since both women have a "deficiency which relates to things sexual" and "a blind spot with respect to an awareness of how men perceive women sexually, how they respond to them, and what they expect from them" (243). Ironically, Cher and Emma, far from being aware of having such a blond spot, proceed as if they are experts in the very subject of which they know next to nothing. Because of the similarity between Emma and Cher in this regard, Mosier suggests that Heckerling's concept of sexual cluelessness "has a rather profound impact on any understanding of the novel" (243).

For Mosier, cluelessness appears to be a trait most commonly found in British and American novels, as opposed to in French or other European novels in which most characters seem to have a greater intuitive grasp of the nature of human sexuality and of courtship rituals. However, Mosier suggests that Austen does not judge Emma for her "cluelessness," but presents the naiveté as a natural stage in a young woman's growing understanding of the world (Mosier 245).

Of course, Mosier confesses that he finds it unlikely that a teenage girl living in a society as sex-obsessed as contemporary America would demonstrate the same ignorance about sex that a twenty-one-year-old woman from Regency England would. While he is essentially correct, there is another way of looking at Cher's innocence that makes it more understandable and realistic. As sexually liberated and progressive as many American teenagers generally seem to be, there are those teens that are so afraid of contracting a sexually transmitted disease that they consider abstinence or serial monogamy the safest possible sex life. In fact, while fear of AIDS is often not enough to prevent teenagers from being sexually active, it is reasonable to suggest that Cher is afraid of sex, and her sexual ignorance/innocence is a natural outgrowth of her decision "to save herself for Luke Perry," an idealized television star who symbolizes white masculinity at its purest and least sexually threatening.

For Melissa Mazmanian, it is the fear of sexually transmitted disease that keeps Cher a virgin and fuels her fear of commitment to a sexual relationship. In "Reviving *Emma* in a Clueless World: The Current Attraction to a Classic Structure," Mazmanian interprets many of the alterations that Heckerling made to the original story—including exaggerating Harriet/Tai's fickleness into an active promiscuity and transforming Frank's suave, effete manners into homosexuality—as signs that Heckerling is interested in using the novel as a means of exploring the ramifications of the AIDS virus on youth culture:

> [*Clueless*] exemplifies how popular culture re-appropriates Austen's novels to serve updated agendas. As a novel of manners, *Emma* creates a space between competing ideological extremes of the late eighteenth century. During this period the traditional 'aristocratic ideology,' based on a hierarchy of social birthright, began to clash with a 'progressive ideology' emerging from burgeoning notions of individualism and capitalism, *Emma* exists as a text enmeshed in this debate and represents a tenuous equilibrium upholding social stability. Correspondingly, *Clueless* creates a guideline for proper sexual relations in a society both obsessed with sex and terrified by the ramifications of sexually transmitted diseases like AIDS....In both cases, the newfound space is extremely narrow and precarious. (1, 7)

After describing *Clueless'* AIDS subtext in detail, Mazmanian explains how the domestic Bildungsroman-style story of Cher's personal growth reflects the film's exploration of issues of "safe sex":

> Essentially, Christian and Tai are subconscious challenges to Cher's virginity. Constructed as the protagonist of a novel of manners, Cher is set up as an ideal character. And in the modern context that prototype denotes virginity. Tai and Christian are subtle projections of the real issue; one has sex and the other implicitly suggests what sexuality can lead to....(6–7)

William Phillips and Louise Heal also suggest that the supporting characters in *Clueless* represent a more dangerous, or less socially desirable, form of human sexuality than Cher, and posit that the resultant moral gulf that is created between Cher and the supporting characters serves as a contemporary equivalent of the novel's interest in class and status distinctions. As convincing as these views are, the fact that the film seems to want the audience to love these characters presents a challenge to the view that their chief function is to symbolically represent sexual deviance. Admittedly, there is a grotesque quality to Tai (the film's Harriet) that seems deliberately built into the character to help audience members excuse Cher's manipulation of her. However, while Dionne and Murray are intended to be funny in the ways that they conform (and *don't* conform) to racial stereotypes, they are charismatic and interesting characters in and of themselves, and can hardly be seen in a purely symbolic light as representative of dangerous sexuality. Christian in particular is a sympathetically presented character, and any reading of the film that views him purely as a warning sign about AIDS robs him of his complexity. As Sue Parrill observes, although "Cher's shock at realizing that Christian is gay" parallels "Emma's shock at Frank Churchill's irresponsibility in coming into the society of young ladies with the appearance of being un-attached...the film attaches no blame to Christian; rather, Cher appears naïve for assuming that he is heterosexual" (121).

In many ways, it is difficult to watch any teenage "sex" comedy without thinking of all of the potential perils of sex that are essentially glossed over by the film, ranging from teen pregnancy to AIDS.[9] The experience of watching *Clueless* is no exception, especially since its handling of sexuality seems to idealistically suggest that lovemaking can be consequence-free if the partners involved love one another enough. However, it is possible to push the AIDS subtext argument too far. Reading the film more literally, it seems feasible to take Cher at her word. She is single, she says, because boys her age are too immature and she has too little in common with them. For Cher, finding someone to date who is intelligent, well-groomed, and sexy is a truly difficult task, especially since the man whose personality is most compatible with hers is gay. However, she learns that sometimes love can come from places where you least expect to find it, and the one she had previously ignored altogether as a possible romantic interest, a former step-brother with whom she engages in comic insult contests, is the very one who can make her most happy.

To one degree or another, all of the critical interpretations of *Clueless* as a domestic Bildungsroman reading of *Emma* are accurate. Cher gradually learns the importance of doing her homework more conscientiously, which signals the possibility that she will learn to elevate the quality of her recreational reading as well. After befriending Christian and becoming romantically involved with Josh, Cher ultimately learns enough about men to accurately boast understanding their wants and needs, thereby shedding the sexual cluelessness that John Mosier sees in her. And Gayle Wald is correct to point out that there are sizable gaps in Cher's knowledge of local and world affairs, which she takes the first steps towards rectifying when she begins watching CNN and finally joining one of Miss Geist's community activist projects. While each of the critics named above emphasizes different thematic strands in the film, their writings on *Clueless* finally complement one another by bringing to light the various ways in which the film dramatizes the maturation of its heroine, Cher Horowitz.

For scholars who see *Clueless* as a successful adaptation of *Emma*, the film finds fascinating contemporary parallels for Austen's ironic narrative tone. Even with its wide array of "high culture" and "popular culture" references, which seem to date *Clueless* as a product of the 1990s (the *Twin Peaks* reference, for example, has not stood the test of time), the film reflects Austen's own interest in critiquing culturally undervalued works of art such as the gothic novels and romance novels of her time. In addition, *Clueless* echoes Austen's concern with the shifting social mores of a turbulent socio-political era, and recreates the novel's ambivalent depiction of provincial life. Perhaps most significantly, if one were to treat the film in the same manner that one might treat a transposition or commentary adaptation of *Emma*, as a reading of the novel, then it may easily be regarded as a domestic Bildungsroman version of the story in which the Emma character learns to grow in understanding of herself and her place in society, and to finally reach her potential as she grows into womanhood.

Overview

Emma on Film: Male and Female Perspectives

Throughout this book, I have discussed each of the individual *Emma* adaptations in detail and have considered the various interpretations of the novel that they represent. While some adaptations offer visions of the novel that are more consistent or more effectively realized than others, each, in its own way, offers a gloss on the text that I find rewarding to contemplate. For example, the first television adaptation from 1948, written by Judy Campbell, anticipates Casey Finch and Peter Bowen's 1990 new historicist interpretation of the novel as a study in gossip and female discourse. Campbell's screenplay shows the gossips of Highbury acting in opposition to Emma: working to reunite Harriet and Robert Martin after Emma drives them apart; drawing attention to Jane Fairfax's suffering when Emma would prefer to ignore it, and expressing hopes that Emma would marry Mr. Elton when she prefers to remain single. Though occasionally funny, the gossips are treated as a serious social force that actively works to shape the outcome of the narrative. In its interest in the Highbury community, and its attention to class and gender issues, Campbell's *Emma* is a social critique.

In contrast, the second adaptation, the NBC Kraft Television Theatre version (1954), echoes some of the views of the novel presented by Maaja A. Stewart and Beth F. Tobin. The Kraft *Emma* teaches its heroine not to take it upon herself to blur class and status distinctions in a highly structured society in which she has no chance of success in marrying the natural-born Harriet to the clergyman, Mr. Elton. In the attention it pays to the pain that Emma causes Elton and the Robert Martin character, this adaptation is more interested in the world of

Highbury than it is in Emma, making it an intriguing social critique despite its frequently distracting use of broad humor.

A dark portrayal of "petticoat government" can be found in Vincent Tilsley's screenplay (1960), which depicts vain upper-class women neglecting (or victimizing) the more socially vulnerable women who depend upon them for support. In a similar fashion, Paul Delaney has written of the novel's portrayal of unjust female rulers, who use their powers to oppress both the men and the women who occupy social positions beneath them. However, Tilsley's screenplay diverges from Delaney's reading when it suggests that Mr. Knightley is just as prone to jealous abuses of his authority as the women of Highbury when he assumes a hostile attitude towards Frank due to the young man's amorous attentions towards Jane and Emma. In granting primacy to issues of class, the Tilsley adaptation is a social critique.

As another social critique, the Glenister-Constanduros film argues that Emma and Knightley need to learn humility and empathy for their romantic rivals by creating a scenario in which the two are briefly compelled to hide their engagement from a disapproving Mr. Woodhouse. The experience of having to endure the trials of an interfering parent and a secret engagement cause the two to recant their former harsh appraisals of Frank and Jane. It also encourages them to be more empathetic towards one another, thereby improving their prospects for a happy marriage as well as enhancing their social awareness. The Glenister-Constanduros adaptation is also the most effective in presenting Highbury as a claustrophobic environment that isolates Emma and stunts her intellectual and emotional growth.

Offering a more idyllic portrait of Highbury and a heroine with a sweeter demeanor, the Douglas McGrath *Emma* presents a reading of the novel as a fairy-tale-like domestic Bildungsroman. Its reading of the novel is akin to Denise Kohn's since it dramatizes the heroine's journey towards "intellectual independence and self-understanding" (46). The film ends with Emma remaining "strong and assertive" but becoming "more caring and sensitive to others" (46). In this adaptation, Emma's seasoning is mirrored by Mr. Knightley's, since he also grows as a character. The two prove themselves worthy of one another when they complete their maturation at the end of the film, and they form an idealized bond of marriage based on equality and mutual respect.

In the Lawrence-Davies film, Emma's vivid imagination and love of romantic literature obscures her vision of the real world, thereby deluding her that she can marry Harriet above her station and leaving her nearly blind to the sufferings of Jane Fairfax. Only through the tutelage of Mr. Knightley, who is often angered by the frivolities of Emma and Frank, does she learn to have a more realistic, and more democratic, view of Highbury society and her place within it.

If some of the period piece adaptations seem too nostalgic and conservative in their staging, and too interested in the novel as British "Heritage," then *Clueless* arguably escapes the trap of traditionalism by setting the story in the present. In effect, *Clueless* faithfully evokes the core thematic concerns of the novel—including education, female friendship, civic responsibility, proper courtship rituals, and provincialism—without recreating Austen's *milieu*. While the film's handling of these issues is very much contemporary and American (especially in its treatment of AIDS, multiculturalism, and sexuality), its interest in these issues is very much in keeping with the spirit of Jane Austen.

Examining the *Emma* adaptations as a group, it becomes fairly clear that they offer diverse and contradictory readings of the novel. In fact, it is both the strength and the weakness of the films that they offer unequivocal visions of the text. For example, the McGrath *Emma* can be praised for its emphasis on romance and comedy, and its retelling of the story of the novel as a domestic Bildungsroman, just as it can be faulted for being too light and too uninterested in social issues. The Lawrence-Davies adaptation, *Jane Austen's "Emma"*, successfully stresses the serious social issues facing Regency England, offering an intelligent reading of the novel as a social critique, but it can be criticized for being too somber and for having too little romance and humor. And yet, as Linda Troost and Sayre Greenfield have indicated, the film adaptations may be stronger when viewed together than they are when screened individually because they complement one another. In fact, viewing both together gives one a more faithful picture of the book than viewing each one separately, as the two bring polar opposite interpretations of the novel to the screen. Based on the experiences of Troost and Greenfield, one might infer that watching any combination of the other adaptations could prove just as interesting to other academics, or even to students in an undergraduate classroom.

However, if, like me, one were to examine *all* of the *Emma* adaptations as a group rather than confine oneself to the 1990s adaptations, then a potential problem comes to light. If there is a weakness with the body of *Emma* adaptations as it exists today, it is that too many of the production teams were dominated by men, and this masculine influence seems to have affected the readings of the novel that the films provide. Of the eight adaptations, only *Clueless* was directed by a woman (Amy Heckerling), and only the Davies-Lawrence version had a female lead producer (Sue Birtwistle). The Kraft adaptation was co-written by a man and a woman (Martine Bartlett and Peter Donat), and three adaptations were written exclusively by women: the 1948 television adaptation (Judy Campbell), the lost American television version from 1960 (Claire Roskam), and *Clueless* (Heckerling). The other four adaptations were written exclusively by men: Vincent Tilsley, Denis Constanduros, Douglas McGrath, and Andrew Davies. Considering the loss of the Roskam script, which cheats modern-day readers of her vision of the novel, and noting that Amy Heckerling is the only female *auteur* with the power of writer-director, then the imbalance seems fairly clear.

A brief comparison of the adaptations written by men with the adaptations written by women makes the difference in sensibilities between "male" and "female" crafted adaptations readily apparent. As a group, male scriptwriters are more likely to emphasize class issues over gender issues and they show more interest in granting interiority to Mr. Knightley than they do in bringing Emma's perspective to the forefront. They tend to cast Mr. Knightley as a lover-mentor and privilege the romantic elements of the story. Also, in screenplays by men, Emma and Mrs. Elton are generally used to exemplify unjust feminine authority whereas Jane Fairfax and Mrs. Weston are depicted more sympathetically because they represent more passive, traditional modes of feminine behavior. Male adaptors also cast Emma as an elitist and a snob, emphasizing her disdain of Robert Martin and the Coles while conveniently forgetting that one of Emma's chief concerns is raising the social status of her female friends, Harriet and Miss Taylor, by seeking to marry them to men of a higher station.

Women scriptwriters, on the other hand, have tended to be more interested in creating a sense of female community and a specific style of women's discourse to bring Highbury to life on screen. Educational concerns are more central to the scripts by Heckerling, Campbell, and Bartlett, all of whom emphasize the importance of Emma's honing her pianoforte skills, improving the quality of the portraits she paints, and finally sitting down to read all the great books that she has earmarked for study. In contrast, based on the adaptations that have been filmed thus far, scripts by men either downplay these concerns or omit them altogether.

Mrs. Elton and Mrs. Churchill are less grotesque and less prominent figures in adaptations by women, and less sympathy and screen time is afforded to Frank Churchill and Robert Martin. Mr. Knightley remains a wise figure, but his flaws are more apparent in dramatizations produced by women. As a case in point, Judy Campbell and Amy Heckerling allow the heroine to tease the Mr. Knightley character: Campbell has Emma tease Mr. Knightley for being too rustic, while Heckerling allows Cher to tease Josh for being pretentious and maudlin. Both screenwriters also have their heroines offer strong cases in defense of the nature of their relationship with Harriet/Tai. In general, Campbell and Heckerling are successful in recreating the witty repartee and the verbal cunning that Austen grants the Emma from the novel. Alternatively, male scriptwriters tend to cast Emma as too much in the wrong to adequately defend herself from Knightley's criticisms; consequently, should she ever have occasion to tease Mr. Knightley, her barbs have a hollow and defensive ring to them.

In pointing out this gender imbalance in the *Emma* film canon, I do not wish to argue against the validity of readings of the novel offered up by men. If I were to do so, I would undermine myself, and call into question my qualifications for writing about Jane Austen on the basis of my gender. However, if one were to compare all of the *Emma* adaptations produced by men to all of the *Emma* adaptations crafted by women, it becomes fairly clear that men and women tend to read the novel differently, and to bring different aspects of the novel to the screen. That being the case, it seems all the more important that women have as many opportunities as men to adapt Jane

Austen's novels to film and television. In fact, given the gender and
the prominence of the author concerned, women should probably
have *more* opportunities to adapt Austen works than men.

Putting aside, for the moment, the issue of the gender of the filmmakers, a second notable criticism can be made of the group of *Emma*
adaptations as a whole: not one of the many film and television
dramatizations of the novel make manifest the radical subtext that
certain scholars have found hidden beneath the surface narrative. In
other words, even the female scriptwriters who make Emma a
stronger and more complex character than she is in most adaptations
by men seem to stop short of making their portrayal of the character
as revolutionary as it could be. Both Allison Sulloway and Claudia
Johnson have contended that the book is far more subversive than it
has often been allowed to be by traditional literary critics. The same
point might be made about the film and television adaptations. For
example, Sulloway has suggested that Mr. Knightley's worldview is
far more flawed than any of the adaptations of *Emma* to date would
lead us to believe. Also, one might argue that no film version of *Emma*
has presented as positive a portrayal of the heroine (including her
matchmaking endeavors and her "masculine" personality traits) as
Johnson does in her scholarly writings. Nor does any film seriously
explore Emma's possibly homoerotic attraction to Harriet, which
Johnson also considers.[1] Many of the individual adaptations have
elements of radical academic readings built into their fabric—
including the Glenister-Constanduros version, which makes something of an antagonist out of Mr. Woodhouse in the final segment—
but none of them provide a thoughtfully subversive reading of *Emma*
in the style of Patricia Roczema's groundbreaking film version of
Mansfield Park. Therefore, should studio executives ever wish to produce another adaptation of *Emma*, they might easily distinguish their
new film from those made before in two obvious ways. First, they
might consider basing their film on more radical scholarly interpretations of the text than have been seen in the past. Secondly, they can
hire women with extensive knowledge of both Jane Austen and film-
making techniques to make the movie rather than, once again, assign-
ing a male screenwriter and a male director to the project.

Of course, as I observed earlier, it is both the strength and the
weakness of the films that they offer imbalanced, unequivocal views

of the text. They tend to emphasize either masculine or feminine concerns and either liberal or conservative politics. They tend to give primacy either to the story of Emma or the story of Highbury. They relate the story either as a domestic Bildungsroman or as a social critique. This tendency to focus on certain aspects of the novel to the detriment of others has been off-putting to critics that expect an adaptation to recreate the effect of the novel in its entirety. On the other hand, Troost and Greenfield have effectively defended the tendency of the film adaptations to "unbalance the novel into...different directions" on the grounds that "a two-hour adaptation cannot and should not try to do everything" (*Filming* 2).

That having been said, perhaps it is time for an adaptation that strikes more of a balance between the conflicting readings of the text, and that comes closer to capturing Ian Watt's view of the novel as both personal and social at the same time. There is always the danger that any film meant to appeal to all audiences will ultimately appeal to none, and that an adaptation that tries to recreate the novel as a whole will fail to do as much justice to it as a less ambitious and less "completist" adaptation. However, in an ideal world, the best possible adaptation of *Emma* is one which strives to recreate the various subtleties and mysteries of the text in a manner that leaves it up to each individual viewer to determine its meaning. A model adaptation would glean influence from both domestic Bildungsroman and social critique readings of the novel and strive to balance the two, just as it would not neglect more iconoclastic readings of the novel in favor of purely traditional interpretations. It would allow the viewers to feel an intimate connection with Emma while keeping them at enough of an objective distance to have a broader view of Highbury as a whole. Therefore, the model adaptation would present viewers with multiple perspectives on characters and events, offering them the opportunity to come to their own conclusions about the story. In doing so, the film would preserve some of the ambiguities found in the novel rather than present possible solutions to the mysteries devised by the production team on behalf of the viewers.

As William Galperin writes in "Byron, Austen, and the 'Revolution' of Irony" (1990):

> ...it is *Emma*'s greatest achievement that its manifest and indirect content are forever separate, if still mutually dependent. Regardless of how we interpret

Emma, in other words, whether as a novel about the proper chastening of a selfish young "imagist" or, more radically, as an allegory about the pressures on women to conform, it is *Emma*'s purpose at some level to show the complicity of these disparate narratives and, with the latter in particular, to suggest the synonymity between a "cover story" and the "story" for which it provides a cover (66).

An ideal adaptation of *Emma* would create a similar effect by juxtaposing complementary and contradictory possible interpretations of characters, themes, and events, simultaneously supporting and undercutting both radical and conservative interpretations (perhaps by dramatizing the same scene more than once—from differing perspectives—in a style akin to Akira Kurosawa's 1950 film *Rashomon*?). Of the adaptations of *Emma* made to date, *Clueless* comes closest to recreating this effect because it has proven to be more open to diversified and conflicting interpretations than any other adaptation. And yet, even the least dramatically successful of the adaptations, the NBC Kraft Theatre special, retains enough of the feel of the novel to cause the viewer to meditate upon issues of class, gender, and education as they are raised in the story.

One of the principal strengths of the novel is its ambiguity and the onus it places on readers to be careful interpreters of events. Like any scholarly reading of the text which attempts the same project, any adaptation which assumes a consistent ideological position regarding the characters and story offers a possible solution to the mysteries of the text but does not recreate the ambiguities and subtle nuances of the text itself. However, the adaptations of *Emma* made thus far are successful, not because they attempt to recreate on film the effect of reading the novel, but because they present coherent, insightful interpretations of Austen's narrative. At their best, these adaptations are dramatically satisfying films that offer an interpretation of Jane Austen's novel that will inspire viewers to read *Emma* for the first time, or to read it again to test the filmmaker's view of the story against their own. Although the films do not *recreate* the novel on screen, they encourage close, consistent readings of the text, and strive to make an early 19th century work relevant to a contemporary audience. In these ways, at least, the *Emma* films are all worthy of Jane Austen.

Adaptations in the Classroom: Final Thoughts

The 1990s Jane Austen adaptations are more than ten years old now, yet they remain an important source of discussion and debate in the academic world, especially since classroom professors are often confronted with the question of whether or not to use them as teaching aids. The hope is that the films will enrich student readings of Austen, but the fear is that the striking visual presentations will distract students from developing an understanding of, and an appreciation for, the artistry and subtleties of the original texts.

Seeking a resolution to the issue, M. Casey Diana conducted a classroom experiment to determine whether students would be better readers of Austen if they saw a film adaptation first or read the novel first. Diana divided the class in half, with one group assigned to watch Ang Lee's *Sense and Sensibility* film before reading Austen's *Sense and Sensibility,* and the other group to read the book first and then see the film. At the conclusion of the experiment, Diana found that those students who had seen the film first were more eager to read the novel, and were better interpreters of the text, than the students who began with the novel and saw the film afterwards.

In my own teaching experience, I have also concluded that film adaptations can be valuable pedagogical tools if used properly. While I have not repeated the experiment, I have found over four years of teaching Mary Shelley's novel *Frankenstein* that my students often have an easier time grasping the complexity of the novel when I use the film adaptations to supplement class discussion than when I made a conscious decision not to screen the films. However, each time I show a film adaptation to my students, I have the nagging doubt that the film is doing the students' work for them, and it is actually harming their understanding of the novel. I am not alone in this fear. Based on his own experiences teaching Austen's novels alongside their respective adaptations, critic Robert Eggleston believes that the primary texts are in danger of being eclipsed by the lush film adaptations that "reduce the novel to a two-hour experience" (4) and are, thus, more easily digestible by current and future generations who are already losing their ability to read with care. The core of Eggleston's argument appears to be that the films visualize and interpret the novel on the students' behalf: the films save the students the trouble of imagining setting and the physical appearances of the characters, and they simplify the story and themes of the source text, bringing a work of high art down to a level that an undergraduate can comprehend with ease. By implication, the films foster lazy and limited readings, as well as offer students the opportunity to avoid reading the novel at all.

Although they are not as concerned with pedagogical issues, Seymour Chatman and Anthony Lane sound much like Eggleston when they assert that films do much (or all) of the work of visualizing and interpreting the source novel on behalf of the audience. Chatman, for example, notes that films conjure up the world of the novel on screen, ensuring that "its appearance is determined for all of us" (101). Also, films take round characters, with whom readers have long felt a strong "sense of intimacy" and who have seemed "virtually inexhaustible objects for contemplation," much "like real-life friends and enemies" (Chatman 132-133), and enforce their visualization on screen. Consequently, "The all too visible player...seems unduly to circumscribe the character despite the brilliance of the performance" (Chatman 118-119). In a similar fashion, *New Yorker* film critic Anthony Lane has suggested that the disadvantage filmmakers face when adapting Austen is that "they have to decide on a tone and stick with it, whereas the atmosphere of the original resists any such definition," thereby dooming those familiar with the novel "to sit through the movie sighing for the lost astringency of the book" (76).

Many other Austen devotees probably experience similar frustrations when watching the adaptations, most likely because they feel as if the films strip them of much of the interpretive power that they held as readers of the source narrative. This would be true even if they essentially agree with an adaptation's conceptualization of the novel, but if readers feel out of sympathy with the film's interpretation then their frustration would likely be even more pronounced. In the case of the *Emma* adaptations, a viewer who has read the novel as a social critique is likely to reject an adaptation that retells the story of the novel as a domestic Bildungsroman, just as one who reads the novel as a domestic Bildungsroman is likely to reject a film version that treats the novel as a social critique. The reasoning is that filmgoers like best those film adaptations that dovetail with their own readings. And yet, it is just as possible that readers will find a film adaptation that challenges their preconceived notions of how to interpret the book to be something of a revelation in the way in which it presents an alternative vision of the story. Therefore, film adaptations can be valuable, not just for students and for those who have never read the book, but also for those who are already familiar with the text.

As John Mosier observes, "Probably the most successful adaptations of literature to film are those which cause the viewer to conclude…that the filmmakers have a point, an interpretation which deserves a hearing" (228).

I agree.

Notes

Introduction

1. A complete guide to all of the film adaptations of *Emma*, including cast and production team lists, can be found in the Appendix.

2. The "independent" film's success story, and the rise of the "women's film," has been chronicled in cinema history books such as *Celluloid Mavericks: A History of American Independent Film* by Greg Merritt (Thunder's Mouth Press, 1999), *Cinema of Outsiders: The Rise of American Independent Film* by Emanuel Levy (New York University Press, 2001), and *Women Who Run the Show: How a Brilliant and Creative New Generation of Women Stormed Hollywood, 1973–2000* by Mollie Gregory (St. Martin's Press, 2002). Many books on the subject agree that 1989 was a banner year for movies emerging from "outside of the mainstream," laying the groundwork for the explosion of independent films produced during the 1990s.

    However, one might also argue that Austen's concern with the social mores and class issues of her time interested a contemporary audience that looked to classic works of 19th century literature (and films based upon them) for a more complex and realistic portrayal of society than had been presented by popular cinema of the recent past. That would explain, in broader terms, the movement to bring classic fiction to the screen that typified European and American cinema of the 1990s.

3. In popular circles, the Academy of Motion Picture Arts and Sciences granted Oscars to *Emma* (1996) for Rachel Portman's music score and to *Sense and Sensibility* (1995) for Emma Thompson's screenplay. Also, *Persuasion* (1995) is featured in *The New York Times' Guide to the Best 1,000 Movies Ever Made*, a 1999 book edited by film critics Vincent Canby, Janet Maslin, and Peter M. Nichols (Three Rivers Press).

4. Wayne Booth popularized the phrase "free indirect style" in *The Rhetoric of Fiction* (University of Chicago Press, 1961). However, some critics have argued that the style itself was first identified by Ian Watt. In *The Rise of the Novel*

(Berkeley, University of California Press, 1957) Watt observes how Austen's writing style successfully combines the satirical narrative voice of Fielding and the personal, psychological storytelling of Richardson. See page 297.

Chapter One

1.   Mosier writes that Austen and her contemporaries considered a "handome" woman to be full-figured, stately, and voluptuous, and supports his definition with a citation from the *Oxford English Dictionary* (235).

2.   As is to be expected, the last ten years of literary criticism of the novel *Emma* has been replete with essays that either allude in passing to the three film adaptations of 1995 and 1996, or which take in-depth looks at the films in comparison to the novel. Some of these scholarly treatments are kinder to the films than others. Many of these essays were written for (or were reprinted in) the following book-length studies: *Jane Austen in Hollywood* (1998) edited by Linda Troost and Sayre Greenfield; *Nineteenth Century Women at the Movies: Adapting Classic Women's Fiction to Film* (1997), edited by Barbara Tepa Lupack, and *"Emma" on Film* (1999), a special edition of *Persuasions*, the Jane Austen Society of North America's periodical. Particularly worthy of note are *Jane Austen and Co.* (2003), edited by Suzanne R. Pucci and James Thompson, and *Film and Literature* (1999) by Timothy Corrigan. In addition to including insightful commentaries on the *Emma* adaptations that will be referred to repeatedly in later chapters, both works feature juxtaposed photographs of Gwyneth Paltrow from *Emma* and Alicia Silverstone from *Clueless* on their covers. [Therefore, I didn't want to follow suit with this book's cover since it has been done twice already. Fortunately, this book is blessed to have a cover rendered by a talented, generous, and immensely likeable cover artist Donald Hendricks.] Paltrow is dressed in pseudo-Regency-period clothing, Silverstone is dressed in chic, 1990s Los Angeles attire, yet both are, ostensibly, playing the same character. Book-length studies of the films by a single author include Anke Werker's *By a Lady: Jane Austen's Female Archetypes in Fiction and Film* (1998), John Wiltshire's *Recreating Jane Austen* (2001), and Sue Parrill's *Jane Austen in Film and Television* (2002). Werker's book concludes by observing that "the general opinion of a certain time influences the reception of the novel that is adapted. But it is also through time that the film gains or loses realistic effect" as in the case of the *Persuasion* adaptation, which was initially criticized as being too grim and gritty for Jane Austen but which has now, less than a decade later, achieved broader acclaim for its stark realism (114). Wiltshire's book is primarily a sociological one concerned with how "Jane Austen" is a cultural icon in Great Britain, and how the Austen films reflect the polarized and one-dimensional views of her as either a prim conservative or a raging revolutionary. Parrill, meanwhile, comprehensively chronicles and reviews every adaptation of Austen's works made to date, concluding that the vast majority of the filmic interpretations are

successful in evoking the spirit of Austen's originals by adhering closely to her plots and keeping most of her dialogue intact (15).

3. In *Novel to Film* (Oxford: Clarendon Press, 1996) Brian McFarlane also cited David Lean's *Great Expectations* as a cinematic auteur's triumph in finding "a visual stylistic verve that may be compared to the novel's peculiar rhetorical power" (105).

4. For example, Douglas McGrath, who wrote and directed the 1996 *Emma* starring Gwyneth Paltrow, chose to make the movie because he had a genuine love of the novel. Despite being an English major, he had never read the novel in school because it was not assigned to him. After electing to read it on his own, and discovering how much he loved it, he wanted to make others aware of the book, as well as to bring his visualization of it to the screen. At every stage, his approach to the project of adaptation was to treat the source novel with great respect. As he explains in an interview in *Screenwriter* magazine: "When you have someone like Jane Austen, who is smarter than I am, you cannot afford to ignore the text, so even when you might blithely change something, if your desire is to be faithful to at least the spirit of the novel, if not the letter, you always go back and look. You do have an ultimate responsibility to her, and even though she cannot verbalize her argument, every time you look at the book her version is there and you're always asking yourself, 'Is my version equal to this or better than this, or am I doing damage to something that survived the test [of time] and tastes of people over almost 170 years?' You ignore that at great peril" ("Douglas McGrath, Screenwriter/Director." *Screenwriter Magazine Online*. http://www.nyscreenwriter.com/article10.htm).

5. A word on the [sic]: Corrigan makes an understandable error at this point in his writing, incorrectly citing the 1932 Clarence Brown film *Emma* as an early Austen adaptation when it shares her novel's title but not her novel's plot. Sue Parrill, the principal cataloger of Austen adaptations, does not list Brown's film as an adaptation of Austen. The Internet Movie Database (www.imdb.com) cites the film as an adaptation of a story by Frances Marion. It describes the film as being about a nanny who marries her rich employer only to fight with his three children for his inheritance money when he dies. Although Corrigan makes a mistake in citing this film as a retelling of the story of Emma Woodhouse, this error does not undermine his overall point. For the quote to read more accurately, one might choose to substitute a genuine early Austen adaptation on DVD, such as John Glenister's 1972 *Emma*.

Chapter Two

1. According to Tobin: "Emma does not understand that to be first in Highbury society involves much more than accepting praise and flattery; it requires exertion and the performance of not particularly pleasant duties such as being

kind to people like the Bateses, inviting them to tea, visiting them in their own home, and providing them with the necessities they lack. As a powerful and wealthy woman, Emma has a social responsibility to assist and protect women who are economically vulnerable and socially disadvantaged. This novel abounds with distressed gentlewomen who by the rights of the old paternal society deserve Emma's protection and benevolence. But failing to grasp her proper role in relationship to these women who are less privileged than she, Emma chooses inappropriate ways to relate to Harriet Smith, Jane Fairfax, and Miss Bates. Eager to form some kind of relationship with Harriet, and claiming she wants to be "useful" and of service (p. 39), Emma adopts Harriet as if she were a pet, and Harriet's grateful and fawning manner encourages Emma's sense of her own superiority. Emma plays with Harriet as if Harriet were a doll, using her to experience vicariously the flirtation and flattery of courtship activities…[And by] assuming the role of match-maker, Emma assumes the right to tinker with the very delicate social and economic adjustments involved in arranging a marriage in a highly structured world" (479–480).

2. A good case can be made that I have inaccurately described Stewart as a critic interested in how Emma reforms during the course of the novel. As a new historicist interested in the social structure of Regency-period Highbury, Stewart may, indeed, have a greater claim to being described as a critic who reads the novel as a "social critique." However, since Stewart so effectively describes the ways in which Emma has mistakenly identified her role within this society, she offers one of the best explanations of why Emma makes so many social "blunders" during the course of the novel; hence Stewart's placement in this discussion of readings of *Emma*.

3. Bharat Tandon, author of 2003's *Jane Austen and the Morality of Conversation*, sees the end of the novel as presenting a moment frozen in time. According to Tandon, "Austen has, throughout the story, threatened the romance by surrounding it with characters unfulfilled within or without marriages, and with possible alternative versions of Emma herself. She then has the audacity to present a romance ending which depends on a marriage, whilst all the time amassing an ever larger weight of equivocal or worrying precedent….Like the marriage which it describes, the last sentence is an act of hope in the ambience and in the teeth of experience. Unlike any relationship, however, it deliberately stops just before the 'ever after,' and remains poised endlessly on the brink" (174–175).

Wayne Booth, who defended the believability of the happy union dramatized at the end in his 1961 work *The Rhetoric of Fiction*, expressed some doubts concerning the marriage when he revisited the topic in his 1988 work *The Company We Keep*. In this follow-up treatment, Booth writes, "In *Emma*, we play doubled roles much more intricate than are demanded by fantastic elements like gold-laying geese. On the one hand, we must see the ending as indeed a happy one, not in the least ironic, given the world of the conventional plot, a world that we are to enter with absolute wholeheartedness. And yet, simultaneously, we are asked to embrace standards according to which the ending can only be viewed as a fairy tale or fantasy" (Company 434–435).

4. Although there is a strong tradition of *Emma* criticism that sees Mr. Knightley as exercising power over *Emma*, either justly or unjustly, some critics have recently taken to suggesting that the relationship should be viewed as an ideal match between intellectual, moral, and social equals. John Hardy, for example, suggests in *Jane Austen's Heroines: Intimacy in Human Relationships* (1984) that Emma and Knightley ultimately achieve a lively union based on trust that does not inspire discontent in either party. According to John Allen Stevenson, author of "Emma: The New Courtship" (1990), the novel features both "old-fashioned" and "new-style" love stories. The first, embodied by Jane and Frank, is a love story in which the opposition to the couple's union is represented by external forces such as the disapproval of a parental figure. The second, represented by Emma and Knightley, is seemingly incestuous in nature and involves two egomaniacal lovers who need to overcome their own internal flaws in order to realize their true love for one another. Laurie Langbauer, however, has offered a strong challenge to the notion of the ideal marriage as represented by Emma and Mr. Knightley by undermining the perception of Mr. Knightley as a successfully realized ideal husband. In *Women and Romance: The Consolations of Gender in the English Novel*, she calls Mr. Knightley "an experiment in constructing the perfect man, pieced together by changing the emphasis on old literary clichés of gender," and the result is a character who is "authoritative, say, rather than overbearing, domestic without being uxorious." He must be considered a failed experiment as a character because the nuances between his amorous and his fatherly traits are not adequately theorized or maintained, Langbauer explains. However, the novel's attempts to "imagine a man that might somehow be different, even though they fail, still point out the need to do so. The attempt to transform what may be an inevitable patriarchal grammar through new inflections reveals the oppressiveness of its categories even when failing to transform them" (Langbauer 174).

5. Many critics over the years have suggested that Emma herself is either asexual, a "masturbating girl," or a closet lesbian. These views of Emma suggest that the character is incapable of having a fulfilling marital relationship with Mr. Knightley. Although none of the film versions of the novel explore the lesbian overtones of the novel, certain critics have written about the issue in scholarly papers, including Susan M. Korba, who wrote "'Improper and Dangerous Distinctions': Female Relationships and Erotic Domination in *Emma*" (1997) and Tiffany F. Potter's "'A Low But Very Feeling Tone': The Lesbian Continuum and Power Relations in Jane Austen's *Emma*" (1994). The theory that Emma is a lesbian also inspired a novel, *Emma in Love: Jane Austen's Emma Continued* (1996) by Emma Tennant (London: Fourth Estate).

6. Although this is as far as I am willing to go in labeling specific interpretations of the novel, it is important to note that some critics have taken to labeling the domestic Bildungsroman readings as ideologically conservative and the social

critique readings as liberal. To me, the labels "conservative" and "liberal" have lost their meanings in recent years due to overuse and the hyperbolic political rhetoric that has been attached to both. However, these labels are occasionally applied, and readers should be prepared to encounter them. For example, Barbara K. Seeber attempts to reconcile the conflicting readings of Austen as both conservative and liberal in her book *General Consent in Jane Austen: A Study in Dialogism* (2000). In a project that compares the "main text" with the "subtext" of Austen's works, Seeber argues that there is "no general consent to be found there" (12) and that novels such as *Emma* are best read as "both conservative and radical at the same time" (14)

Chapter Three

1. Despite the regrettable fact that Watt makes these observations about Austen's narrative style during the course of only one page, he nevertheless offers *Emma* a place of great prominence in the traditional literary canon as the author of the first "complete" novel.

2. Interestingly, the narrator is often not present for large sections of the novel, and there are key scenes in which the action is viewed only through Emma's perspective. The result is that readers are sometimes left with a less-than-reliable impression of key events and characters. As Janet Todd has indicated, characters such as Harriet are presented to the reader almost solely through Emma's perspective, which is biased in Harriet's favor. "We perceive that Harriet's face has been reflected in Emma's mind—so notoriously prone to alter with its own lighting; of Harriet's real countenance and feelings we have scarcely a hint" (283). The same could be said of Jane Fairfax, who may only seem cold and distant to the reader because that is how Emma herself views Jane.

3. Or, more appropriately, "with 'Cher' and at 'Cher'" since the Emma character has a different name in *Clueless*. Meanwhile, Patricia Rozema's *Mansfield Park* also cleverly attempts to recreate Austen's ironic voice by collapsing the character of Fanny Price and Jane Austen into a single whole that narrates the story, and much of the humor and political commentary comes from the thoughts heard via voice-over or in the moments when Fanny (played by Frances O'Connor) looks into the camera and directly addresses the audience.

4. For example, adaptations that grant primacy to the Harriet Smith storyline and are told primarily from Emma's perspective tend to be more comic in tone. Adaptations that focus on the plight of Jane Fairfax and are told from the perspective of the less wealthy and lower class residents of Highbury tend to be more serious.

5. Transposition adaptations bring traditional readings of the novel to the screen, often as a result of a given production team's intent to achieve complete tonal and thematic fidelity to the mother text despite the absence of certain characters and scenes from the novel. For example, the stated goal of the production team of the 1972 BBC miniseries *Emma* was "total fidelity" to the source material (Lauritzen 112). As we will later see, while the producers did not succeed in creating a cinematic experience that is directly equivalent to reading *Emma*, they did provide a thoughtful interpretation of Austen's novel.

6. See the appendix for the full cast list and production team information.

7. Since the film has been lost, Campbell's screenplay, complete with a full cast list and a credit for producer Michael Barry but no directorial credit, remains the most significant extant evidence of the nature of this particular adaptation. Of the eight *Emma* adaptations, only the most recent four are readily available to be viewed by the public on DVD and VHS. Of the previous four, only one version, the *NBC Kraft Television Theatre* production of 1954, still exists in a viewable form. This is on a videotape made available to scholars who present a letter of introduction to Rosemary Hanes of the Motion Picture and Television Reading Room of the Library of Congress, and who travel to the Madison Building for a special viewing of the program. The hour-long *CBS Camera Three* production from 1960 no longer exists in any format, since the footage has been lost and the original screenplay is no longer available. The remaining two adaptations, a live, 180-minute BBC miniseries written by Vincent Tilsley that was broadcast in 1960 and a live, 105-minute BBC TV broadcast from 1948, exist only in screenplay form as the original prints have been lost. (This is not unusual, especially for the live BBC television adaptations, because the BBC spent years destroying archive copies of old broadcasts, not realizing that they would be of interest to later viewers and historians. For example, the BBC is most notorious for destroying more than three years worth of episodes of its venerable science fiction program *Doctor Who*.) With the help of Sue Parrill, author of *Jane Austen on Film and Television* (2002), I have obtained copies of these screenplays, which were on file in the BBC Written Archives Centre, and have used them as the basis for my analysis of the two "lost" television adaptations. The two scripts are: 1) Judy Campbell. "Emma." Unpublished screenplay. BBC TV. 1948. In the BBC Written Archives Centre. Television Drama Scripts Microfilm 31/32. 2) Vincent Tilsley. "Emma." Unpublished screenplay. BBC TV. 1960. In the BBC Written Archives Centre. Television Drama Scripts Microfilm. Note: Much of the above *Emma* adaptation information comes from Austen adaptation archivist Sue Parrill, author of *Jane Austen on Film and Television* (McFarland & Company, 2002), and from the Internet Movie Database at http://www.imdb.com.

8. Scacchi, though uncredited as narrator, also plays Mrs. Weston in the film. While the identity of the narrator is not known, it is most likely not Mrs. Weston herself. Still, the narrator, who tells the story as if it takes place in a distant, fairy-tale past, shares Mrs. Weston's approval of Emma in her dialogue and inflection. For a more thorough discussion of the identity of the narrator in the McGrath

version and the motivation of said narrator, see Christine Colon, "The Social Constructions of Douglas McGrath's *Emma*" in *Persuasions: The Jane Austen Journal On-Line*, Occasional Papers No. 3 (1999).

9. This is especially true of the two adaptations from 1996 (featuring Gwyneth Paltrow and Kate Beckinsale as Emma), neither of which make Mr. Weston's or Mr. Cole's position in society clear enough.

10. Naturally, this observation is based on my reading of the script, since the performances of the actors are not available for examination. Their vocal inflection and facial expression, combined with a general manner, would more firmly set the tone for the gossipy dialogue as either farcical or something more serious.

11. Emma's attitude towards gossip in the original novel seems inconsistent. While she is angered at Jane Fairfax for refusing to gossip with her about Frank Churchill, and while she enjoys gossiping with Mrs. Weston, she is also capable of voicing displeasure with the local gossipers when she feels that they have revealed too much to Mr. Knightley about her plans for Harriet. In Chapter VIII she exclaims, "Highbury gossips!—Tiresome wretches!" (63) when Knightley predicts that Harriet will soon receive an offer of marriage.

12. The sudden shifts of topic during these debates are cause for some measure of confusion and the transitions read awkwardly in the screenplay, making one wonder if the scenes were easier to follow when acted out on television. If the actor who played Knightley (Ralph Michael) had enough finesse, he could conceivably make these scenes work. Even then, however, one is never sure of where the lion's share of Knightley's displeasure is coming from, since he keeps mentioning Jane Fairfax when he should be concerned with more immediate issues.

13. Wayne Booth suggests that Austen deliberately avoids directly depicting Jane's inner life because the inevitable consequence is a sharp loss in reader sympathy for Emma, who would suffer in comparison to Jane. *The Rhetoric of Fiction* (Chicago: University of Chicago Press, 1961), p. 249.

14. A forerunner of *Masterpiece Theater*, the *Kraft Television Theatre* (1947–1958) program regularly broadcast live, hour-long dramatizations of classic works of literature. Those who want a sense of what kind of program it was may get some idea by viewing the vintage, 60-minute adaptation of the first James Bond adventure, *Casino Royale*, originally broadcast on the live television series "Climax!" This rare adaptation, currently available as a special feature on the *Casino Royale* DVD (the 1967 version with David Niven, not the 2006 one with Daniel Craig) features an American James Bond played ineptly by Barry Nelson, a rewritten, happy ending (!) in which Bond defeats the villain and "gets the

girl" (in the book the villain is killed by another villain and "the girl" kills herself). The action of the novel is compressed, and the production is necessarily "stagey." However, in this Ian Fleming adaptation, as in the Kraft *Emma* adaptation, the main supporting character is played by the most talented actor in the production. Both Roddy McDowall in the Kraft *Emma* and Peter Lorre (the villainous LeChiffre) in the "Climax!" *Casino Royale* steal the show from the protagonist, who is played less skillfully by a less famous actor.

15. The live nature of the broadcast renders this incarnation of Knightley even less plausible since Cookson repeatedly flubs lines in important speeches from Volume I Chapters V and VIII—in which Knightley expresses concern to Mrs. Weston about the nature of the friendship between Emma and Harriet, and in which he defends his farmer tenant as a worthy suitor for Harriet. (Cookson also misspeaks Emma's name at one point and refers to her as "Harriet.")

16. Simple-minded and effusive, William Larkins' portrayal appears to have been somewhat inspired by the biased and uncharitable description that Emma offers of Robert Martin in the novel:

> "He is very plain, undoubtedly—remarkably plain:—but that is nothing compared with his entire want of gentility. I had no right to expect much; but I had no idea that he could be so very clownish, so totally without air. I had imagined him, I confess, a degree or two nearer to gentility....I am sure you must have been struck by his awkward look and abrupt manner—and the uncouthness of a voice, which I heard to be wholly unmodulated as I stood here." (Austen 44)

17. The only invented moment of comedy that works revolves around Emma's portfolio of portraits, which is deliberately made to look like the work of a fifth-grader rendered in black crayon, and Emma's hurt expression when Mr. Elton (Roddy McDowall) misidentifies a portrait of Emma's Cousin Isabella (yes, it is "Cousin" Isabella, here) as Mrs. Weston, but the joke works primarily because the actor's delivery is so adept.

18. In the previous adaptation of 1948, Mrs. Goddard introduces Harriet to Emma and inquires whether Harriet might be brought to Hartfield for cards. Emma agrees, shaking Harriet's hand. After Emma's departure, Harriet stands amazed and says to Mrs. Goddard, "She actually shook hands with me." This seems a lovely dramatic moment that works towards a similar purpose to the scenes described above, (in which Harriet approaches the opulent world of Emma Woodhouse tentatively,) but handles the characterization with greater finesse.

19. Indeed, Chapter XVI in the novel opens with Emma reflecting darkly on Elton's motivations in proposing to her:

> Contrary to the usual course of things, Mr. Elton's wanting to pay his addresses to her had sunk him in her opinion. His professions and his proposals did him no service. She thought nothing of his attachment, and was insulted by his hopes. He wanted to marry well, and having the arrogance to raise his eyes to her, pretended to be in love; but she was perfectly easy as to his not suffering any real disappointment that need be cared for. There had been no real affection in his language or manners. Sighs and fine words had been given in abundance; but she cold hardly devise any set of expressions, or fancy any tone of voice, less allied with real love. She need not trouble herself to pity him. He only wanted to aggrandize and enrich himself; and if Miss Woodhouse of Hartfield, the heiress of thirty thousand pounds, were not quite so easily obtained as he had fancied, he would soon try for Miss Somebody else with twenty, or with ten. (Austen 121)

In marrying the heiress Augusta Hawkins shortly thereafter, Elton proves Emma's thoughts prophetic, surprising Emma only with the speed with which she was replaced. However, the novel presents Elton's proposal, and the aftermath, purely from Emma's perspective, leaving open the possibility that she has misjudged his motivations—possibly out of snobbery, possibly out of shock and disappointment. The Kraft production explores this possibility admirably in a manner that need not conflict with the source. It may, in fact, suggest an intriguing alternative way of reading the Elton storyline.

On the subject of Mr. Elton, Claudia Johnson writes, "Implying a counter discourse of 'true feeling,' Emma suggests in a most unBurkean way that 'humanity' and gallantry are two different things. The 'gallant' Mr. Elton by contrast damns himself when he avows that it is impossible 'to contradict a lady' (p. 51)' when he takes care 'that nothing ungallant, nothing that did not breathe a compliment to the sex should pass his lips (p. 73), and when he 'sigh[s] and languish[es] and stud[ies] for compliments" (p. 57). As presented here, gallantry is intrinsically nonsensical: artificial and disingenuous, taking on the very femininity it courts. No man, as the logic of the novel would have it, talks or believes such rubbish. When Mr. Elton is alone among men, as Mr. Knightley informs us, he makes it clear that he wants to marry into money and that his attentions to the fair sex are only a means to an end, that he is not really a man of feeling at all" (451). From "'Not at all what a man should be!': Remaking English Manhood in Emma" (451)

20. In the novel, reader perception of Mrs. Elton is, primarily, filtered through the heroine's view of the character, which is essentially antagonistic from the outset. First laying eyes on Mrs. Elton in church, Emma decides on the basis of appearance that:

> She did not really like her. She would not be in a hurry to find fault, but she suspected there was no elegance;—ease, but not elegance.—She was almost sure that for a young woman, a stranger, a bride, there was too much ease.

Her person was rather good; her face not unpretty; but neither feature, nor air, nor voice, nor manner, were elegant. Emma thought at least it would turn out so. (Austen 219)

When Mrs. Elton paid a visit to Emma at Hartfield shortly thereafter, and Emma was able to speak with her alone for fifteen minutes, the conversation merely served to confirm these poor initial impressions.

[T]he quarter of an hour quite convinced her that Mrs. Elton was a vain woman, extremely well satisfied with herself, and thinking very much of her own importance; that she was meant to shine and be very superior, but with manners that had been formed in a very bad school, pert and familiar; that all her notions were drawn from one set of people, and one style of living; that if not foolish she was ignorant, and that her society would certainly do Mr. Elton no good. (Austen 221)

Shortly after this passage, Austen presents the conversation to readers to judge for themselves whether Emma is being too harsh. Most, if not all, of Mrs. Elton's dialogue is indeed damning, as she spends much of the conversation bragging of her wealth, her worldliness, and her selflessness. Worse still, Mrs. Elton makes tactless allusions to the personal defects of all of Emma's loved ones, making a quick succession of loaded observations about Mr. Woodhouse's ill health, Mr. Knightley's rustic background, Mrs. Weston's past as a governess, and Emma's own provincialism. While it is possible to interpret Mrs. Elton's dialogue as being friendly in tone and well meant, it seems more likely that her remarks are calculated to inflate her own self-importance and/or to wound Emma. However, some readers might well view the scene when Emma encounters Mrs. Elton for the first time from Mrs. Elton's perspective and see a genuine overture of friendship and an invitation to form a musical club turned away by a narrow-minded snob. Such readers are less likely to see Emma as a heroine keeping a cold-hearted social opportunist at bay and more likely to view Emma a self-appointed guardian of the establishment whose chief interest is in preventing new blood from becoming part of the community.

21. While the Harriet character in *Clueless* (called "Tai") eventually begins to turn on, and even socially surpass the Emma character ("Cher"), this was not her goal for most of the film.

22. Before the proposal comes there is an intriguing moment when Emma is showing her sketch of Mr. Knightley to Harriet. Emma observes that she was displeased with it because she "had made him too pretty, you see." Harriet disagrees, cooing "Oh, Miss Woodhouse, I think it is just like him," in a dreamy tone that could only be interpreted as a declaration of love for Knightley that Emma does not notice. In addition, when Emma first meets William Larkins, she observes, "Well I thought he looked very respectable and hard-working," to which Harriet replies, "Of course, he is not so genteel as a real gentleman,"

already thinking of Mr. Knightley. And, during the debate over Larkins' proposal, the camera is off of Harriet's face and on Emma's for much of the conversation, so it is unclear how much of what Emma says is greeted with consternation. What is clear, however, is the primacy she gives Knightley and the offhand manner in which Harriet ultimately considers Larkins' disappointment: "I must admit that since my coming here I have seen people ... one is so handsome and agreeable [smile]... but William is very amiable ...and he has written such a letter...." Emma then reminds her that a tolerable letter should not be inducement enough to marry, to which she replies, "I wonder if he will be unhappy. I wonder if ... well ... and it is but a short letter, too."

23. Interestingly enough, the 1995 film *Clueless*, which transported the tale to contemporary Los Angeles, flirted with the idea that "Harriet" could indeed rise to greater social heights than "Emma" by allying herself with "Mrs. Elton." This seeming alteration in the story takes excellent advantage of the dramatic opportunities opened up by transporting the plot to a more "democratic" time and society, but the Kraft adaptation, which takes similar liberties with the source material for less reason, makes no such intriguing adjustment to the storyline.

24. Like the previous British adaptation written by Judy Campbell, this adaptation no longer exists on film, but Vincent Tilsley's screenplay still exists, and it is based on this screenplay that I will be making my observations. (Tilsley, Vincent. "Emma." Unpublished screenplay. BBC TV. 1960. In the BBC Written Archives Centre. Television Drama Scripts Microfilm.)

25. In the novel, when Emma reveals to Mr. Knightley her suspicions that he loves Jane Fairfax, Austen writes the following:

> Mr. Knightley was hard at work upon the lower buttons of his thick leather gaiters, and either the exertion of getting them together, or some other cause, brought the color into his face as he answered,
>
> "Oh! Are you there?—But you are miserably behind-hand. Mr. Cole gave me a hint of it six weeks ago."
>
> He stopped.—Emma felt her foot pressed by Mrs. Weston and did not know herself what to think. In a moment, he went on—
>
> "That will never be, however, I can assure you. Miss Fairfax, I dare say, would not have me if I were to ask her—and I am very sure I shall never ask her."...
>
> ...he was thoughtful—and in a manner which shewed him not pleased, soon afterwards said, "So you have been settling that I should marry Jane Fairfax."
>
> ...Mr. Knightley was thoughtful again. The result of his reverie was, "No, Emma, I do not think the extent of my admiration for her will ever take me by surprise.—I never had a thought of her in that way, I assure you."

And soon afterwards, "Jane Fairfax is a very charming woman—but not even Jane Fairfax is perfect. She has a fault. She has not the open temper which a man would wish for in a wife."

Emma could not but rejoice to hear that she had a fault. "Well," said she, "and you soon silenced Mr. Cole, I supposed?"

"Yes, very soon. He gave me a quiet hint; I told him he was mistaken; he asked my pardon and said no more. Cole does not want to be wiser or wittier than his neighbors." (233)

Tilsley's screenplay suggests that Mr. Knightley's red face and long, thoughtful pauses in this scene reveal that he is either not honest with himself or not honest with Emma when he denies his attraction to Jane Fairfax. Such a reading is possible. It is also just as possible to take Mr. Knightley at his word when he claims that he "never thought of her in that way."

26. Why is Emma so jealous of Jane? Some critics have suggested that Emma has an inferiority complex since she is well aware of Jane's superior talents. Others have argued that the primary reason for the jealousy is Emma's fear that Jane will win Mr. Knightley away from her. Concerning the first of these theories, Beth Fowkes Tobin writes that Emma "is threatened by Jane's talents, recognizing that without her inherited status and wealth, she would fall short of Jane Fairfax. Envious of Jane's real accomplishments, Emma cannot tolerate equality with a woman who, without property or position, lays claim to elegance and gentility. Preferring the nonthreatening and clearly inferior Harriet, who is without property, position, gentility or accomplishments, Emma rejects Miss Bates' niece as too cold and reserved for her taste, thus preserving her sense of superiority" (480). Concerning the second of these theories, Janet Todd argues, "The fear that Mr. Knightley loves Jane starts Emma on her path to self knowledge. Only when Harriet declares herself does Emma understand her own heart, but already her extravagant hostility must hint the truth. At the mere suggestion of Mr. Knightley's interest, she exclaims, 'Jane Fairfax mistress of the Abbey!–Oh! No, no;–every feeling revolts' (p. 225). The match would be, she asserts, 'shameful and degrading.' Yet the woman in question is one whom Emma has declared to be all that is elegant and accomplished, and her only disadvantages have been the reserve Mr. Knightley esteems in moderation and her loquacious aunt. Certainly Emma's own unconscious desires intrude here to make the horror, and the match further repulses by its uniting of social status and worth, a combination which threatens to top Emma herself. 'A Mrs. Knightley for them all to give way to!' she muses bitterly" (292).

27. In fact, I am surprised that not one of the adaptations presented the death of the first Mrs. Weston and the delivery of Frank into the hands of the Churchills as a form of dramatic, pre-credits segment since that event, like Wickham's seduction of Darcy's sister in *Pride and Prejudice*, influences the events that occur during the course of the story proper, despite taking place long beforehand. Such a backstory would certainly make the Frank Churchill-Jane Fairfax storyline easier

to grasp, as well as make Emma more sympathetic by suggesting that she has finally brought Mr. Weston the happiness he lost at the death of his first wife by promoting his marriage to Miss Taylor.

28. Most film adaptations of *Emma* have tended to portray Frank as merely phony in the blandest and most obvious possible way instead of in a more interesting fashion as sinister or charming. Even the likeable Ewan McGregor, who was solid in the part in the Douglas McGrath adaptation, fails to evoke much reaction. Although it is not possible to know exactly how David McCallum (*Sapphire and Steel, Billy Budd*) played the part in the Tilsley adaptation, the screenplay would tend to suggest that this was the version that strove the most noticeably to make Frank a graspable and sympathetic character.

    The screenplay dramatizes certain scenes from Frank's point of view in order to bring his character more fully to life. One example of this is Frank's meeting with Jane as she departs from the strawberry-picking outing, which is only referred to in the novel, but which Tilsley dramatizes. Frank and Jane's dialogue is suitably coded and Frank seems about to make a direct plea to his fiancé when the two are interrupted. As a consequence of scenes such as this, the secret engagement between Frank and Jane is a little too strongly hinted at, but that is typical of the British television adaptations, which tend to favor creating a memorable Jane Fairfax to preserving the mystery.

29. Certainly Andrew Davies, screenwriter of the ITV/A&E version from 1996, saw it in this fashion (Birtwistle 7).

30. This scene is included in the 1975 version, this version, and the 1996 ITV/A&E version with Kate Beckinsale.

31. Unlike the previous versions discussed, only one of which exists on film (and it can only be viewed in the United States by those eager to visit the Library of Congress' viewing room), this production is readily available on DVD and VHS through major distributors such as Amazon.com and Barnes and Noble. Although originally broadcast in five installments, the VHS version has only one set of credits, the opening credits of part one and the closing credits of part five, and edits together all of the episodes to make one long, feature-film version. This is a different viewing experience from the original broadcast as it eliminates many of the effects of the original "cliffhanger serial" feel of the presentation. For example, in its original broadcast, episode one ended with a dramatic close-up of Emma dictating Harriet's refusal letter to Robert Martin. Viewers of the VHS tape do not have to wait a week to see what happens next as viewers back in 1972 did.

32. Austen aficionados interested in a purely faithful adaptation would be pleased by this version remaining faithful to the novel in its presentation of the proposal scene, cutting away to another scene before Emma gives her response to Knightley and refraining from melodramatic music and soft lighting, but

viewers hoping for a little more physical passion in their romantic fiction are bound to be disappointed. In contrast, Mr. Knightleys from more recent adaptations, most notably Mark Strong and Jeremy Northam, have been described as too young and too glamorous, pointing to the possibility that Knightley is a difficult part to cast, as he is markedly older than Emma, but still described through Emma's eyes as young-looking, "tall, firm, upright" (Austen 261) during the Crown Inn ball. But while their physical types are not ideal for the character, it is possibly more important that both Carson and Northam are naturals in the role, and performance quality is a critical consideration.

33. Ultimately, Lauritzen concludes that the production succeeds on its own terms—that it will most likely encourage viewers over the years to read a novel that they never would have otherwise (154) and that those who already appreciate the novel will derive the most pleasure from the serial's "dramatic effectiveness, the directness and emotional force of the performance (153), especially in the Box Hill segment, which lends itself to dramatic staging and, done properly, can eclipse the novel in dramatic potency. Still, Lauritzen observes that the serial "falls short of the original...with regard to subtlety and precision, and this has an effect both on the characterization and on the articulation of the main themes of the story" (154).

   Two more recent reviews of the Glenister-Constanduros film were written by David Monaghan and by William Phillips and Louise Heal. David Monaghan's 2003 article "*Emma* and the Art of Adaptation" takes the Glenister-Constanduros version to task for relying too heavily on "historically accurate costumes and settings" and bread-and-butter direction to present a faithful onscreen rendering of the Regency period novel. For Monaghan, this *Emma*, and other "televised versions of Austen function as illustrated supplements to the original novels rather than as independent works of art" (Monaghan 197) primarily because, "pleasing as it has been to millions of viewers, the 'verisimilitude' carefully cultivated by televisual renderings of the Austen canon is usually 'superficial' and serves as a substitute for any attempt to point up complexities of character and theme that lie beneath the polished surface of her novels. Pre-1990 BBC adaptations also tend to make use of unobtrusive and conservative camera and editing techniques that reflect their creator's unwillingness to rethink Austen's novels in visual terms" (Monaghan 197).

   William Phillips and Louise Heal observe in "Extensive Grounds and Classic Columns: *Emma* on Film" that the Glenister-Constanduros film is unimaginative in its staging and does little more than dramatize the novel, except offer more time than it should to the male characters (Phillips and Heal 7).

34. Lauritzen calculated that, "In the novel, Emma is alone on about 21 out of 355 pages. This means that Austen devotes about 1/16 of her text to this type of scene. In the serial, Emma is alone during about 5 of 270 minutes, which is only about 1/54 of the total viewing time. This radical modification of an important type of situation is bound to have a negative effect on the articulation of Emma's development, which is the central subject of the novel....An explanation of the reduction of the scope of this type of situation may no doubt be found in the

transition from prose narrative to drama, and in the known expectations of the television audience.…It should be added, however, that Constanduros' presentation of Emma herself, when it occurs, shows a lack of imagination, which is possibly related to his respect for the original text. Rather than using any of the available techniques for rendering interior monologue like letter-writing, voice-over or straight monologue, he refrained from articulating the content of the text verbally. Paradoxically, it could therefore be argued that Constanduros could have attained greater faithfulness to the original if he had allowed himself to depart more from it" (Lauritzen 81).

Chapter Four

1. Although Haskell is a film critic and not a literary scholar, echoes of her view can be found in literary criticism. In "Not Subordinate: Empowering Woman in the Marriage Plot" (1992), Julie Shaffer argues that the traditional lover-mentor marriage-plot novels of the eighteenth and nineteenth centuries that were made popular by the success of Charlotte Lennox's *The Female Quixote* (1752) presented females as socially ignorant—if not asocial or antisocial—and in desperate need of education from a wise masculine figure. However, Shaffer writes, Austen worked to subvert the conservative conventions of these lover-mentor novels by writing stories in which the lover-mentor learns as much from the heroine as she learns from him.

    In another example, John Hardy suggests in *Jane Austen's Heroines: Intimacy in Human Relationships* (Boston: Routlegde & Kegan Paul, 1984) that Emma and Knightley ultimately achieve a lively union based on trust that does not inspire discontent in either party. In *The British Novel, Defoe to Austen: A Critical History*, John Allen Stevenson writes that the novel features both "old-fashioned" and "new-style" love stories. The first, embodied by Jane and Frank, is a love story in which the opposition to the couple's union is represented by external forces such as the disapproval of a parental figure. The second, represented by Emma and Knightley, is seemingly incestuous in nature and involves two egomaniacal lovers who need to overcome their own internal flaws in order to realize their true love for one another (Boston: Twayne, 1990, pp. 110–28). Perhaps most famously of all, Wayne Booth asserts in "Control of Distance in Jane Austen's *Emma*" (1961) that "[m]arriage to an intelligent, amiable, good, and attractive man is the best thing that can happen to this heroine, and the readers who do not experience it as such are, I am convinced, far from knowing what Jane Austen is about—whatever they may say about the 'bitter spinster's' attitude towards marriage" (Rhetoric of Fiction 260).

2. Douglas McGrath initially wrote a scene in which Emma and Mr. Knightley competed against one another at croquet. When the film's production designer, Michael Howells, informed him that croquet was not invented until years later, archery was substituted. (http://www.nyscreenwriter.com/article10.htm)

3.	As Claudia Johnson wrote, in "'Not at all what a man should be!': Remaking English Manhood in *Emma*:" "It is the work of *Emma* to make Mr. Knightley seem traditional. Combining as it does the patron saint of England with the knight of chivalry, his name itself conduces to his traditional-seeming status. But as I hope I have indicated, he is not a traditional and certainly not a chivalric figure, and far from embodying fixed or at the very least commonly shared notions of masculinity, there is nothing in Scott, Burney, More, Burke, Radcliffe, or Edgeworth remotely like him. On one hand, Knightley is impeccably landed, a magistrate, a gentleman of 'untainted' blood and judicious temper, and as such emphatically not the impetuous, combustible masculine type Burke so feared, the mere man of talent who is dangerous precisely because he has nothing to lose. But on the other hand, Knightley avows himself a farmer and a man of business, absorbed in the figures and computations Emma considers so vulgar, a man of energy, vigor, and decision, and as such emphatically not an embodiment of the stasis onto sluggishness Burke commended in country squires. The exemplary love of this 'humane' as opposed to 'gallant' man is fraternal rather than heterosexual. If Emma has difficulty in realizing that Knightley is in love with her, it is not because she is impercipient, but rather because he is highly unusual in loving a woman in the same manner he loves his brother rather than the other way around...." (452)

4.	Douglas McGrath on the Americanisms: "The funniest kind of problem we had was many English people complained, or Boston scholars complained. Knowing I was American, they'd say, 'there are dreadful Americanisms in the script.' I'm not 100% faithful to the dialogue because there were places I couldn't be, but I love the dialogue. I'm all for taking what is pre-typed and putting it right in the script, but every so often you need to throw in a little something. The thing they always sighted as an obvious Americanism was at a number of points in the movie Emma says, 'Good God.' The first time I read the complaint, I think it was in *The New Yorker*, I thought, 'Good God.' And I've been known to say 'Good God' myself, so I don't think it was impossible that I thought of that, but I thought, I'm sure that's from the book, and I looked it up and it indeed is in the book. Well, somebody from England set a letter to the editor of a magazine which had reviewed the film with that very complaint that there were these Americansisms and the one they sighted again was 'Good God.' The letter writer says, 'You can find the phrase 'Good God' on the following pages of Miss Austen's book,' and the letter writer was Alec Guinness. So I was very happy about that. [Her fans] are very devoted—and rightly so—she's a wonderful, wonderful author who has inspired near maniacal devotion from many readers, but when you're making a transition from the book to the screen, you have other considerations besides merely how it's done in the book. You want to be faithful and that's why you're drawn to the material, because you love it. But there are a lot of things you have to think about besides just how it is in the book." From *Screenwriter Magazine Online*. (http://www.nyscreenwriter.com/article10.htm)

5.	This was the core argument of an essay by Moya Luckett called "Image and Nation in 1990s British Cinema."

Although Luckett is concerned primarily with Paltrow's performance as a modern-day British woman in the film *Sliding Doors*, the comments remain salient in an evaluation of her performance as an archetypal Regency period heroine. For Luckett, any time that Paltrow plays a British character, especially in a film such as *Sliding Doors*, she causes a displacement that "leaves a vacuum at the center of the nation" suggesting "that national identity is always elsewhere, a paradox that seems to be echoed in the current efforts of audiences to find the nation in the images of British cinema." Since a false Brit such as Paltrow cannot uncover the truth of "Britishness," *Sliding Doors'* "attempts to find the truth of the nation rest on supporting characters who have strong regional identities." Luckett concludes that, "After all, Gwyneth Paltrow is American, and despite her appearances in films like *Emma* (Douglas McGrath, 1996) and *Shakespeare in Love* as "the quintessentially British" heroine, her star image undermines her authenticity" (Luckett 98).

6.   Mining magazine articles and newspaper reviews published at the time of the release of *Emma*, James Thompson presented a montage of tabloid descriptions of Gwyneth Paltrow as both the ultimate Jane Austen heroine and the personification of silver screen "class": "The new representations of Austen, then, present an aristocracy as attractive to nominal or residual democrats, an aristocracy at the point of its moralization and anesthetization into an abstract hierarchy, an aristocracy of the plucky, of the good, and the elegant, in which we perceive morality as style. This operation turns on the transcoding of class from brute exclusionary practice to class as elegance in grace, to class in a commodity culture. This is an Austen superimposed with the look and feel of Ralph Lauren nostalgia for an available aristocracy, old money and class in the consumer sense of the term. The language of class is most evident in the marketing of Gwyneth Paltrow." (Thompson 24).

7.   See http://userpages.umbc.edu/~jpeck1/films/emma.html

8.   The uncertainty of the identity of the female narrator, and the lack of ascertainable physical presence of the narrator on screen, is one of the things that makes this film rare. Kaja Silverman explains in her 1984 essay "Dis-Embodying the Female Voice" that male film viewers are disturbed by a disjunction between a woman's voice and a woman's body, so a female narrative voice is almost unheard of in cinema. "To allow her to be heard without being seen...would disrupt the specular regime upon which mainstream cinema relies; it would put her beyond the control of the male gaze, and release her voice from the signifying obligations which the gaze sustains. It would be to open the possibility of woman participating in phallic discourse and...to challenge every conception by means of which we have previously known her, since it is precisely as body that she is constructed....Thus (with the exception of music) there are no instances within mainstream cinema where the female voice is not matched up in some way, even if only retrospectively, with the female body....The female voice almost never functions as a voice-over, and when it

does it enjoys a comparable status to the male voice-over in film noir—i.e. it is autobiographical, evoking in reminiscent fashion the diegesis which constitutes the film's 'present,' a diegesis in which the speaker features centrally" (135–136).

9. In "'The Duty of Woman by Woman': Reforming Feminism in *Emma*," Devoney Looser describes Mrs. Elton as the novel's "gravest warning against female/female paternalism," a central theme of the book filled with student-teacher relationships that range from the fruitless to the nightmarish. "Mrs. Elton is Emma's nemesis but she is also a sign of what Emma—if unrepentant—could become....If Mrs. Elton selects a more class appropriate and deserving humble companion in Jane than Emma does in Harriet, she more egregiously oversteps her boundaries as patron in her attempted machinations. Mrs. Elton's finding employment for Jane as a governess poses as a selfless act. It is, however, an attempt to force an unwanted agenda on Jane and to prove to her new community (and to her beloved Maple Grove relatives) that she has power in Highbury" (Looser 588).

    Paul Delany writes in "'A Sort of Notch in the Donwell Estate': Intersections of Status and Class in *Emma*" that the novel stigmatizes all efforts made by ambitious members of the rising classes to purchase status. This disapproval of "consumption" is presented most noticeably in scenes in which John Knightley casts a disdainful eye on Mrs. Elton's lace and pearls, and in which Emma mocks Mrs. Elton's sister's barouche-landau. Meanwhile, the narrator of the story pays little attention to clothing worn by Emma or purchases made by characters with old-world status, minimizing the importance of ostentatious displays of wealth to Highbury's upper crust, Delaney observes (515).

10. Galperin's view of the novel will be given greater coverage in the discussion of *Clueless*.

11. Critics generally cite *Clueless*, which was released before *Jane Austen's "Emma,"* as the most daring treatment of the source material since it acts as a post-modern re-visioning of the story set in an America of the "present." Since *Clueless* is the only adaptation of the story that does not attempt to visually recreate the Regency period setting in which it was originally intended to take place, I have chosen to discuss that particular film last. It is important to note, however, that *Clueless* was released in the United States on July 19, 1995, before both the McGrath film (which was released on August 2, 1996) and the Meridian-ITV/A&E film *Jane Austen's "Emma,"* written by Andrew Davies and directed by Diarmuid Lawrence, which aired on British television in 1996 and which was released in the United States on February 16, 1997. If I had organized this survey of adaptations purely chronologically, the Meridian-ITV/A&E film would be discussed last because it was the most recent of the adaptations.

12. In *Sensibility*, Janet Todd explains that "One of the most sustained attacks on the female sentimental novel came from Jane Austen, all of whose works, from the juvenile parodies to the final unfinished *Sanditon*, form part of the debate of

sentimentalism. In her novels the clichés of sentimental fiction are overturned: mothers are vulgar and limited, sentimental friends are a sham, and orphans prove not noble but lower-middle class. Families exist not as images of harmonious society, infused with sentimental female values, but as constricting forces, embarrassments to the few sensible offspring they produce. Heroines do not fight against their fathers to marry beyond their power, but choose as spouses paternal men who have helped bring them up and who are often already within the family" (144).

13. It is also important to note that the gypsy segment is rarely so faithfully recreated as it is here, with the all-important satire of romantic fiction present in the original text preserved for posterity on film. The Glenister-Constanduros version also makes Harriet seem suitably ludicrous during the "attack," in which she trips and hits her head while running from several small children. The tone of the scene in that version is in keeping with the satirical tone of the scene in the novel. Otherwise, in general, the gypsy segment suffers badly in transference from the novel to the screen. Judy Campbell treats the attack seriously, but at least she uses it as an intriguing opportunity to bring Robert Martin back into the spotlight. The McGrath film is noteworthy as being particularly bad at realizing the gypsy segment. It is presented seriously and falls flat; it is most definitely the worst scene in the entire film.

14. Each film has struggled with finding a means of bringing the two characters together dramatically, and all have fallen flat in the attempt. The novel presents their first meeting in a primarily narrated manner. Mrs. Goddard, who forms a part of Mr. Woodhouse's regular whist party along with Mrs. Bates, brings Harriet to Hartfield one evening and Emma is taken with her. It works well enough in the novel, but has proven a difficult scene to realize dramatically on screen. Vincent Tilsley's screenplay skips the meeting and begins the story after they are already friends. The Glenister-Constanduros film has Mrs. Goddard introduce Harriet to Emma in the hallway at Hartfield and the Kraft version has Mrs. Goddard bring Harriet with her to the Weston wedding.

15. And the film, through the use of the "objective" camera, is able to show the audience the disjunction between Emma's perceptions of reality and reality itself quite dramatically. In the book, the narrator serves a similar purpose, often with a humorous and dramatic result. However, Emma's perspective dominates large portions of the novel's narrative, leaving readers less certain of where her ideas end and reality begins than the Lawrence-Davies version would have viewers be.

16. This running joke may not seem funny, but it is laugh-out-lough hilarious by about the mid-point of the novel. (I just wanted to insert a gratuitous opinion here. Thanks for flipping to the back of the book for this. And for reading the book, actually. I hope you are enjoying it.)

17. Most of the other adaptations, like the novel itself, de-emphasize the presence of servants. One notable exception to the rule is the Kraft broadcast featuring Roddy McDowall, which shows servants taking pains to decorate for the Weston wedding and which develops the friendship between Mr. Knightley and the Woodhouse butler, Serle, both of whom enjoy complaining to one another of Miss Woodhouse's excesses. Of course, part of the issue is not whether servants are shown but how they are shown as well. In the Kraft version Serle is a figure of fun, and the other servants are really just window dressing to give the audience a sense of the Woodhouse wealth.

    Commenting on the presence of servants in the Glenister-Constanduros version, Monica Lauritzen observes that "servants appear in a number of scenes, where they are not explicitly referred to in the novel. It is possible that he [Constanduros] has introduced this adjustment with a view of making the *milieu* seem as authentic as possible, but it hardly means a violation of Austen's text. It may be assumed, on the contrary, that servants were so much taken for granted among the upper classes at the time that even a scrupulous writer like Jane Austen included references to their existence only as an exception and for specific purposes" (Lauritzen 78).

18. It is important for any adaptation interested in portraying Emma as an imagist to render Jane Fairfax in a starkly realistic and compelling fashion, and the Lawrence-Davies film does just this. It is important because the audience needs to be able to see that the real Jane Fairfax is a far more interesting and loveable woman than the Jane Fairfax that Emma constructs in her mind. While Beckinsale's Emma learns the hard way that she needs to democratize her sensibilities, she also learns that seeing people as they are can be an even more rewarding experience than seeing them as she would prefer them to be.

19. "Actress Lucy Robinson's portrayal of Mrs. Elton with a suggested Somerset accent whose heavy post-vocalic 'r' (perhaps intended to remind viewers of certain American accents) certainly helps establish a growing irritation in the viewer parallel to the same irritation that is amply shown in Kate Beckinsale's portrayal of Emma" (Phillips 2).

Chapter Five

1. Heckerling made these comments during a Harold Lloyd Seminar, which was, at one time, available on-line, but the link no longer functions. The web address *used to be* http:// www.afionline.org/haroldlloyd/heckerling/script.1.html.

2. Geoffrey Wagner's other categories of adaptation include the transposition, an adaptation "in which a novel is given directly on the screen, with the minimum of apparent interference" (222) and the commentary, in which the original is

"either purposely or inadvertently altered in some respect" causing "a re-emphasis or re-structure" (223)

3. The entry on *Clueless* in the appendix includes a guide to the *Clueless* characters and the corresponding characters in *Emma* upon whom they are based.

4. Making Cher a high-school student instead of a 21-year-old woman almost seems to necessitate making the film's Mr. Knightley younger as well. Had Josh retained Knightley's age while Cher became markedly younger, the film would start to seem more like an adaptation of *Lolita* than of *Emma*.

5. In this manner, both films have an advantage over the earlier, made-for-television British adaptations, which took less pains to make Emma's thoughts and feelings known to the audience, often resulting in portrayals of Emma that appeared too cold and calculating.

6. In "Emma Becomes Clueless," Suzanne Ferris writes that, "Cher's first-person voice-over neatly captures the contradiction between actual events and her perceptions. As a commentary on events, a voice-over is always temporally distinct from the visually realized events, occurring in narrative time necessarily after the events pictured have unfolded. Simultaneously, the voice-over illustrates the disjunction between Cher's perceptions and reality, and her confidence in her own misguided views of it emphasizes her outspokenness" (124).

7. This moment, like others in the film, is self-referential—it is *Clueless* discussing its own cultural significance as a film adaptation of a classic literary text. Another significant way in which the film discusses its own value as a work of art is through Christian Stovitz, a character who is complex enough to serve multiple functions in the narrative. In one of his many functions in the story, Christian serves as a symbolic vehicle through which previously undervalued products of popular culture might achieve greater status and acclaim. In this fashion, Christian represents one of the film's arguments in favor of itself; that is to say, his love of revered pop culture of the past offers the promise that, one day, the teenager movie, the comedy film, and the film adaptation of the classic novel, will find greater respect in the eyes of the arbiters of good taste. Denise Fulbrook writes: "Christian and the venerable history he represents is in a sense 'trash' culture already redeemed, already 'classic;' it is his character who most overtly moves popular culture in the film into the terrain of 'high' or 'classic' art. To the stylish, Christian is the connoisseur of fashion. His character not only has a passionate knowledge of high art and an awareness of how one could capitalize on art; he loves movies now considered 'classic' such as *Spartacus*, clothes that pay tribute to 'classic' queer icons and music that identifies him with Billie Holiday, Judy Garland, and Barbara Streisand. Finally, he drives a 'classic' convertible and calls Cher from art museums where cartoons hang, framed

behind him. This last scene provides the film with a recognizable script for the movement of popular culture to the hallowed halls of high aestheticism" (198).

8. Some critics have cited Emma's claim to have made the Weston match to be pure hubris on Emma's part, and agree with Mr. Knightley that the claim is unsubstantiated. Certainly, at no point in the novel does either Mr. Weston or Miss Taylor ever offer an opinion on this issue, so the mystery is not resolved by them. However, Denise Kohn has demonstrated how Emma could be seen as being correct in her assertion.

9. Tom Doherty, discussing the often unintentional subtext of the traditional teenage sex comedy, contends that "the lightweight banter and the *Tiger Beat-*puppy love in *Clueless* is not without its darker cultural historical resonance. Since the blithe, orgiastic days of *Risky Business*, sex has become just that. The deep background is AIDS, the horror now nascent in real-life sex. The recreational adolescent fornication celebrated and spied through peepholes in *Animal House, Porky's, Private School* (1983), *Revenge of the Nerds* (1984), and other exemplars of what William Paul has dubbed the "animal comedy" of the late Seventies/early Eighties now seems less a passage to adulthood than a jump into the fire" (3).

Chapter 6

1. The writings of Sulloway and Johnson are explored in greater detail in Chapter 2.

Appendix

Adaptation Reference Guide

Information from the Internet Movie Database
(http://www.imdb.com)
and Sue Parrill's *Jane Austen on Film and Television:
A Critical Study of the Adaptations.*
London, McFarland & Company, Inc. 2002.

I. Emma (TV)

Original Broadcast Date: May 24, 1948
Channel: BBC
Running Time: 105 minutes
Description: Live, black and white, television play. Footage lost.
Director/Producer: Michael Barry
Scriptwriter: Judy Campbell. Screenplay extant.

Cast

Emma Woodhouse	Judy Campbell
Mr. George Knightley	Ralph Michael
Miss Bates	Gillian Lind
Mr. Elton	Richard Hurndall
Mr. Woodhouse	Oliver Burt
Mrs. Elton	Mirian Spencer
Frank Churchill	McDonald Hobley
Harriet Smith	Daphne Slater
Jane Fairfax	Joyce Heron

II. Emma (TV)

Original Broadcast Date: November 24, 1954
Channel: NBC
Running Time: 60 minutes
Description: Live, black and white *Kraft Television Theatre* production
    archived in the Library of Congress, NBC Television Collection
Dramatized by: Martine Bartlett and Peter Donat

Cast

Emma Woodhouse	Felicia Montealegre
Mr. George Knightley	Peter Cookson
Mr. Elton	Roddy McDowall
Mrs. Elton	Martine Bartlett
Mr. Woodhouse	Stafford Dickens
Harriet Smith	Sarah Marshall
Mrs. Weston	Nydia Westman
Mr. Weston	Robinson Stone
Mrs. Goddard	Nancie Hobbs
William Larkins	Peter Donat
Searle	McLean Savage

III. Emma (TV)

Original Broadcast Date: February 26 – April 6, 1960
Channel: BBC
Running Time: 180 minutes
Description: 6-part miniseries, live, black and white. Footage lost.
Director/Producer: Campbell Logan
Scriptwriter: Vincent Tilsley. Screenplay extant.

Cast

Emma Woodhouse	Diana Fairfax
Mr. George Knightley	Paul Daneman
Miss Bates	Gillian Lind
Mr. Elton	Raymond Young
Harriet Smith	Perlita Smith
Mr. Woodhouse	Leslie French
Jane Fairfax	Petra Davies
Mrs. Bates	May Hallatt
Frank Churchill	David McCallum
Mrs. Weston	Thea Holme
Mr. Weston	Philip Ray

IV. Emma (TV)

Original Broadcast Date: August 26, 1960
Channel: CBS
Running Time: 60 minutes
Description: Installment of *Camera Three.* Footage lost.
Director: John Desmond
Scriptwriter: Claire Roskam. Screenplay not extant.
Producer: John McGiffert

Cast

Emma Woodhouse	Nancy Wickwire

V. Emma (TV)

Original Broadcast Date: 1972
Channel: BBC-2
Running Time: 257 minutes
Description: Color. Originally broadcast as 5-part miniseries.
Director: John Glenister
Scriptwriter: Denis Constanduros
Producer: Martin Lisemore

Cast

Emma Woodhouse	Doran Godwin
Mr. George Knightley	John Carson
Harriet Smith	Debbie Bowen
Frank Churchill	Robert East
Jane Fairfax	Ania Marson
Mr. Weston	Raymond Adamson
Robert Martin	John Alkin
Miss Bates	Constance Chapman
Mrs. Weston	Ellen Dryden
Mr. Woodhouse	Donald Eccles
Mrs. Bates	Mary Holder
Mr. Elton	Timothy Peters
Mrs. Goddard	Mollie Sugden
Mrs. Elton	Fiona Walker
Mrs. Cole	Hilda Fenemore
Isabella Knightley	Meg Gleed
John Knightley	John Kelland
Mrs. Ford	Lala Lloyd

VI. Emma

Original Release Date: August 2, 1996 (US), September 13,
    1996 (UK)
Studio: Columbia/Miramax
Running Time: 120 minutes
Description: Color, motion picture
Director/Screenwriter: Douglas McGrath
Producer: Patrick Cassavetti, Steven Haft
Original Music: Rachel Portman
Cinematography: Ian Wilson
Film Editing: Lesley Walker
Art Direction: Joshua Meath-Baker, Sam Riley
Set Decoration: Totty Whately
Costume Design: Ruth Myers

Cast

Emma Woodhouse	Gwyneth Paltrow
Mr. George Knightley	Jeremy Northam
Harriet Smith	Toni Collette
Mr. Weston	James Cosmo
Mrs. Weston	Greta Scacchi
Mr. Elton	Alan Cumming
Mrs. Elton	Juliet Stevenson
Mr. Woodhouse	Denys Hawthorne
Miss Bates	Sophie Thompson
Mrs. Bates	Phyllida Law
Mr. Martin	Edward Woodall
Mrs. Goddard	Kathleen Byron
John Knightley	Brian Capron
Isabella Knightley	Karen Westwood
Jane Fairfax	Polly Walker
Frank Churchill	Ewan McGregor

VII. Jane Austen's "Emma" (TV)

Original Broadcast Date: February 16, 1997 (US), 1996 (UK)
Channel: Meridian-ITV / A&E
Running Time: 107 minutes
Description: Color. Television movie.
Director: Diarmuid Lawrence
Scriptwriter: Andrew Davies
Producer: Sue Birtwistle
Original Music: Dominic Muldowney
Cinematography: Remi Adefarasin
Film Editing: Don Fairservice
Casting: Janey Fothergill
Production Design: Don Taylor
Art Direction: Jo Graysmark
Set Direction: John Bush
Costume Design: Jenny Beavan

Cast

Emma Woodhouse	Kate Beckinsale
Mr. George Knightley	Mark Strong
Mr. Woodhouse	Bernard Hepton
Mrs. Weston	Samantha Bond
Mr. Weston	James Hazeldine
Mr. Elton	Dominic Rowan
Harriet Smith	Samantha Morton
Miss Bates	Prunella Scales
Mrs. Bates	Sylvia Barter
Jane Fairfax	Olivia Williams
Frank Churchill	Raymond Coulthard
John Knightley	Guy Henry
Isabella Knightley	Dido Miles
Mrs. Elton	Lucy Robinson
Mrs. Goddard	Judith Coke
Robert Martin	Alistair Petrie
Mr. Perry	Peter Howell
Elizabeth Martin	Phoebe Welles-Cooper
Miss Otway	Tabby Harris

VIII. Clueless

Original Release Date: July 19, 1995 (US), October 20, 1995 (UK)
Studio: Paramount
Running Time: 113 minutes
Description: Color, motion picture
Director/Screenwriter: Amy Heckerling
Producer: Robert Lawrence, Scott Rudin
Original Music: David Kitay
Cinematography: Bill Pope
Film Editing: Debra Chiate
Casting: Marcia Ross
Production Design: Steven J. Jordan
Art Direction: William Hiney
Set Direction: Amy Wells
Costume Design: Mona May

Cast

Emma Woodhouse/Cher Horowitz	Alicia Silverstone
Mrs. Weston (I)/Dionne	Stacey Dash
Harriet Smith/Tai Frasier	Brittany Murphy
Mr. George Knightley/Josh	Paul Rudd
Mr. Weston (I)/Murray	Donald Faison
Mrs. Elton/Amber	Elisa Donovan
Robert Martin/Travis Birkenstock	Breckin Meyer
Mr. Elton/Elton	Jeremy Sisto
Mr. Woodhouse/Mel Horowitz	Dan Hedaya
Miss Bates/Lucy	Aida Linares
Mr. Weston (II)/Mr. Hall	Wallace Shawn
Mrs. Weston (II)/Miss Geist	Twink Caplan
Frank Churchill/Christian Stovitz	Justin Walker

Bibliography

Armstrong, Nancy. "The Rise of the Novel." *Desire and Domestic Fiction: A Political History of the Novel*. New York: Oxford University Press, 1987. 96 – 160.

Ascher-Walsh, Rebecca. "EW Entertainers of the Year: Jane Austen." *Entertainment Weekly* 22 Dec. 1995.

Austen, Jane. *Emma: Case Studies in Contemporary Criticism*. Ed: Alistair M. Duckworth. New York: Bedford/St. Martin's, 2002.

Beja, Morris. *Film and Literature: An Introduction*. New York: Longman, 1979.

Belasz, Bela. "The Close-Up." *Film Theory and Criticism* (fifth edition). Ed: Leo Braudy and Marshall Cohen. London: Oxford University Press, 1999.

Benjamin, Walter. "The Work of Art in the Age of Mechanical Reproduction." *Illuminations*. Translater: Harry Zohn. New York: Random House, 1998. 217-251.

Birtwistle, Sue and Susie Conklin. *The Making of Jane Austen's "Emma"*. London: Penguin Books, 1996.

Bloom, Harold. "Canonical Memory in Early Wordsworth and Jane Austen's *Persuasion*." *The Western Canon*. New York: Harcourt Brace, 1994.

Blum, Virginia L. "The Return to Repression: Filming the Nineteenth Century." *Jane Austen and Co*. ed. Suzanne R. Pucci and James Thompson. Albany: State University of New York Press, 2003.

Boose, Lynda E. and Richard Burt "Totally Clueless? Shakespeare goes Hollywood in the 1990s." *Film and Literature*. Ed: Timothy Corrigan. New Jersey: Prentice Hall, 1998.

Booth, Wayne. *The Company We Keep*. University of California Press, 1988.

——.*The Rhetoric of Fiction*. Chicago: University of Chicago Press, 1961.

Bradley, A.C. "Jane Austen: A Lecture." Parrish, Stephen M. *Emma: A Norton Critical Edition* (3rd edition). New York, London: W.W. Norton, 2000.

Butler, Marilyn. "Introduction to *Emma*." *Emma: Everyman's Library Edition*. New York: Knopf, 1991. Revised and reprinted in *Emma: Case Studies in Contemporary Criticism*. Edited by Alistair M. Duckworth. Boston: Bedford/St. Martin's, 2002.

——. *Jane Austen and the War of Ideas*. Oxford: Clarendon, 1975.

Calvino, Italo. "Why Read the Classics?" *The Uses of Literature*. Translated by Patrick Creagh. Harcourt Brace and Company, 1986. 125-135.

Campbell, Judy. "Emma." Unpublished screenplay. BBC TV, 1948. In the BBC Written Archives Centre. Television Drama Scripts Microfilm 31/32.

Canby, Vincent and Janet Maslin and Peter M. Nichols. Ed. "Persuasion." *The New*

York Times' Guide to the Best 1,000 Movies Ever Made. Three Rivers Press, 1999.

Cantor, Paul A. "A Class Act: *Persuasion* and the Lingering Death of the Aristocracy." *Philosophy and Literature* 23.1 (1999):127-137.

Carroll, Laura. "A Consideration of Times and Seasons: Two Jane Austen Adaptations." *Literature/Film Quarterly* 31.2 (2003): 169-176

Casillo, Robert. "Moments in Italian-American Cinema: From *Little Caesar* to Coppola and Scorsese." *From the Margin: Writings in Italian Americana*. Edited by Anthony Julian Tamburri, Paolo A. Giordano, and Fred L. Gardaphe. Indiana: Purdue University Press. 1994.

Chatman, Seymour. "What Novels Can Do That Films Can't (And Vice Versa)." *Film Theory and Criticism* (fifth edition) ed. Leo Braudy and Marshall Cohen. London: Oxford University Press, 1999

———. *Story and Discourse: Narrative Structure in Fiction and in Film*. Ithaca and London: Cornell University Press, 1978.

Clueless. Writer and director Amy Heckerling. With Alicia Silverstone and Paul Rudd. Paramount, 1995.

Colon, Christine. "The Social Constructions of Douglas McGrath's *Emma*: Earning a Place on Miss Woodhouse's Globe." *Persuasions: The Jane Austen Journal On-Line*, Occasional Papers No. 3, 1999.

Copeland, Edward and Juliet McMaster. *The Cambridge Companion to Jane Austen*. New York: Cambridge University Press, 1997.

Corrigan, Timothy. *Film and Literature: An Introduction and Reader*. New Jersey: Prentice Hall, 1998.

Cunningham, Valentine. "Games Texts Play." *In the Reading Gaol: Postmodernity, Texts, and History*. Cambridge, Massachusetts: Blackwell, 1994. 259-336.

Davies, J.M.Q. "*Emma* as Charade and the Education of the Reader." Philological Quarterly 65 (1986): 231-242.

Delany, Paul. "'A Sort of Notch in the Donwell Estate': Intersections of Status and Class in *Emma*." *Eighteen-Century Fiction* 12.4, July 2000: 533-548. Revised and reprinted in *Emma: Case Studies in Contemporary Criticism*. Edited by Alistair M. Duckworth. Boston: Bedford/St. Martin's, 2002.

Diana, M.Casey. "Emma Thompson's Sense and Sensibility as Gateway to Austen's Novel." *Jane Austen in Hollywood*. Ed: Linda Troost, Sayre Greenfield. University Press of Kentucky, 1998. 140-147.

Diengott, Nilli. "Neo Impressionism? Some Examples of Austen Criticism and Their Import for Current Critical Discourse." *AUMLA: Journal of Australasian Universities Language and Literature Association*. No. 88: November 1997.

Dixon, Rebecca. "Mis-Representing Jane Austen's Ladies." *Jane Austen in Hollywood*. Ed: Linda Troost, Sayre Greenfield. Lexington: University Press of Kentucky, 1998.

Doane, Mary Ann. "The 'Woman's Film': Possession and Address." *Re-Vision:Essays in Feminist Film Criticism*. LA: University Publications of America, 1984.

Doherty, Tom. "Clueless Kids." *Cineaste*. New York, 1995.

Dole, Carol M. "Austen, Class, and the American Market." *Jane Austen in Hollywood*.

Ed: Linda Troost and Sayre Greenfield. Lexington: The University Press of Kentucky, 1998.

Duffy, Joseph M. "*Emma*: The Awakening from Innocence," *Journal of English Literary History*, 21, March 1954.

Eckstut, Arielle and Dennis Ashton. *Pride and Promiscuity: The Lost Sex Scenes of Jane Austen*. New York: Simon and Schuster, 2001.

Eggleston, Robert. "*Emma*, the Movies, and First-year Literature Classes." *Persuasions: The Jane Austen Journal Online, Occasional Papers No. 3*, 1999.

"Emma." Dramatized by Marine Bartlett and Peter Donat. *NBC's Kraft Television Theatre*, Nov. 24, 1954. Library of Congress, NBC Television collection. 1-inch videotape.

Emma. Writer Denis Constanduros. Director John Glenister. BBC TV, 1972. DVD.

Emma. Writer and director Douglas McGrath. With Gwyneth Paltrow and Jeremy Northam. Miramax, 1996. DVD.

Emma (a.k.a. *Jane Austen's "Emma"*). Writer Andrew Davies. Director Diarmuid Lawrence. With Kate Beckinsale and Mark Strong. Meridian (ITV)/A&E, 1996.

Everett, Nigel. "The View of Donwell Abbey." *The Tory View of Landscape*. New Haven: Yale University Press, 1994. 183-203.

Farrer, Reginald. "Jane Austen, ob. July 18, 1917." *Quarterly Review* 228 (July 1917): 23-25.

Ferriss, Suzanne. "Emma Becomes Clueless." *Jane Austen in Hollywood*. Ed: Linda Troost and Sayre Greenfield. Lexington: The University Press of Kentucky, 1998.

Finch, Casey and Peter Bowen. " 'The Tittle-Tattle of Highbury': Gossip and the Free Indirect Style in *Emma*." *Representations* No. 31, Summer 1990. 1-18. Revised and Reprinted in *Emma: Case Studies in Contemporary Criticism*. Ed: Alistair M. Duckworth. (Bedford/St. Martin's, 2002): 441-455.

Fletcher, Loraine. "*Emma*: The Shadow Novelist." *Critical Survey* 4 (1992): 36-44.

Fulbrook, Denise. "A Generational Gig with Jane Austen, Sigmund Freud, and Amy Heckerling: Fantasies of Sexuality, Gender, Fashion, and Disco in and Beyond *Clueless*." *Jane Austen and Co.* ed. Suzanne R. Pucci and James Thompson. Albany: State University of New York Press, 2003.

Gallop, David. "Jane Austen and the Aristotelian Ethic." *Philosophy and Literature* 23.1 (1999): 96-109.

Galperin, William. "Byron, Austen, and the 'Revolution' of Irony." *Criticism: a Quarterly for Literature and the Arts*. Volume XXXII, number 1. Winter 1990. 51-80.

Geduld, Harry M. *Authors on Film*. Bloomington: Indiana University Press, 1972. 88-90.

Gilbert, Sandra M. and Susan Gubar. *The Madwoman in the Attic: The Woman Writer and the Nineteenth-Century Literary Imagination*. 2nd edition. London: Yale University Press, 1979. 1984. 2000.

Goldsworthy, Kerryn. "Austen and Authenticity." *Australian Humanities Review*. July. 1996.

Gregory, Mollie. *Women Who Run the Show: How a Brilliant and Creative New Generation of Women Stormed Hollywood*. New York: St. Martin's Griffin, 2003.

Griffith, James. *Adaptations as Imitations*. Newark: University of Delaware Press, 1997.

Hardy, John. *Jane Austen's Heroines: Intimacy in Human Relationships*. Boston: Routlegde & Kegan Paul, 1984.

Harris, Jocelyn. "A Review of Three Austen Adaptations." *Eighteenth Century Fiction* 8:3 (April 1996).

Haskell, Molly. *"Emma." Holding My Own in No Man's Land*. Oxford, New York: Oxford University Press, 1997. 172 – 181.

———. *From Reverence to Rape: The Treatment of Women in the Movies*. 2nd edition. University of Chicago Press, 1973, 1987.

Hopkins, Lisa. "Emma and the Servants." *Persuasions: The Jane Austen Journal On-Line, Occasional Papers No. 3*. 1999.

———."Mr. Darcy's Body: Privileging the Female Gaze." *Jane Austen in Hollywood*. Ed: Linda Troost and Sayre Greenfield. Lexington: University Press of Kentucky, 1998.

Johnson, Claudia. "Austen Cults and Cultures." *The Cambridge Companion to Jane Austen*. Ed. Copeland and McMaster. New York: Cambridge University Press, 1997. 211-26.

———. "The Divine Miss Jane: Jane Austen, Janeites, and the Discipline of Novel Studies." *Boundary 2: An International Journal of Literature and Culture* 23, Fall 1996. 143-163.

———.*Equivocal Beings*. Chicago: University of Chicago Press, 1995. 191-203.

———.*Jane Austen: Women, Politics, and the Novel*. London/Chicago: University of Chicago Press, 1988.

———. "'Not at all what a man should be!': Remaking English Manhood in *Emma*." Revised version of chapter from *Equivocal Beings*.) *Emma: Case Studies in Contemporary Criticism*. Ed: Alistair M. Duckworth. Boston: Bedford/St. Martin's, 2002. 441-455.

Kohn, Denise. "Reading *Emma* as a Lesson on 'Ladyhood': A Study in the Domestic Bildungsroman." *Essays in Literature*; Macomb; Spring 1995.

Lane, Andy. "The Dumbing of Emma," *The New Yorker*, August 5, 1996.

Langbauer, Laurie. *Women and Romance: The Consolations of Gender in the English Novel*. Itaca and London: Cornell University Press, 1990.

Lauritzen, Monica. *Jane Austen's Emma on Television: A Study of a BBC Classic Serial*. Sweden. Minab, 1981.

Litz, A. Walton. *Jane Austen: A Study of Her Artistic Development*. New York: Oxford University Press, 1965.

Lloyd, Trevor. "Myths of the Indies: Jane Austen and the British Empire." *Comparative Criticism* 21 (1999): 59-78

Looser, Devoney. "'The Duty of Woman by Woman': Reforming Feminism in *Emma*." *Emma: Case Studies in Contemporary Criticism*. Edited by Alistair M. Duckworth. Boston: Bedford/St. Martin's, 2002.

Lubrano, Alfred. *Limbo: Blue-Collar Roots, White Collar Dreams*. Hoboken, NJ: John Wiley and Sons, Inc, 2004

Luckett, Moya. "Image and Nation in 1990s British Cinema." *British Cinema of the 90s*.

Ed. Robert Murphy. London. BFI Publishing, 2000.

Lynch, Deidre. "Clueless: About History" *Jane Austen and Co.* ed. Suzanne R. Pucci and James Thompson. Albany: State University of New York Press, 2003.

Mallett, Phillip. "On Liking Emma." *The Durham University Journal* 53 (1992): 249–54.

Mansell, Darrel. *The Novels of Jane Austen: An Interpretation.* London: Macmillan, 1973.

Marie, Beatrice. "*Emma* and the Democracy of Desire." *Studies in the Novel* 17 (1985): 1-13.

Martin, Wallace. *Recent Theories of Narrative.* Cornell University Press,1986.

Maslin, Janet. "So Genteel, So Scheming, So Austen." *New York Times* 2 Aug. 1996: C1.

Mazmanian, Melissa. "Reviving *Emma* in a Clueless World: The Current Attraction to a Classic Structure." *Persuasions: The Jane Austen Journal On-Line*, Occasional Papers No. 3, 1999.

McGrath, Douglas. "Douglas McGrath, Screenwriter/Director." *Screenwriter Magazine Online.* http://www.nyscreenwriter.com/article10.htm

Medhurst, Andy. "That Special Thrill: Brief Encounter, Homosexuality, and Authorship." *Screen*, vol. 32, no. 2, Summer 1991, p. 198.

Meyersohn, Marylea. "Jane Austen's Garrulous Speakers: Social Criticism in *Sense and Sensibility, Emma,* and *Persuasion.*" *Reading and Writing Women's Lives: A Study of the Novel of Manners.* Ed. Bege K. Bowers and Barbara Brothers. London: UMI Research Press, 1990. 35-48.

Miller, D.A. "Austen's Attitude." *The Yale Journal of Criticism: Interpretation in the Humanities.* Spring 1995. Volume 8. Number 1.

Mitry, Jean. *Aesthetics and Psychology of the Cinema.* Translated by Christopher King. Bloomington and Indianapolis: Indiana University Press, 1997.

Monaghan, David. "*Emma* and the Art of Adaptation." *Jane Austen on Screen.* Ed: Gina Macdonald and Andrew F. Macdonald. Cambridge: Cambridge University Press, 2003.

Morrison, Sarah R. "*Emma* Minus Its Narrator: Decorum and Class Consciousness in Film Versions of the Novel." *Persuasions: The Jane Austen Journal On-Line*, Occasional Papers No. 3 (1999).

Mosier, John. "Clues for the Clueles." *Jane Austen on Screen.* Ed: Gina Macdonald and Andrew F. Macdonald. Cambridge: Cambridge University Press, 2003.

Mukherjee, Meenakshi. *Women Writers: Jane Austen.* New York: St. Martin's Press, 1991.

Mulvey, Laura. "Visual Pleasure and Narrative Cinema." *Film Theory and Criticism* (fifth edition) ed. Leo Braudy and Marshall Cohen. London: Oxford University Press, 1999

Nachumi, Nora. "'As If!': Translating Austen's Ironic Narrator to Film." *Jane Austen in Hollywood.* Ed: Linda Troost, Sayre Greenfield. University Press of Kentucky, 1998.

Naremore, James. *Film Adaptation.* New Jersey: Rutgers University Press, 2000.

O'Farrell, Mary Ann. "Jane Austen's Friendship." *Janeites: Austen's Disciples and Devotees.* Ed. Deidre Lynch. Princeton, NJ: Princeton University Press, 2000.

Page, Alex. "'Straightforward Emotions and Zigzag Embarrassments' in Austen's

Emma." *Johnson and His Age*, ed. James Engell. Harvard English Studies 12. Cambridge, Mass.: Harvard University Press, 1984. 559-74.

Paget, Derek. "Trainspotting: Speaking Out." *Adaptations: From Text to Screen, Screen to Text.* New York: Routledge, 1999.

Palmer, Sally. "Robbing the Roost: Reinventing Socialism in Diarmuid Lawrence's *Emma.*" *Persuasions: The Jane Austen Journal On-Line*, Occasional Papers No. 3, 1999.

Parrill, Sue. "The Cassandra of Highbury: Miss Bates on Film." *Persuasions: The Jane Austen Journal On-Line*, Occasional Papers No. 3, 1999.

———. *Jane Austen on Film and Television: A Critical Study of the Adaptations.* London: McFarland & Company, Inc, 2002.

———. "Metaphors of Control: Physicality in *Emma* and *Clueless.*" *Persuasions On-line* V. 20, No. 1.

Phillips, William and Louise Heal. "Extensive Grounds and Classic Columns: *Emma* on Film." *Persuasions: The Jane Austen Journal On-Line.* No. 3, 1999.

Pickrel, Paul. "*Emma* as Sequel." *Nineteenth-Century Fiction*, Vol. 40, No. 2, 1985. 135-153.

Poovey, Mary. "Address to the Jane Austen Society in Philadelphia, October 8, 1983." Printed in *Persuasions* 5: 48-51.

———. *The Proper Lady and the Woman Writer.* University of Chicago Press, 1984. 1995.

Pucci, Suzanne R. and James Thompson, editors. *Jane Austen and Co.* Albany: State University of New York Press, 2003.

———. "The Return Home." *Jane Austen and Co.* Albany: State University of New York Press, 2003.

Restuccia, Frances L. "A Black Morning: Kristevan Melancholia in Jane Austen's *Emma.*" *American Imago: Studies in Psychoanalysis and Culture* 51 (1994): 447-469.

Said, Edward. "Jane Austen and Empire." *Culture and Imperialism.* New York: Vintage Books, 1994.

Schor, Hilary. "Emma, interrupted: speaking Jane Austen in fiction and film." *Jane Austen on Screen.* Edited by Gina Macdonald and Andrew F. Macdonald. Cambridge. Cambridge University Press, 2003. (144-174.)

Schorer, Mark. "The Humiliation of Emma Woodhouse," *Jane Austen: A Collection of Critical Essays*, ed. Ian Watt. Englewood Cliffs: Prentice-Hall, 1963.

Scott. Sir Walter. "Review of *Emma.*" Parrish, Stephen M. *Emma: A Norton Critical Edition* (3rd edition). W. W.Norton. New York, London, 2000.

Searle, Catherine. "Outdoor Scenes in Jane Austen's Novels." *Thought* 59 (1984): 419-431.

Sedgwick, Eve Kosofsky. "Jane Austen and the Masturbating Girl." *Critical Inquiry* 17 (1991): 818-37.

Seeber, Barbara K. General Consent in *Jane Austen: A Study in Dialogism.* Montreal: McGill-Queen's University Press, 2000.

Shaffer, Julie. "Not Subordinate: Empowering Woman in the Marriage Plot – the Novels of Frances Burney, Maria Edgeworth, and Jane Austen." *Criticism: A Quarterly for Literature and the Arts*, Volume XXXIV, number 1. Winter, 1992. 51-

73.

Silverman, Kaja. "Dis-Embodying the Female Voice." *Re-Vision: Essays in Feminist Film Criticism.* Ed: Mary Anne Doane, Patricia Mellencamp, Linda Williams. LA: University Publications of America, 1984.

Skal, David J. *The Monster Show.* Faber and Faber, Inc, 1993.

Stevenson, John Allen. "*Emma*: The New Courtship in the British Novel, Defoe to Austen: A Critical History." *Twayne's Critical History of the Novel.* Boston: Twayne, 1990. 110-28.

Stewart, Maaja A. *Domestic Realities and Imperial Fictions: Jane Austen's Novels in Eighteenth-Century Contexts.* Athens and London: The University of Georgia Press, 1993. 137-168.

Sulloway, Alison G. *Jane Austen and the Province of Womanhood.* University of Pennsylvania Press, 1989.

Sutherland, John. "Apple-blossom in June-again" *Who Betrays Elizabeth Bennet? Further Puzzles in Classic Fiction.* New York: Oxford UP, 1999. 28-34

———. "How Vulgar is Mrs. Elton?" *Can Jane Eyre Be Happy? More Puzzles in Classic Fiction.* Oxford: Oxford University Press, 1997.

———. "Jane Austen, *Emma*: Apple-Blossom in June?" *Is Heathcliff a Murderer? Great Puzzles in Nineteenth-Century Literature.* New York: Oxford University Press, 1996. 14-19.

Tandon, Bharat. *Jane Austen and the Morality of Conversation.* London: Anthem Press, 2003.

Tennant, Emma. *Emma in Love: Jane Austen's "Emma" Continued.* London: Fourth Estate Limited, 1996.

Thompson, Emma. *The Sense and Sensibility Screenplay and Diaries: Bringing Jane Austen's Novel to Film.* Newmarket Press, New York, 1995.

Thompson, James. "How to Do Things with Austen." *Jane Austen and Co.* Albany: State University of New York Press, 2003.

Tilsley, Vincent. "*Emma*." Unpublished screenplay. BBC TV, 1960. In the BBC Written Archives Centre. Television Drama Scripts Microfilm.

Tobin, Beth Fowkes. "Aiding Impoverished Gentlewoman: Power and Class in *Emma*." *Criticism* 30, Fall 1998. 413-31. Revised and Reprinted in *Emma: Case Studies in Contemporary Criticism.* Ed: Alistair M. Duckworth. Bedford/St. Martin's, 2002. 441-455.

Todd, Janet. *Sensibility: An Introduction.* Routledge, 1986

———. *The Sign of Angelica: Women, Writing, and Fiction, 1660 – 1800.* New York: Columbia University Press, 1989.

———. *Women's Friendship in Literature.* Columbia University Press, 1980.

Tomalin, Claire. *Jane Austen: A Life.* Vintage Books, New York, 1997, 1999.

Trilling, Lionel. "Introduction." *Emma.* Boston: Houghton Mifflin, 1957.

Troost, Linda and Sayre Greenfield. "Filming Highbury: Reducing the Community in *Emma* to the Screen." *Persuasions: The Jane Austen Journal On-Line*, Occasional Papers No. 3 (1999).

———. ed. *Jane Austen in Hollywood.* Lexington: University Press of Kentucky, 1998.

Turim, Maureen. "Popular Culture and the Comedy of Manners: *Clueless* and Fashion Clues." *Jane Austen and Co.* ed. Suzanne R. Pucci and James Thompson. Albany: State University of New York Press, 2003.

Wagner, Geoffrey. *The Novel and the Cinema.* Cranbury, NJ: Associated University Presses, Inc., 1975.

Wald, Gayle. "Clueless in the Neo-Colonial World Order." *The Postcolonial Jane Austen.* Ed. You-me Park and Rajeswari Sunder Rajan. London and New York: Routledge, 2000.

Waldron, Mary. *Jane Austen and the Fiction of her Time.* Cambridge: Cambridge University Press, 1999.

Warner, Marina. *From the Beast to the Blonde: On Fairy Tales and Their Tellers.* New York: The Noonday Press, 1994

Watt, Ian P. *The Rise of the Novel.* Berkeley, University of California Press, 1957.

Williams, Raymond. *The Country and the City.* New York: Oxford University Press, 1973.

Wiltshire, John. *Recreating Jane Austen.* Cambridge: Cambridge University Press, 2001.